MW00910205

Steps to Success

Global Good Practices in Tourism Human Resources

Helen Williams
World Travel & Tourism Council

Christy Watts
Capilano College
World Travel & Tourism Council

Prentice
Hall

Toronto

National Library of Canada Cataloguing in Publication Data

Williams, Helen, 1965–
    Steps to success : global good practices in tourism human resources

Includes index.
ISBN 0-13-041960-5

1. Tourism—Personnel management—Case studies. 2. Hospitality industry—Personnel management—Case studies. I. Watts, Christy, 1963– II. Title.

G155.A1W54 2002   338.4'791'0683   C2001-901376-0

Copyright © 2002 Pearson Education Canada Inc., Toronto, Ontario

All Rights Reserved. This publication is protected by copyright, and permission should be obtained
from the publisher prior to any prohibited reproduction, storage in a retrieval system, or transmission
in any form or by any means, electronic, mechanical, photocopying, recording, or likewise. For information regarding permission, write to the Permissions Department.

ISBN 0-13-041960-5

Vice-President, Editorial Director: Michael Young
Acquisitions Editor: Sophia Fortier
Marketing Manager: Sharon Loeb
Developmental Editor: John Polanszky
Production Editor: Cheryl Jackson
Copy Editor: Carina Blafield
Production Coordinator: Wendy Moran
Page Layout: Heidi Palfrey
Art Director: Mary Opper
Cover Design: Sarah Battersby
Cover Image: PhotoDisc

1 2 3 4 5   06 05 04 03 02

Printed and bound in Canada.

Helen Williams

To Dale for your continued support and to both
my mother and father for the strength and the wisdom
you each gave me to go out into the world.
And, to my children Gillian and Hilary for your tolerance
during my many long hours in front of the computer.

Christy Watts

To my family, near and far, for their unwavering support, belief,
and encouragement in all I do; and to my young daughter Kaitlyn,
who sustains my balance between work, play, and dreams.

To our mentors in the industry, who have shared
their passion, expertise, and vision.

In particular, we thank Dr. Brian P. White—
our friend and colleague.

Contents

4 Building a Performance Culture: Improving Performance Service, Evaluations, Appraisals, Monitoring, and Accountability   72

5 Leading Change for Tourism Organizations: Communication, Partnerships, Organizational Leadership, Decision Making, and Empowerment   103

8 Setting Workplace Standards: Skill Certification, Occupational Standards, Workplace Safety, Risk Management, and Liability Issues   219

PREFACE

Steps to Success: Global Good Practices in Tourism Human Resources provides a snapshot of what's really happening all around the world in human resource management. Organizations from across the travel and tourism industry are realizing a need to change the way they do business, attract customers, or reward their employees. In each of the 55 "good practice" case studies, an organization shares its experiences and its results after implementing new, adapted, or in-house human resource management policies, training programs, and philosophies. These good practices are real-life success stories that illustrate a positive, practical outcome to a specific challenge.

As the world's largest provider of services, travel and tourism is restructuring to provide more lifetime career prospects to attract and retain the industry's most valuable asset—a trained, professional workforce. Whether you are about to enter the travel and tourism industry for the first time or are upgrading your skills for re-entry, we want you to have a fresh understanding of workplace issues and challenges.

Book Objective

The objective of this book is to present real-life examples of travel and tourism human resource strategies used in small, medium-sized, and large businesses today. The case studies explain why and how each business implemented a strategy to restore, build, or maintain competitive advantage within the travel and tourism industry. Generalities and trends can be drawn from these examples, as well as practical applications that can be implemented in the workplace.

Book Structure

Chapters—All of the case studies have been grouped into eight chapters, each of which reflects a current theme in the global travel and tourism workplace.

Learning Outcomes—The learning outcomes summarize the key concepts and ideas presented in each case study.

Overview—In the overview, the nature and scope of the organization is profiled along with its challenges, specific concerns, or opportunities encountered.

Implementation—The implementation section explains the human resource management strategy used by the organization to resolve its challenge.

Results—Each article concludes with a results section that provides a snapshot of the action taken and outcome achieved.

WTTC Human Resource Centre Comment—The World Travel & Tourism Council's (WTTC's) Human Resource Centre summarizes each case study in a short comment suggesting the impact of the actions taken by the organization, and looks at the broader implications for other travel and tourism agencies.

Key Terms—Near the end of each good practice article there is a list of key terms. These terms are often sector specific—that is, unique to the tourism area in which the study is concentrated. To fully comprehend the article, review these words and clarify unfamiliar terms prior to reading each case study.

Discussion Questions—The discussion questions found at the end of each case study encourage you to further explore the topics identified in the learning outcomes section. They should challenge you to think critically on an individual basis and on a group basis, inviting you to ask, "*What would I do if faced with a similar situation?*"

Chapter Summaries

Chapter One: Finding Your People
Whether by seeking employees via the Web or through more traditional avenues such as career trade fairs, companies must first attract individuals to their organizations. It is the job of management to attract, train, and retain quality people to gain competitive advantage. The philosophy behind hiring criteria is changing, reflective of a shrinking worker pool and a widening skills gap. Chapter One examines success stories in recruitment, selection, and hiring.

Chapter Two: Building Job Skills and Values
To provide more lifetime career prospects to attract and retain a professional workforce, employers are focussing more on building employee and management job skills and values. New recruits are being hired more for their attitude than for their skills, and employers often prefer to develop the necessary skills in-house. Chapter Two features case studies discussing job readiness, basic skills development, and employee relations.

Chapter Three: Recognizing and Rewarding Your Team
Employers recognize that if their people are competent, well managed, and well motivated, they are better able to delight consumers. To retain quality staff, employers are creating different methods to recognize employee achievements through lifelong learning, incentives, and rewards. Chapter Three presents case studies that explore team building, morale boosting, incentive programs, and compensation.

Chapter Four: Building a Performance Culture
To develop a team that provides quality work performance and customer service, employers are providing on-site training in many different formats. Self-paced learning packages, interactive computer programs, and skill-building exercises help create a strong performance culture. Chapter Four highlights companies that have improved their performance and service through evaluation systems, performance appraisals, monitoring, and accountability.

Chapter Five: Leading Change for Tourism Organizations
Tourism organizations leading change are often those creating partnerships and blending existing company practices with local communities. Chapter Five highlights organizations that are working to improve communications, both internally and within their community or region. Organizational leadership, effective decision making, and employee empowerment are topics targeted by large and small companies featured in this section.

Chapter Six: Celebrating Cultural Differences

Countries with shrinking populations are opening their borders to immigration. The influx of peoples with different cultural backgrounds and the ever-increasing volume of international travel have persuaded many travel and tourism companies to focus on cross-cultural sensitivity issues and language training. Employers are celebrating culture by incorporating multicultural skills and awareness in their training programs, while still maintaining their national identity. Chapter Six highlights companies that have developed programs and strategies focussed on cross-cultural training, multicultural skill building, and cultural interpretation.

Chapter Seven: Training for Service Quality

Both large and small businesses benefit from multi-skilled workers who are also able to provide quality customer service and cross-sell products and services. Establishing clear expectations, defined goals, and an accepted training system are key to developing the talents and skills required to maintain high standards. Chapter Seven outlines successful customer service training programs that use techniques such as mentoring, coaching, peer training, and multi-skill training.

Chapter Eight: Setting Workplace Standards

Writing accurate job descriptions, defining required certifications, and establishing firm performance standards are fundamental to building a strong employee base. Although the travel and tourism industry encompasses a variety of sectors, each with its own unique needs, accreditation systems have proved invaluable in defining and monitoring basic requirements. Chapter Eight features companies from across the globe that have successfully implemented systems to encourage and manage skill certification, increase workplace safety, address risk management and liability issues, and define occupational standards.

We Welcome Your Comments

We appreciate feedback from instructors, students, and industry professionals to learn how this book was used in the classroom and workplace. If you have suggestions for future editions or comments on the present edition, please address them to the

WTTC Human Resource Centre
c/o Capilano College—Tourism Management Department
2055 Purcell Way
North Vancouver BC V7J 3H5
Canada

E-mail: wtthrc@direct.ca

ACKNOWLEDGMENTS

Most of the research and writing for this book was undertaken at the World Travel & Tourism Council's (WTTC's) Vancouver-based Human Resource Centre. The authors would like to thank the WTTC for its financial support, as this book would not have been possible without its vision and commitment to travel and tourism. Since its founding in 1990, the WTTC has promoted travel and tourism to governments and the business community around the world, and has presented a positive image of this industry as a provider of jobs and career opportunities. We would also like to thank Capilano College and the Tourism and Outdoor Recreation Management Department for their support in housing the WTTC Human Resource Centre.

We gratefully acknowledge the work of the many individuals who took the time to share their human resource success stories with us. This book is a tribute to their hard work, commitment, and vision. The authors would like to recognize the following individuals, some of whom have changed careers since the outset, who were instrumental in supporting our research: Franco Anglesio, Darrell Ballard, Graeme Benn, Nancy Brenner, Allen Brown, Raymond Chan, Witchuda Chookittipong, Carol Chu, Amanda Close, Jorge Delarbre-Rodal, Belinda Dusbaba, Cathy Eber, Marian Fisher, Ian Graham, Andrew Henry, Juan Kock, Rick Lemon, Stephen Lewis, Gen McKenzie, Olivia Mortimer, Thelma Oldak, Steven Palombo, Preeya Pramukkul, Ajay N. Rajguru, Jacqueline Richardson, Sasithorn Saipiroonpetch, Bill Shields, Ian Sykes, Michiru Tamanai, Dave Weitsz, Rebecca Wilson-Mah, Ron Wolf, and Maureen Wright.

THE WORLD TRAVEL & TOURISM COUNCIL

The World Travel & Tourism Council (WTTC) is the global business leaders' forum for Travel & Tourism. Its Members are Chief Executives from all sectors of the industry, including accommodation, catering, entertainment, recreation, transportation and other travel-related services. Founded in April 1990, WTTC policies are set and implemented by a Member Executive Committee, a President and a small staff in London, with representative offices in North and South America, India, Asia/Pacific and Europe. WTTC research identifies the potential for Travel & Tourism to generate 252 million jobs by 2010—an increase of 60 million new jobs across the world economy. WTTC's Seven Strategic Priorities are the organization's guiding policy platform. WTTC promotes public/private sector cooperation within its policy framework, Seven Strategic Priorities:

1. Vision the future for Travel & Tourism—a future for everyone.
2. Measure and promote the economic importance of Travel & Tourism.
3. Communicate a positive image of the industry as a provider of jobs and career opportunities.
4. Encourage free access, open markets, open skies and the removal of barriers to growth.
5. Match infrastructure development and customer demand.
6. Facilitate access to capital resources and technological advancement.
7. Promote responsibility in natural, social and cultural environments.

Representing the private sector, the World Travel & Tourism Council works with governments to implement these Seven Strategic Priorities.

INTRODUCTION

The research for this book started in 1995 when the World Travel & Tourism Council (WTTC) established the WTTC Human Resource Centre at Capilano College in Vancouver, Canada, with support from American Express. In response to the need for greater activity in the industry's human resource field, the Human Resource Centre began collecting travel and tourism human resource management success

WORLD TRAVEL & TOURISM COUNCIL
HUMAN RESOURCE CENTRE

stories from around the world. This collection of "good practices" is distributed globally to national government organizations, academia, and management personnel working in travel and tourism through the centre's publication *Steps to Success: Global Good Practices in Travel and Tourism Human Resource Development*. As the publication has evolved, so has the scope of the articles. Today, the WTTC Human Resource Centre houses a database of success stories, featuring human resource management challenges and achievements from large and small companies and organizations.

As governments around the world gain a greater understanding of travel and tourism as a key industry for economic growth, developing a professional and highly skilled workforce is becoming a higher priority of national human resource development strategies. *Steps to Success* was created with this in mind. This collection of updated and newly discovered good practices provides a current look at struggles and solutions as they relate to "people management" in travel and tourism.

A Dynamic Global Workforce

Travel and tourism is more than a service industry. Through networks, partnering, and consortium initiatives, it is a huge social and cultural phenomenon that creates employment and spreads skills, wealth, and innovation while stimulating community development. At the same time, global factors such as population change, new technologies, immigration, and ethnic and cultural diversity are all impacting local tourism workforces.

The travel and tourism industry is dependent on a multi-skilled and well-educated workforce. The tourism workforce must employ a wide variety of occupational tasks and complex skills to deliver quality tourism experiences and services to the customer. Despite the traditional view that tourism provides low-paying front line and seasonal employment, the industry actually offers a higher proportion of entrepreneurial, supervisory, and management positions than most other sectors.[1]

Changing demographics are altering workforces globally, causing changes to human resource policies and programs. These variables have materialized in the form of increasing skills gaps, a shrinking workforce, and, in many developed economies, an aging population. The labour shortages emerging in some regions may, in time, lead to industry requests for increased immigration.[2] While many governments are beginning to recognize the economic importance of travel and tourism, in many cases this sector still receives an inadequate share of government policy, attention, and resources.

The need to attract, develop, and retain a tourism workforce that can meet emerging labour market challenges has never been greater. Throughout all the travel and tourism sectors, the focus is common: recruiting talented, well-educated, and trained individuals from front line to senior management who will contribute to the success of the business and the industry. One might argue that employees do not merely create the product—they *are* the product. Management needs to develop the abilities of its employees as a resource, which will in turn shape its recruitment procedures and training practices. According to Gallup, poorly managed workgroups are, on average, 50 percent less productive and 44 percent less profitable than well-managed groups. In many cases, employment workplace practices are directly linked to industry performance.

As access to newly discovered destinations has improved and target markets have gained more knowledge of alternative travel opportunities, human resource development for the travel and tourism industry has become a significant factor in maintaining national competitiveness. The travel and tourism industry will continue to show strong global growth despite shifts in demand, labour force issues, and political uncertainty. To keep pace with rising global expectations, all countries must address tourism labour force needs with effective education, training, and human resource development strategies.

HR Challenges for the 21st Century

According to WTTC research, human resource development challenges for the 21st century require practical solutions to overcome a number of complex barriers:

- Travel and tourism must compete for skilled human resources with other growth sectors such as finance and information technology, but often lacks a sufficient reputation as an employer to attract and keep the best employees.
- Policy makers often do not recognize that travel and tourism redistributes national wealth by creating part-time and full-time employment opportunities for people of all ages, races, and skill levels in both urban and rural areas.
- While most emerging economies have growing populations, the workforce in many developed countries is shrinking. The availability of human resources is further constrained by aging populations.
- Labour shortages will lead to immigration, potentially impacting the social balance of local communities.
- The skills gap in travel and tourism is widening as technology and customer service needs evolve and insufficient resources are made available to maintain national competitiveness.[3]

While the economic and social benefits are numerous, the approach that national governments should take to maintain competitive advantage is less obvious. Frequently, a lack of funding and a shortage of qualified instructors, teaching materials, and educational facilities have prevented strategic travel and tourism education and training plans from producing significant improvements. Attention has often been focussed on capital spending and destination marketing, with human capital development treated as a secondary consideration.

The evidence of travel and tourism's economic and social benefits—provided by organizations such as the WTTC, the Economic Social Commission for the Asia Pacific, the Organization for Economic Co-operation and Development, and the World Tourism Organization—has added travel and tourism education and training initiatives to many national policy agendas. Such policies can help provincial, regional, and local authorities to harmonize conflicting objectives.

Travel and tourism organizations are turning more frequently to human resource development strategies to maintain competitive advantage and viability. In the former Soviet Union, "smile training" and telephone etiquette are in big demand, as businesses make the link between customer satisfaction and profit.[4]

Globalization Issues

Travel and tourism companies and agencies are defined by the quality of their workforces. The product delivered is a service: on the spot, right now, and often outside of management's immediate control and direction. Bad service cannot be undone, so it is crucial to provide quality service in the first place.

In an increasingly competitive international market, travel and tourism products need to provide good quality and high value to meet customers' expectations. Businesses cannot assume that they know what the customer wants, but must do research to understand customer demands and provide appropriate employee training.

Many factors drive the emerging need for education and training investment in the travel and tourism industry. Globalization and international competition are particularly significant factors. Decentralized and downsized decision-making structures—operating out of several countries—can create huge challenges in developing a common workplace culture. Paradoxically, while we may travel to experience the differences the world has to offer, we expect quality and consistency in the services we find. Given that, does "world-class" have to mean homogenized and blandly consistent? More likely than not, we treasure the uniqueness of our global human encounters more than the similarities to home. We must meet the challenge of educating and training for excellent quality service, and, at the same time, celebrate the cultural diversity that makes travel stimulating and exciting.

While the featured good practices have different business strategies, each focusses on human resource management as the key to sustaining competitive advantage. As the tourism industry develops in the global community, labour markets will increase their demand for qualified professionals. And, concurrently, employee workplace quality expectations will rise.

Finding, developing, and retaining the best people are essential elements in building a competitive advantage for travel and tourism companies. As more and more companies realize the link between customer satisfaction and success, a stronger focus on human resource development is likely to occur in both large and small companies. The authors hope that the good practices illustrated in this book will help you make a difference in creating a quality workplace for all participants in the travel and tourism industry.

---

1 WTTC (1999). "Millennium Vision: Strategic Economic & Employment Priority" *Progress & Priorities 1999*, London.
2 WTTC/WEFA (1999). "Travel & Tourism's Economic Impact" *Progress & Priorities 1999*, London.
3 WTTC (2000). Web site: **www.wttc.org**, London.
4 Industry Canada—Commercial Education and Training, (1998). "Growth Prospects for the Industry" Sector Competitiveness Framework Series Education and Training Services.

chapter one

Finding Your People: Recruitment, Selection, and Hiring

Canada
Intrawest Corporation

Submitted by: Chris Wrazej

WE WORK 2 PLAY

… Using a corporate brand approach to hire employees via the Internet helps build this company's desired employee profile, as well as staff loyalty and commitment.

LEARNING OUTCOMES

1. Identify approaches for using corporate lifestyle as a recruitment incentive.
2. Explain how Intrawest uses a corporate branding approach to build its desired employee profile.
3. Describe approaches within Intrawest's corporate culture that build employee loyalty and commitment.

> *"Imagine a PERFECT DAY. Now imagine getting PAID for it."*
>
> *Intrawest Corporation*

OVERVIEW

Intrawest Corporation is the leading developer and operator of village-centred destination resorts across North America. Headquartered in Vancouver, British Columbia, Intrawest is committed to building a network of destination resorts and resort clubs that are second to none. Intrawest Corporation (Intrawest) acknowledges its success in developing world-class villages, and feels it is equally famous for developing world-class people!

The company credits this success to its energy, passion, and level of commitment to the people that work for it. Due to the seasonal nature of the business and the short time frame to produce revenues, Intrawest has created an environment, philosophy, and culture to provide incredible memories for its guests and employees again and again.

A backstage pass to Intrawest's Copper Mountain Resort Jobfest 2000

Intrawest offers a number of seasonal and full-time management career opportunities. In peak season, the company employs over 16 000 people, uniquely positioned to service 6.2 million skier visits and 546 000 golf rounds. Employment positions include:

- resort lodging
- sales and marketing
- finance
- golf and ski operations
- ski and snowboarding school

- food and beverage
- human resources
- real estate development
- retail operations
- information technology

IMPLEMENTATION

What does Intrawest do to attract nearly 11 000 seasonal employees, and retain almost 5 000 year-round employees? According to Intrawest, to truly understand how, you must visit one of its resorts or properties. An employee's "day at the office" could literally be spent in no office at all. Walls are mountains, and front yards are golf greens and the ocean. Every day is a casual day! A lunch break may be spent carving fresh tracks on the ski hill, or hitting a bucket of balls at the driving range.

However, Intrawest must offer more than great surroundings to secure excellent employees. Given the locations and economies of many of its resorts, competition for employees is fierce. Intrawest has designed a unique strategy to ensure it attracts the best employees.

Attracting the right employees involves elaborate efforts in its "own back yards" and around the globe (including Australia, South America, and Jamaica). Employee skills are important, but, for the most part, Intrawest seeks those with the kind of motivation, interest, and drive that will ensure success with the company. Successful employees understand Intrawest's corporate culture, and learn how to interpret that culture to guests through service and attitude.

A Branded Approach

Intrawest operates 10 resorts, three divisions, and numerous subdivisions (including retail, golf, and destination travel). This kind of diversification requires a significant base of employees working both in seasonal and year-round positions. Managing the employee resource base is a complex job for human resources.

To understand just how tough competition for employees can be, consider this: Right now, a person looking for a job in Summit County, Colorado, could walk into a McDonald's restaurant and secure a wage that is two to four dollars higher than minimum wage, and get a ski pass at local mountains! In 2001, this city's unemployment level was below two percent.

Each division is responsible for its own recruitment strategies, and for ensuring employee retention. To maintain some consistency in hiring, Intrawest recruits people using a branded approach. By using this approach under the umbrella of "WeWork2Play," Intrawest has created a unique identity that complements its corporate image, and also functions as a stand-alone program.

The WeWork2Play recruitment program is a complete package, with its own Internet domain name: **www.wework2play.com**. On the front end, the Web portal provides a "one-stop shop" where potential employees can review job positions and apply for any and all employment opportunities at Intrawest. The site also offers detailed job descriptions, provides information about Intrawest's company culture, outlines benefits of working for Intrawest, and highlights frequently asked questions. Employee real-life testimonials, in day-to-day jobs, lend additional credibility to the site. The site is linked with third-party vendors who assist with collecting résumés and managing job-fit assessments, which are received over the Internet.

Intrawest's challenge is how to best attract potential employees to the Web site. To market the program, WeWork2Play is printed on business cards, brochures, and banners. Intrawest also plans to integrate the message, and the wordmark, in non-traditional recruiting formats. This will be done by highlighting the phrase on employee uniforms, on restaurant menus, on trail maps, and through in-house television channels. The marketing of the phrase will be done in collaboration with some of Intrawest's corporate sponsors and partners.

The benefits of creating a recognizable recruiting brand and Web portal are numerous. In establishing a solid recruitment format, the following is achieved:

- The company lifestyle of work and play is marketed continuously.
- A company-wide look, feel, and experience is consistently expressed.
- Employment and lifestyle opportunities at Intrawest are clearly and consistently defined.
- All divisions and subdivisions will encompass and market the brand.

- Smaller business units are able to access a large applicant pool.
- Recruiting efforts can be leveraged on a larger scale. (This would not be possible if individual business units looked for their own employees.)

Job Fairs

The Web portal allows Intrawest to showcase the company, but it is at the job fairs that potential candidates get to experience what the company has to offer first hand. Fierce competition for employees continues to drive Intrawest to provide applicants with value-added experiences.

To entice potential employees, Intrawest job fairs can be elaborately staged events complete with activities and themed décor. At one location, portable climbing walls are available for applicants to try out before their interviews. Full-size snowmen may be staged as greeters (indoors!), and recruiters on rollerblades are a common sight. Balloons have been used to colourfully display the perks and benefits of working for the company. Food service, beer gardens, and dance music are often featured at Intrawest job fairs.

Because much of Intrawest's employment application process is Web-based, computer labs (with as many as 20 terminals) and support personnel are available for those without access.

The selection process incorporates multiple or panel interviews with some of the company's current stars. These employees, who epitomize the ideal Intrawest employee, are trained in the skill of Behavioural Descriptive Interviewing. Personality and cognitive assessments are benchmarked against top-performing employees and guest-service stars. In this way, Intrawest is able to match candidates with a job they will most likely find satisfying and rewarding.

Managers and leaders with Intrawest are well versed in the importance of employee job satisfaction, and in the concept of the service profit chain. Providing value to the employee experience is the key to fuelling Intrawest's financial and business success. Intrawest believes this will lead to employee satisfaction and loyalty, and, in turn, guest satisfaction and loyalty.

"It's a way of life ..."

Intrawest Corporation

Orientation Training

Once hired, employees partake in a fun, interactive, and animated orientation training (complete with fake red noses for new participants, scavenger hunts, and guest speakers). The orientation is mandatory for all employees. Training focusses around Intrawest's four core values: employee experience, teamplay, customer loyalty, and striving to be the best.

A high percentage of employees (91 percent) feel that the company effectively communicates its philosophy of how Intrawest guests should be treated.

Cross-Training

A good training program for full-time employees provides Intrawest with growth opportunities. With this in mind, training and development is a high priority.

Due to the seasonal nature of many of Intrawest's properties, maintaining a committed staff on a year-round basis is a challenge. Although the company strives to create a continuous four-season experience for both guests and staff, at times business requires that resorts operate seasonally. Consistency and quality in service is therefore accomplished through cross-training. By creating a multi-skilled workforce, the company reduces recruitment costs and is able to operate with a core group of employees who can function well in many areas, and at many different properties.

Cross-training occurs between Intrawest resorts by sharing staff. For example, during their peak winter season, Intrawest's United States resorts in California, Colorado, and West Virginia recruit employees from off-season properties in northern Florida. In spring, other local businesses and operators outside the company are invited to interview Intrawest resort employees so that employees can remain in the same geographical area. Opposing business cycles help many winter lift operators, housekeepers, and car parkers find opportunities in the summer on golf courses and at water parks. The goal of cross-training is to assist employees in finding summer employment, so that they will return to Intrawest when needed in the fall. Providing alternative work experiences also builds staff loyalty. When financial realities make it difficult to operate a resort fully staffed at all times, Intrawest strives to provide employees with as close to full-time work as possible.

RESULTS

Intrawest understands that not all employees will be (or want to be) with them forever. Many seasonal employees are simply looking for an opportunity to get away from the drudgery and responsibilities of jobs in the "real world." Many front line employees have traditional backgrounds as physicians, lawyers, accountants, engineers, and teachers. For a season or two, they take a job loading chairlifts, ski patrolling, ski instructing, waiting tables, or manicuring greens, with the sole desire of recharging their "life batteries."

Many of those who do make a career out of working with Intrawest have worked their way up through the ranks. For example, the president of the Resort Operation Group, Hugh Smythe, is now responsible for the strategic planning and operation of all Intrawest destination resorts. At the age of 19 in 1966, Smythe started at Whistler Mountain as a lift operator.

Intrawest's corporate priority is a commitment to hire and promote from "within." The company has also established a company-wide employee referral program called PERPL CRAZE (Passionate Employee Referral Program Lottery). This program allows employees from all levels to win cash and prizes for referring new employees. Although still in its infancy, the program is becoming more and more successful, with some employees cashing as many as four or five referral cheques per season. When seasonal employees are invited to come back for a second season, their package includes registration and instruction forms for use in recruiting a friend or acquaintance. By including all employees in the recruitment process, and by having employees recommend like-minded individuals, blanket recruiting costs are reduced. As a result of these savings, some of the funds allocated for recruitment costs are redistributed to referring employees.

Intrawest benefits include free multi-area ski passes for employees and their families, golfing privileges, food and beverage discounts, and significant retail discounts at many of its stores. Top-performing employees take part in staff celebrations such as toboggan parties, slush cups, bonfires, and pig roasts. Other recognition programs provide cash prizes, trips, heli-skiing, and various ski or golf packages.

Despite all its efforts to remain an employer of choice, Intrawest knows that providing employment opportunities in world-class settings does not solve all of its recruiting challenges. It does, however, remain strategic and focussed on what works, and embrace technology and smart thinking. In Intrawest's own words, "it makes the 'race' a whole lot easier."

WTTC HUMAN RESOURCE CENTRE COMMENT

Intrawest's job fairs are almost a form of entertainment on their own, as they woo applicants to join the Intrawest team. Equally exciting is the WeWork2Play Web site, designed to attract applicants to send in their résumés electronically. The rollerblading recruiters, balloons with benefits info, good food, and lively music all sound like fun, but as Intrawest has indicated, it is all part of thinking strategically to meet the challenges of recruiting.

The high school or college student, or the late bloomer needing a break from the "real world," can continue to enjoy a carefree lifestyle suited to the great outdoors at one of Intrawest's mountain or beach resorts. Intrawest expects employees to provide guests with memorable experiences that will keep them coming back. By treating its employees well, and providing good incentives, benefits, and opportunities, Intrawest also hopes it is building a winning team that will return the next year. Intrawest's branded approach is a unique strategy to ensure it attracts the best employees, and this is reflected in its orientation training, cross-training, job fairs, promotions, and benefits.

KEY TERMS

Web portal	competition
wordmark	recognition programs
recruiting	cross-training
hiring	incentive
destination resorts	value-added
motivation	referral
multi-skilled	branding

www.intrawest.com

www.wework2play.com

DISCUSSION QUESTIONS

1. As an employee seeking a management position with a company like Intrawest, what questions would you ask a recruiter to help you in finding out if a front line job with this company is worth pursuing, and if moving up within the ranks is possible?

2. Employee sharing between resorts has many benefits. List four benefits for the corporation, the employee, and the surrounding community.

3. If looking for a job online, what Web site features would convince you the company is a good employer to work for and entice you to submit your résumé?

4. Discuss why some employees consider lifestyle an important component in selecting a front line job with a resort.

5. List the pros and cons of sharing your trained employees with other companies during shoulder seasons.

United Arab Emirates
Department of Tourism and Commerce Marketing—Dubai

Submitted by: Abdul Hakim Thani

Government of Dubai حــكـــومـــه ديـــــي
DEPARTMENT OF TOURISM دائـــــره الســـياحـــة
AND COMMERCE MARKETING والــتـــسـويــو الــجـــاري

A STATE-OF-THE-ART HUMAN RESOURCE MANAGEMENT SYSTEM

… With the use of a confidential personal profiling computer system, recruitment, hiring, and team building within this organization have been simplified. A training needs analysis was established and monitored, thereby effectively matching employee skills and duties.

LEARNING OUTCOMES

1. Explain the benefits of matching individual skill sets with job requirements.

2. Describe an approach where employee skills and behaviours are systematically identified.

3. Describe the process by which a government agency responds to an industry's training requirements.

Government of Dubai, Department of Tourism and Commerce Marketing

Tourism business is increasing in the United Arab Emirates.

OVERVIEW

Dubai's Department of Tourism and Commerce Marketing (formerly the Dubai Commerce and Tourism Promotion Board) operates as the principal authority for planning, supervising, and developing tourism throughout the United Arab Emirates. The organization has also been responsible for promoting Dubai's commerce and tourism interests internationally since 1997.

Today, with the increase in travel to the United Arab Emirates and the concern for providing quality standards, the Department of Tourism and Commerce Marketing (DTCM) oversees the licensing of hotels, hotel apartments, tour operators, tourist transport companies, and travel agents. Its supervisory role also covers all tourism-related archaeological and heritage sites, tourism conferences and exhibitions, the operation of tourist information services, and the organization and licensing of tour guides.

The DTCM is committed to:

- establishing systems that expand training opportunities;
- raising front line service standards; and
- increasing the cultural skills of Dubai's tourism industry personnel to meet the needs of an increasing number of foreign visitors.

Despite cultural restrictions, statistics show that tourism is an important component of Dubai's economy. In 1999, total accommodation occupancy within Dubai was over three million. This was an increase of 13.6 percent over the previous year's figure of 2.5 million.

From 1998 to 1999, tourism accounted for 11 percent of the Emirates' gross domestic product (GDP). The increase in tourism-related revenue offset the Emirates' decreased oil revenues for 1998 to 1999, which were down by 8 percent.

Even though the United Arab Emirates' travel and tourism industry has only recently developed, the DTCM did not find it difficult to recruit qualified staff for departmental job positions. Applicants had generally worked in the travel and tourism industry prior to applying to the DTCM.

The DTCM's head office in Dubai began using the computer-based Thomas International Personal Profiling System to better match employee talents with the appropriate job, and to help in coordinating tourism ministry staff training. This system helped in the areas of recruiting, training, and placing employees.

The Personal Profiling System is a "psychometric" management tool that has evolved over the last 50 years. The system assists management in recruiting and placing the best possible people in the best possible positions within their organization. The system software is designed to evaluate the personal qualities of an employee against the requirements of the job. In this way, the system offers an "objective" focus in assessing employee skill sets and on-the-job requirements. The key component of the system is linking the behavioural requirements of the job to the behavioural traits of the employee.

The DTCM's department of human resources adopted the Personal Profiling System because the most commonly repeated and costly mistakes occur in the area of personnel selection. Recruiting the right person for the right job is what the DTCM hopes the system will ensure.

> *"The main objective of this system is to help managers in all disciplines do their jobs effectively and more efficiently by giving them a better understanding of themselves and their subordinates. This enables the managers to improve the motivation, performance, and effectiveness of their staff, and assists them in building winning teams."*
>
> *Abdul Hakim Thani*
> *DCTM, Manager, Human Resources*

IMPLEMENTATION

A consulting company provided training on the Personal Profiling System during the first month that the system was running and continues to provide technical support to DTCM staff managing the system. Set-up required no additional computer hardware purchases. However, the DTCM is exploring the possibility of linking the system to an intranet environment.

One of the reasons the DTCM chose the Personal Profiling System is that it is easily adapted to large-, medium-, and small-sized businesses. Currently, the system is operated in more than 25 different languages and is being used in over 40 different countries worldwide, with an active client base of over 40 000 organizations.

Recruitment and Selection

The two key elements of the Personal Profiling System are the Human Job Analysis (HJA) and the Personal Profiling Analysis (PPA). The system aids in staff recruitment and provides a formal analysis of individual training needs. After employees complete a questionnaire, the information is processed through the system and reports are produced which make it possible to predict (with a high degree of accuracy) how a person is likely to behave.

The system is able to provide information and results in approximately 10 minutes. Results and recommendations are confidential and used only for management review. The department of human resources works with management in other DTCM departments to best place employees.

With better employee selection, it is then the task of the DTCM's department of human resources to oversee in-house training activities, as the system notes training needs and monitors the effectiveness of training. The department of human resources is able to identify training needs by using the system's PPA program, and the Training Needs Analysis program. To monitor the effectiveness of ministry training programs, the DTCM uses a training course assessment questionnaire.

> *"At the DTCM, we realize the importance of training and staff development. This new system will help us in identifying the behaviour traits of employees as well as new recruits, and help us to place the right person in the right position."*
>
> *Khalid A. bin Sulayem*
> *DTCM, Director General*

Training

DTCM staff training includes courses in languages, computers, telephone skills, customer care, public relations, and translation. Course topics were chosen after reviewing the information generated by the Training Needs Analysis program. The program also provided necessary information for designing the goals and objectives for each topic.

For example, the telephone skills training course teaches professional telephone manners, explains how to be efficient on the telephone, and discusses effective customer communications. This course also addresses how each employee contributes to the overall image of the department.

The public relations and customer care course was designed to address the DTCM's "business culture" by improving general communication skills throughout the organization. This course explains how staff can have a positive effect on the way customers view their department and illustrates how an individual plays an important role in the overall success of promoting Dubai worldwide.

Training courses and programs are generally organized and coordinated in-house by the DTCM's training and development department. Trainers and teachers are brought in from established universities and training institutes worldwide.

Most courses are conducted during working hours and held on-site. These in-house training courses average 15 to 25 participants, and are offered at no cost to the employee. Depending on the content and the number of participants, courses are designed as one- or two-day seminars, weekend workshops, or as training held over several weeks. Training is conducted both on a one-to-one basis and in a group or classroom setting. Teaching tools include videotapes, manuals, and role-playing. The course presenter designs the individual course material, such as manuals, workbooks, or guides.

The DTCM also offers training to tourism industry operators. This ensures that the travel and tourism industry continues to grow as an up-market destination. Working with leading hotel managers throughout Dubai, the DTCM organizes best practice workshops, wherein training directors in top hotels share winning strategies in customer service and employee training.

These best practice workshops are industry driven, targeting topics which the management considers important. Sample topics include customer care training, youth management, and service industry training. On occasion, workshops will include employees. Generally, workshops are free and held in full-day sessions at the DTCM's head office training facility. This allows the DTCM to act as a training facilitator and to focus on critical topics as identified by industry leaders.

General tourism courses are also offered by the DTCM. One such course is a certificate program covering general tourism topics specific to the United Arab Emirates. This subsidized, three-day course includes information on area history, tourism attractions, and general visitor information. There is also a nine-day training course for tour guides. To work as a tour guide in the Emirates one must successfully complete a written and oral exam.

> *"Employees reflect the most expensive assets in organizations today, and a company's success or failure almost uniformly depends upon management's ability to recognize and develop people skills, and to find the best person available to perform important assignments."*
>
> *Abdul Hakim Thani*
> *DTCM, Manager, Human Resources*

RESULTS

For Dubai's Department of Tourism and Commerce Marketing, the Thomas International Personal Profiling System is a very effective tool for recruiting, selecting, and training new employees. The system enables managers to help employees develop their individual skills and plan a career. Internally, the system has provided a framework for team management and corporate communications. The system has also helped the DTCM improve performance and gain a competitive edge in the marketplace. Through the use of best practices and technology, return on human investment has been maximized.

Specifically, the Personal Profiling System has:

- enhanced the overall corporate performance by improving the productivity and profitability of the organization;

- identified leadership potential more effectively and maximized the management capacities of existing staff;
- identified individual training needs, assisting in the preparation of more meaningful career development plans;
- improved communications and interpersonal relationships within the organization;
- enhanced and improved the employee performance appraisal system;
- recruited a higher quality of staff, over time; and
- better identified stress factors and provided recommendations for counselling when appropriate.

WTTC HUMAN RESOURCE CENTRE COMMENT

Worldwide, human resource departments use interviews and résumés to determine if individuals are well suited to both a company and a position. Hiring is one component. Placing individuals in the right environment, based on their skills, is another. The Personal Profiling System utilized by Dubai's Department of Tourism and Commerce Marketing (DTCM) is tailored for large public and private corporations. What this good practice illustrates is the DTCM's commitment to strategies that expand training opportunities, raise front line standards, and expand the cultural skills of tourism industry personnel to meet the needs of foreign visitors.

KEY TERMS

employee profiling
recruitment
hiring

behavioural traits
training needs analysis
career development

 **www.dubaitourism.co.ae**

DISCUSSION QUESTIONS

1. List five behavioural attributes (e.g., friendliness, reliability, assertiveness, etc.) and explain how these attributes might be applied to particular tourism jobs.
2. What are the benefits of the "best practice workshops" described in this case study?
3. What is the key objective of the DTCM?

United States
The Broadmoor Hotel

Submitted by: Cindy Clark

THE MENTOR PROGRAM

… For up to 18 months at a time, this hotel adds well-trained, highly motivated international students to its staff through a quality on-site mentoring program.

LEARNING OUTCOMES

1. Identify the steps involved in building an international student training program.
2. Define the benefits of a partnership approach in providing an in-house training program.
3. Describe strategies for integrating international students into ongoing staff training.

OVERVIEW

The Broadmoor Hotel is a 700-room resort nestled at the base of Colorado's Rocky Mountains. Founded in 1918, The Broadmoor Hotel is the oldest five-star, five-diamond resort in the United States and has maintained this status since the award ratings were first established. The eighty-one-year-old resort employs a staff of 1 600 employees to maintain the property's nine restaurants, convention facilities, three 18-hole championship golf courses, and on-site European spa and fitness centre.

As a leader in the hospitality industry, The Broadmoor Hotel developed an on-site training program for international students actively pursuing an education in the hospitality industry. By participating in the program, students learn firsthand many aspects of world-class hotel service standards. In turn, the program participants share their experiences and enthusiasm for the hotel profession.

In 1995 The Broadmoor Hotel began working with the Association for International Practical Training (AIPT) to develop a year-round training program. AIPT (a non-profit organization) promotes international understanding through on-the-job, practical training exchanges for students and professionals. AIPT's mission is to be a leader in international human resource development by conducting high quality experiential training exchanges. These exchanges aim to enhance the ability of all involved to meet the opportunities and challenges of the global economy.

The training program offers students a global training opportunity complementing the hotel's focus on world-class service. The Broadmoor Hotel gains a global perspective, broadens its network of international contacts, and adds well-trained, highly motivated students to its staff for up to 18 months.

IMPLEMENTATION

Students from countries around the world—including Hungary, the Netherlands, Switzerland, Australia, Malaysia, Ireland, France, and the United Kingdom—have been accepted into The Broadmoor Hotel's training program. Most participants are in their third year of an established hospitality program that requires training abroad as part of its curriculum. Other students hold a certificate or degree in hospitality management, but seek skills acquired through on-the-job training in an international setting.

The Broadmoor Hotel accepts approximately 100 students per year (about 20 students over five intake periods). The application process begins when student curricula vitae are sent directly to the hotel's human resource department by participating schools, or through AIPT. Initially, hotel management interviewed students over the phone via a 15- to 20-minute interview conducted in English. Today, hotel staff travel to participating schools to conduct interviews in person. Direct interviews have proved to be more successful at determining a student's work experience, attitude, and language ability. They also provide an opportunity for the students to ask questions. The result is a better "fit" for both the student and the property. (Smaller properties unable to incur such travel costs can contact AIPT about possible assistance in developing a successful selection process.)

On acceptance to the program, The Broadmoor Hotel offers students an advance on program fees and insurance costs, and provides hotel housing for up to 45 days while students locate permanent housing. The hotel provides assistance in finding student lodgings through referrals. Students are responsible for their own travel costs.

The Broadmoor Hotel's human resource department and AIPT developed guidelines for the training program. The program's overall objective is to provide students with an in-depth experience in delivering five-star, five-diamond service at a destination resort. The program is structured so that training opportunities match student interests within the hotel's existing operational structure.

The Broadmoor Hotel's human resource department is credited with developing, monitoring, and evolving the program on-site. Individual training outlines were developed for: the overall training program; training department managers; and each staff position. Specialized training classes were also created for international students requiring English as a second language tutoring and additional training in operations.

AIPT reviews—and must approve—all training outlines and the overall training program as designed by The Broadmoor Hotel.

In preparing department managers for working with international students, key topic areas covered include:

- a student's school
- school curriculum and objectives
- cultural elements of the student's home country
- student expectations
- management's responsibility
- varied training opportunities appropriate to individual student requirements.

AIPT does not visit students on-site. Many schools, however, have representatives visit the hotel to personally review student progress and to discuss future placements. Department managers are required to meet with the school placement officer during these site visits.

The first training positions open to students included food and beverage (both staff and supervisory positions), front office, concierge, and reservations. Today, the program also offers students work in the culinary department.

Students are paid the same rate as their United States counterparts, thus encouraging 100 percent effort in each position. All employees are evaluated at the end of their first 90 working days. AIPT provides a form, which must be completed separately by both student and manager. The Broadmoor Hotel conducts its own 90-day review for each new employee, including all international trainees. Subsequent evaluations fall in line with regular hotel policy.

Specific training programs operate under different time frames, relative to the complexity of the position. Training programs average 12 months each. The shortest training program lasts 11 months. Although a trainee is based out of their home department for the duration of their work experience, students are allowed to shadow or work in other departments of their choice. As most visiting students are travelling with a J-1 training visa, internships can only last 18 months. After completing the 12-month program in their core department, a student may rotate to another of the 20 departments for an additional six months.

Students are also expected to participate in free classes offered in conjunction with the Educational Institute of the American Hotel and Motel Association (AH&MA). Required courses are:

- The Broadmoor Orientation
- Departmental Training
- Keeping the Stars—Five-Star, Five-Diamond Guest Service Training.

Optional class topics include:

- Introduction to the Hospitality Industry
- Hospitality Supervision
- Hospitality Sales and Marketing
- Hospitality Law
- Hospitality Accounting.

There are numerous specialized training courses, which are department-specific.

Classes average 10 weeks in length and are held twice a week in The Broadmoor Hotel's human resources training facilities. Students receive monthly training calendars and may sign up at any time for a class. Students are not limited to certain class subjects, but may find supervisors encourage enrolment in particular classes. Students are not paid for attending these classes, but are eligible for tuition reimbursements from the hotel. The courses contribute towards earning the Educational Institute Certificate in Resort Operations and may also count towards credit at community colleges.

Course instructors include hotel managers, department heads, and executive committee members. These instructors consider the unpaid teaching role as a mentoring role and generally enjoy it. Textbooks are provided by the Educational Institute of the AH&MA. The

Broadmoor Hotel provides additional materials and resources. Bimonthly progress tests and chapter tests are used for class evaluation.

In addition to the class offerings, a special seminar series, initially created for the international students, provides instruction in facilities management, hotel operations, finance, sales and marketing, food and beverage, and human resources. These seminars are offered every six months and last two hours each. The department head, or an executive committee member of the area, teaches each seminar and focusses entirely on how The Broadmoor Hotel operates in these critical areas. Seminar attendance is not mandatory, though a record of attendance is kept and student participation is documented as part of their individual accomplishments. There is no fee to attend the seminar, and students are not paid for attending class. The seminar series is open to all trainees and hotel employees.

RESULTS

After successfully completing their work training, students receive a formal letter of recommendation and a certificate of completion. Although students receive formal credit while training with The Broadmoor Hotel, they do not receive individual grades. AIPT sends student evaluation forms to each manager who then provides feedback on a student's progress. The Broadmoor Hotel also completes individual forms as required by the schools.

Student trainees are given an invaluable experience, learning what it takes to provide and maintain the level of service associated with a five-star and five-diamond rating. Many trainees report that service-level demands far exceed any work that they have experienced in their own country.

The Broadmoor Hotel has benefited from the enthusiasm and energy shared by international students who possess the poise, professional standards, and desire to succeed in their chosen career. Students are keen to develop their guest service skills, language skills, and cultural skills. Over 250 students have trained at The Broadmoor Hotel. This experience has helped many gain a good management position in their home countries.

WTTC Human Resource Centre COMMENT

Student exchange programs have been around for decades. With the assistance of associations like AIPT, and with current communication and access, hotels and resorts can bring in the best and brightest from around the world. The human resource department at The Broadmoor Hotel has shown how it has benefited from the intake of students from hospitality management programs worldwide. By having departmental managers from various hotel departments serve as mentors and providing a structured training program, this hotel has brought an international perspective to its business and helped to broaden its network of international contacts.

KEY TERMS:

exchange program
mentoring
vocational training
on-the-job training
evaluation

cross-cultural initiatives
training visa
world-class
curricula vitae

 **www.broadmoor.com**

DISCUSSION QUESTIONS

1. What advantages does a graduate from this program have on return to his/her home country?
2. List five major benefits to The Broadmoor Hotel in providing the international student work/experience program.
3. List two partnerships in this good practice and identify the benefits to each side of the partnerships.

Canada
Westin Nova Scotian

Submitted by: Carol Thorn

EMPLOYEES CUSTOMIZE THE SERVICE CULTURE

… For a hotel situated off the beaten track, in a not so convenient area of the downtown core, it is the associates' "can do" attitude and desire to meet guest expectations that creates a service culture like no other.

> *"The Westin Nova Scotian is dedicated to 100 percent guest satisfaction. We take that pledge very seriously and our efforts continue to pay off. As we strive to meet the challenges that come our way, we will stay focussed on our service and training strategies as strictly as we do on our business and financial goals. The business cycle is fluid; training at the Westin Nova Scotian is also fluid and ever changing, yet still permanent."*
>
> *Management, Westin Nova Scotian*

LEARNING OUTCOMES

1. Explain why staff attitude is an important component of a hotel's service culture.
2. Discuss ways that training encourages staff to exceed customer expectations.
3. Describe how the human resource department tracks property training.

OVERVIEW

The Westin Nova Scotian is a completely renovated landmark hotel offering elegant accommodations in the heart of downtown Halifax. This seventy-year-old heritage property has 296 guest rooms and suites and the largest hotel meeting facilities in the downtown region.

Situated off the beaten track, the hotel has had to rely on more than location or physical plant amenities to succeed. In fact, many local competitors dismissed the property as a contender for the lucrative business traveller and convention group market. To entice guests to stay at the property, and win repeat business, the Westin Nova Scotian understands that its competitive edge is in the ambience of the heritage property and its choice of uniquely sociable employees.

Staff at the Westin Nova Scotian is enthusiastic, dedicated, and works with a can-do attitude! This is a direct result of the hotel's recruiting and hiring practices, departmental training, motivational and incentive programs, and ongoing training opportunities for career development. The hotel maintains a culture where associates offer their very best service to each guest, with encouragement and ongoing support from supervisors.

IMPLEMENTATION

Due to its location, the Westin Nova Scotian needed to distinguish itself from its competitors. Operating as a historic landmark property was not enough to attract guests and win repeat business. The hotel needed a strong competitive advantage.

The hotel could offer the cheapest prices in the marketplace, but management wanted to win customer recognition by developing a valued product—not through a "price war." Management thus chose to build clientele through exceptional guest service. Employee training in customer service excellence was therefore considered a top priority.

Standardized training was an option, and has worked for many global corporations and franchises. But the Westin Nova Scotian was unique in the Westin chain. By tailoring its hiring and recruiting systems, it would supplement standardized training. To complement the ambience of the historic building, management customized the Westin Nova Scotian's service culture. Successful training would start with the hiring of service-minded individuals.

Recruiting and Hiring

The Westin Nova Scotian believes that it is an individual's desire to serve that will make them successful in the hotel business. Teaching staff to perform required jobs is the easy part. It's finding the right person who will fit in with the service culture that is the challenge!

When recruiting new associates, the human resource department at the Westin Nova Scotian first looks for people who "light up" when they talk about serving guests.

Applicants are screened in advance so that managers are able to quickly find a "fit" when looking to hire staff. Managers have the final hire decision, as they are accountable for staff performance.

Departmental Training

New hire orientation sessions teach new associates the company's core values and its guest commitment: "To you we pledge 100 percent service excellence." Employees themselves pass this service message on to new hires. Employees demonstrate the message through their service, and talk about it as being the hotel's most important selling point. All new employees receive a free night's stay at the hotel so that they can experience the guest service and sample the property's services and amenities.

Standards-based programs (procedural, cleanliness, and physical plant-based) developed by the Westin Corporation are focussed on exceeding the Westin customer's expectations. Westin Corporation offers these programs to franchisees like the Westin Nova Scotian to assist hotels in meeting guest service expectations. These standards, which are audited by the Westin Franchise division, are used as topics for five-minute pre-shift training "mini sessions" in all Westin Nova Scotian's departments. This allows staff to understand topics and issues that are not only departmentally specific, but have an impact over the entire property, such as:

- up-selling
- using the guest's name
- video checkout
- changing folio style
- feature menu item of the day
- up-selling room service
- recording due-backs
- taking phone orders
- holiday functions
- water testing
- minibar procedures
- rate strategy
- quoting times for room service orders

Every month, the department management team outlines topics to be covered and documents this training in the property-wide training summary. This summary is prepared monthly and submitted to New Castle Hotels' corporate vice-president of human resources.

Ongoing Training

While these sessions and orientation are important and do contribute to the hotel's success, associate training goes further. The property publicizes monthly training calendars that allow all associates, at every level of the organization, to enhance learning and future professional status. Topics include:

- Service 101
- Back to Basics and Then Some
- Managing Time
- Stress Management
- Writing and Conducting Performance Appraisals.

Different classes are available for different audiences. Classes noted as "open" are available to all associates who would like to learn new skills and prepare themselves for possible advancement within the company. Other classes are audience-specific. For example, labour relations training courses are restricted to managers to create an environment where they feel comfortable discussing sensitive issues in an open forum, without line associates present. In contrast, classes such as Writing and Conducting Performance Appraisals, Managing Time, and Stress Management are open to all staff. Open classes are free to employees and attendance is voluntary.

These in-house educational opportunities are developed specifically for Westin Nova Scotian associates, and are based on the results of a needs assessment completed in 2000. Classes are fine-tuned to departmental schedules and the different professional disciplines on site. Training is delivered by the hotel's master trainer, or by certified trainers on staff. All programs are developed using a combination of purchased videos, "home grown" case studies, PowerPoint material, quizzes, and even homework assignments.

> *"As a trainer, I have worked in other jurisdictions, and I have never seen the enthusiasm for education that I have experienced in Nova Scotia. Locally, there is a strong interest in tourism as a career. The employee base tends to be well educated and values ongoing education in the workplace."*
>
> *Carol Thorn, Master Trainer*
> *Westin Nova Scotian*

Motivational and Incentive Programs

The Westin Nova Scotian supports a variety of reward and recognition programs. The Gottcha program is a corporate-wide initiative that recognizes the "right" service noted "on-the-spot." Employees earn coupons redeemable for prizes. The purpose of this program is to "catch the associate doing something right—instantly."

Along with the Gottcha program, the hotel supports an Associate of the Month and a Leader of the Quarter initiative. There is also an annual celebration for "of the year" winners, service awards, and attendance awards. To continuously acknowledge the value of recognition programs, the hotel's reward and recognition program committee carefully reviews these programs and makes improvements on an ongoing basis.

> *"We get letters every month from guests who are thrilled with our service and their experience at our hotel.*
>
> *One guest recently wrote to say, 'I was very impressed with your demeanour and overall handling of my call and questions. You are to be commended on your professionalism and abilities.'*
>
> *Another stated upon his departure, 'You are a skilled negotiator in dealing with guests and taking care of their needs,' referring to one of our associates who helped him deal with a problem he needed resolving."*

RESULTS

The Westin Nova Scotian is proud of its reputation and attributes many of its awards to the can-do attitude of its associates. The hotel has twice won the prestigious Conde Naste Traveler's Award (1998 and 1999) acknowledging the property as one of the "Top Hotels in the World." In 2000, the Northwest Travellers Association named the hotel the "Best Business Hotel in Nova Scotia."

At the Westin Nova Scotian, all staff are guaranteed to have at least eight hours of training opportunities available to them each year. This is the hotel's training guarantee. To better meet the needs of all associates, classes are offered in the evening and on Saturdays.

The human resource department tracks all on-property training. Behaviours and skills learned in the classroom are directly tied to performance expectations. Associate files reflect training and educational efforts. The department also looks at how the hotel's training plans impact on guest service and employee satisfaction by comparing results from the guest satisfaction index and employee satisfaction surveys of previous years.

WTTC HUMAN RESOURCE CENTRE COMMENT

Given the location of this property and the historical ambience it provides, providing better service was considered to be the best way to gain market share and build value in the hotel experience. Hiring service-minded people is an important factor in the Westin Nova Scotian's success. Tying its guest and employee satisfaction survey results to a flexible training strategy is necessary in a changing marketplace. The hotel's commitment to provide further training creates a more qualified and loyal staff, thereby reducing turnover.

KEY TERMS

hiring	career development
interview process	on-the-job training
departmental training	competitive advantage
service culture	franchisee
reward and recognition programs	performance expectations

 **www.newcastlehotels.com**

DISCUSSION QUESTIONS

1. As the hotel's human resource director, prepare a list of interview questions helpful in targeting the kind of employee the Westin Nova Scotian seeks.

2. What other kinds of open classes would you consider valuable to an employee working at the Westin Nova Scotian?

3. Discuss the incentive program in reference to short-term and long-term benefits to the employees. What would you suggest as additional ideas or approaches?

Building Job Skills and Values: Job Readiness, Basic Skills Development, and Employee Relations

Australia
Melbourne Airport

Submitted by: Janice Jordan

MELBOURNE AIRPORT

MELBOURNE HOSTS PROGRAM–
INNOVATIVE AIRPORT TRAINING

… In a joint venture with private and public tourism industry partners, Melbourne Airport facilitated a program that provided unemployed workers in the community with valuable training experience in tourism visitor services. In this win-win situation, Melbourne Airport benefited from having a motivated team of staff-in-training able to welcome travellers at the departures, arrivals, and international baggage hall desks.

LEARNING OUTCOMES

1. Identify the key curriculum components in a tourism job re-entry training program.
2. Illustrate how mentoring and on-the-job training are effective tools in an employment re-entry curriculum.
3. Design approaches to on-the-job training which incorporate confidence building and motivational elements.

4. Recognize the advantages of a nationally accredited curriculum that provides for future educational opportunities and job mobility.

OVERVIEW

Melbourne Airport, located in Victoria, Australia, is one of the world's leading airports, and serves an increasing number of inbound foreign travellers. As a predominantly destination airport, the international terminal has become a central focus of airport services. To meet the needs of inbound traffic, Melbourne Airport has expanded airport visitor services to include:

- **Travellers Information Service Desk**—a full-service information centre with daily hours corresponding to flight schedules.
- **Groups and Tours Desk**—offering reception facilities to serve passengers attending local conferences, conventions, and major events.
- **Welcome to Melbourne Gallery**—showcasing local artwork and photography while highlighting Melbourne and the region of Victoria.

In a joint community initiative, Melbourne Airport also helped to develop and implement the Melbourne Hosts program—an Australia Certificate Level 1 training course in tourism (visitor services) at the airport. It is a work experience development program designed to provide coordinated training and skill development to local, unemployed people seeking jobs in tourism. It is currently the only tourism services training program in Victoria combining classroom study with four months of work experience.

IMPLEMENTATION

The Melbourne Hosts program was developed in collaboration with Melbourne Airport, Tourism Training Victoria, local technical school Kangan Batman Technical and Further Education (TAFE), and Tourism Victoria. The objective of the program is to support the local community (which has been experiencing high unemployment since the mid-1990s), and to provide quality customer service at Melbourne Airport. Each of these tourism partners donated time, sponsorship, and expertise to create the program, and each continues to provide peer guidance and input by having a representative on the Consultative Committee overseeing the program.

Melbourne Airport identified the need for expanded visitor services and approached Kangan Batman TAFE (a government-funded college) to provide subject lecturers and administrative support for the educational component of the program. Both Kangan Batman TAFE and Melbourne Airport developed the program's course content and Tourism Training Victoria provided the curriculum guidelines. Melbourne Airport donates the facilities, overall coordination, and both supervisory and support staff training free of charge. Program participants pay Kangan Batman TAFE regular attendance fees for the program, which includes classroom tuition and practical on-the-job training. Government support is through Tourism Victoria which contributes a great deal of industry support and advice. Tourism Victoria also covers the cost of the uniforms, thereby further reducing costs to participants.

Melbourne Airport

A Melbourne Hosts participant provides visitor service at Melbourne Airport.

The program, now in its third year, took approximately one year to develop, beginning with an intake of 20 students. Once operational, the program was placed under the direction of a full-time management employee in the airport operations department at Melbourne Airport. In addition to other duties within the department, the Melbourne Hosts coordinator oversees the operations of the program and works on-site interviewing potential participants, training, managing, and mentoring. The coordinator also provides job-seeking assistance to each participant throughout the 16-week program.

Participants in the nationally accredited program develop skills in the following:

- knowledge of Australian tourism destinations;
- knowledge of accommodation and tour booking procedures;
- effective cross-cultural communication; and
- personal confidence and presentation.

Each course subject is structured around a designated set of learning outcomes, allowing flexibility for course modification as the program gains maturity. To ensure that industry standards continue to be met, participants are supervised on a weekly basis by the program coordinator, and the overall program is monitored by the sponsor's Consultative Committee, which meets on a quarterly basis.

All areas of study are nationally accredited tourism subjects, with the exception of personal confidence and presentation—a specially developed subject where students receive approximately six hours of training on the importance of image, personal hygiene, and professional dress. The program advertises for participants in Melbourne newspapers and local community papers. Approximately 20 to 24 participants are accepted at each intake period, following an application process and interview. The program is delivered over a 16-week period, combining classroom education with practical on-the-job experience. Through the course, the program delivers approximately 150 hours of classroom instruction and 150 hours of work training experience. Classroom instructors and work experience trainers differ, allowing for variety in training techniques.

Local colleges provide program instructors for certificate subjects. Melbourne Airport specialists instruct in the areas of:

- airport familiarization, safety, and security (including the Airport Emergency Plan)
- customs and immigration
- airlines' schedules
- survey techniques
- mobile-radio use
- retail
- environment awareness
- workplace behaviour, personal presentation, and self-esteem.

Classroom instruction averages 12 hours per week, delivered in four separate three-hour sessions, three days a week during normal business hours. Classes are held in a designated homeroom/training room at Melbourne Airport. Instructors have access to such training tools as video equipment, whiteboards, and flipcharts, and classroom activity includes role-play, lectures, guest speakers, group assignments, and presentations.

As part of the program, 12 hours per week are devoted to unpaid work experience within the airport. Because Melbourne Airport is open 24 hours per day, seven days a week, hands-on training hours are widely distributed and take place concurrently with classroom study. Airport information desks at both the arrivals and departures halls (public areas) are staffed by both airport employees and program participants. Melbourne Hosts participants also work in the baggage reclaim hall (a secure area).

Students are responsible for assigned reading and assignments, making up an estimated 40 hours of out-of-classroom study per week. Program enrolment is continuous, with a new intake approximately every 16 weeks. Classes overlap for two weeks so that the outgoing group supports the new group over the initial training period. Participants must be 18 years of age. Overall, the age of participants varies widely and most students attending have had no previous work experience in tourism.

Participants who complete the program receive counselling to help them find a job either within the airport, or in the local community. Graduation from the program does not guarantee students a position with Melbourne Airport or retailers, and the airport does not require employees to have Certificate Level 1 as a job requirement. However, knowledge of the facility and student visibility throughout the program are definitely advantages. According to an April 1999 survey finding, approximately 35 percent of program graduates have obtained employment at Melbourne Airport (many in the retail sector) while approximately 25 percent have found employment in the local tourism industry.

"We have actively developed the services and facilities available to all airport users and continually look to improve what is on offer at the airport. Passengers have ranked us highly for these initiatives, but recognition from peers and colleagues in such a competitive industry is always a fantastic feeling."

Terry Morgan, Chief Executive
Melbourne Airport

RESULTS

Melbourne Airport authorities consider quality customer service an integral part of excellence in airport operations. The Melbourne Hosts program is only one of many initiatives put in place to improve customer satisfaction.

Up to the year 2000, 161 participants had completed the program, with approximately 97 percent gaining successful employment. Graduates are encouraged to continue their education and training through additional certificate programs, leading up to a diploma in tourism offered through a number of area colleges.

In 1998 and 1999, Melbourne Airport won the Victoria Award for "General Tourism Services" and the Australian Airports Association voted Melbourne Airport the "Major Australian Airport of the Year" in 1999. These tourism awards focus on quality of facilities, provision of services, marketing of the tourism product, and customer service.

WTTC HUMAN RESOURCE CENTRE COMMENT

We can list numerous benefits of this nationally accredited certificate program in visitor services. In the short term, graduates gain invaluable, practical hands-on experience in Australia's tourism industry. Similar welfare reform programs suggest that possibly more important to the participant is the confidence gained through the peer counselling during the program and after graduation. Graduates can choose to immediately seek front line entry into the tourism industry, or make a long-term career decision and further their studies by completing a diploma in tourism services. This is a peer-training good practice, illustrating a community initiative that works jointly at public, private, and educational levels.

Note: The Melbourne Hosts program operated for three and a half years, by which time local colleges had established contacts to manage their own work experience programs. The Consultative Committee is no longer needed, but participants in past programs still have access to the coordinator for personal references. Melbourne Airport was delighted with the success of the Hosts program, and is now investigating other community-based initiatives.

KEY TERMS

visitor services

training partnerships

employment re-entry

occupational skills training

peer guidance

sponsorship

mentoring

national accreditation

 www.melbourne-airport.com.au

DISCUSSION QUESTIONS

1. List the major benefits gained through employment re-entry training as described in this good practice, as they apply to the employer, the community, and the participant.

2. Why is peer guidance a central part of this program, and how do you think it improves the success rates for students?

3. What advantage does this program offer in terms of future job mobility and employment? Provide examples.

Canada
Fairmont Hotels & Resorts

Submitted by: Lyle Thompson

HOTELS & RESORTS

GREEN PARTNERSHIPS PROGRAM

… A hotel making an environmental difference is dependent upon the willingness of its staff.

LEARNING OUTCOMES

1. Explain how listening to staff feedback and encouraging employee commitment affects the success of a company program.

2. Explain why standardizing Green Teams was necessary for the success of the Green Partnership Program.

3. Describe the international model Fairmont Hotels & Resorts has set in creating environmentally friendly hotel properties.

"I bring you good news from a company that has one of the most comprehensive programs in the industry: Once you make the commitment towards strong environmental stewardship, you will find that your employees will feel better about their jobs, your guests will appreciate your efforts, you will save money in all sorts of unexpected ways, and you will help keep your destination competitive."

Ann Layton, Vice President Public Affairs & Communications
Fairmont Hotels & Resorts

OVERVIEW

In 1991 Canadian Pacific Hotels (now known as Fairmont Hotels & Resorts) conducted a nationwide survey of its 10 000 employees. The survey researched interest levels for an employee-based hotel environmental program. A total of 2 472 questionnaires were returned, representing 28.9 percent of the employees in Canada.

Survey responses revealed that:

- 95.6 percent of employees considered environmental protection an important public issue;
- 92.2 percent felt it was important for their hotel to become more environmentally responsible;
- 91.9 percent strongly supported the introduction of more environmentally friendly practices within their hotel;
- 88.8 percent were proud that their hotel wanted to be recognized as environmentally friendly;
- 82.3 percent said they were willing to give extra time and effort without compensation in support of on-the-job environmental improvements; and
- 64 percent expressed concern about the impact of their job-related duties on the environment.

The survey results clearly indicated that Fairmont Hotels & Resorts could expect employee support in the design and introduction of what soon became known as the Green Partnership Program. Since the initial concept in 1991, Fairmont Hotels & Resorts has established itself as a worldwide leader in the environmental management of hotels.

IMPLEMENTATION

The first step in developing the Green Partnership Program was for hotel management to establish a Canada-wide network of environmental committees called "Green Teams." Green Teams were simply a group of employees who collected conservation-related ideas from others working at that property. The Green Teams, formed on-site at all participating properties, were thus a key communication tool and became the foundation for the program.

For all Green Teams to be consistent, a standard format was refined in 1997. Each team has a maximum of 10 elected members. Members come from a variety of departments, including engineering, public relations, and food and beverage. The "environmental champion," who makes sure that meetings are scheduled 10 times yearly, for a period of one hour, chairs each team. Meeting minutes and agendas are recorded and submitted to the corporate office.

As a result of standardizing Green Teams across the nation: employee participation and commitment increased; a diverse, cross-functional team developed; and property-level goals were established and streamlined.

In 1997, Fairmont Hotels & Resorts launched a campaign to "renew" employee commitment to the Green Partnership Program. The company wanted employees involved in establishing future program objectives. Once again, employees were interviewed and surveyed, this time focussing on "property-specific" environmental successes and challenges. Phase II was born out of employee responses and an in-depth survey of industry-wide best environmental practices.

In-room recycling programs have been successful at Fairmont Hotels & Resorts.

Green Partnership Program—Phase II

Information gathered in the second survey helped Fairmont re-address important issues and update goals and objectives, which were found to be important to employees. An outline of 10 initiatives—recorded and distributed to all environmental committees—included the following suggestions:

1. Inform new employees of the company-wide Green Partnership Program during orientation.
2. Obtain full Audubon accreditation for all Fairmont Hotels & Resorts golf courses.
3. Offer an environmentally sensitive meeting option to guests in the form of an "Eco-Meet" product.
4. Have standardized in-room environmental materials in all guest rooms.
5. Ensure that all used soaps and amenities are being donated to charity or returned to suppliers for recycling.
6. Divert organic waste from landfill through the use of industrial composting alternatives.
7. Donate more unused food and prepared meals to food banks.
8. Develop local ecotourism partnerships and promote them as "Fairmont Green Tours."
9. Participate actively in Seeing the Forest AND the Trees incentive program.
10. Encourage all Canadian properties to participate in "Be My Beluga" program to help protect the endangered beluga whales in the St. Lawrence River. (Properties are encouraged to participate in programs to protect severely endangered species in their area.)

Corporate initiatives in Phase II included suggestions to:

1. Establish an office of environmental affairs.
2. Formalize the environmental committees' role at hotels.
3. Conduct a national review to determine "where we are now," and solicit feedback on Green Partnership—Phase II direction.
4. Identify best practices for benchmarking purposes.
5. Create a new list of property-level goals based on best practices and employee feedback.
6. Motivate employees to continue making positive changes.
7. Create a national Environmental Management Systems (EMS) program.
8. Create standardized in-room guest information materials for use nationally.
9. Establish an environmental charitable donation project.

Environmental Review

A five-month environmental review identified progress and challenges associated with the Green Partnership Program. The review examined existing practices and critiqued already established EMS standards. Topics focussed on included: waste management; pollution prevention; hazardous waste management; energy conservation; water conservation; environmentally responsible procurement; employee awareness; public communications; community outreach; and design issues.

The environmental review consisted of:

- property visits to all hotels;
- individual interviews with key personnel;
- meetings with each environmental committee to review the Green Partnership Program—Phase I, and to present Phase II;
- a review of corporate and property environmental practices, achievements, and opportunities; and
- developing an environmental database and benchmarking system for the purpose of information exchange.

The environmental review concluded with a report highlighting environmental practices taking place throughout the hotel chain, including an environmental profile of each hotel property.

Environmental review results, and the new goals and initiatives for Phase II, were presented in 1998 at the company's inaugural Environmental Conference and Science Fair, held at the Fairmont Royal York in Toronto, Canada.

The conference was attended by an international panel of guest speakers—from Walt Disney World, Accor Hotels, Green Globe, and Negril, Jamaica—as well as participants from each Fairmont property. Seminar topics covered composting, purchasing initiatives, energy efficiency, and environmentally friendly meeting planning. The Science Fair was a unique chance for Fairmont Hotels & Resorts to display its best environmental practices to management, company employees, and the public.

Seeing the Forest AND the Trees—Employee Motivation

The evaluation and benchmarking process developed during Phase I helped to establish realistic goals and initiatives for many Fairmont properties. The process also revealed a need for an employee motivation program.

Seeing the Forest AND the Trees is the Fairmont Hotels & Resorts employee incentive program. Throughout the program, properties' Green Teams earn "Fairmont Trees" reward stickers when they achieve predetermined environmental goals. These stickers are awarded for a wide variety of activities, such as reducing solid waste, conserving energy, donating amenities to women's shelters, or conducting a recycling tour for a local school.

Annually, the hotel with the largest "forest of Fairmont Trees" is named the "Environmental Hotel of the Year." All 10 committee members of that hotel's Green Team receive an all-expenses-paid eco-exchange to the Caribbean. Working with partners from the Jamaican Hotel & Tourism Association (JHTA) and the Caribbean Hotel Association (CHA), this program rewards active Green Team members while encouraging the exchange of ideas and information about conservation.

Seeing the Forest AND the Trees is a completely self-sustaining program supported by suppliers with a strong commitment to environmental stewardship. To date, participating companies include Ecolab, Stannair, BC Hydro, Unisource, Panasonic Canada, and TerraChoice Environmental Services. The Fairmont properties are now in heavy competition to outdo one another with their environmental initiatives, and employees are hard at work "growing their forests."

RESULTS

Efforts by both hotel management and staff have allowed the company to reap significant cost savings in all aspects of hotel operations. For example:

- Through the optional sheet and towel exchange program for guests, in 1999 the Fairmont Chateau Whistler saved $126 000 in laundry fees.
- The Fairmont Jasper Park Lodge separates 313 130 kilograms of organic wastes a year through the hotel's composting program. This saved the hotel $17 537 in 1998 alone.
- Fairmont Le Chateau Frontenac saves $14 667 yearly by using linen hats rather than disposable ones for kitchen chefs.
- In a building with over 34 050 light fixtures—1 920 bulbs in the guest bathrooms and 5 500 bulbs in the guest rooms—the Fairmont Royal York has switched from incandescent to compact fluorescent bulbs, saving $57 135 annually. In public areas and staircases, over 773 bulbs have been switched with an additional savings of $23 095 each year.
- To decrease excess packaging, Fairmont Chateau Lake Louise has eliminated the purchase of individual servings of yogurt. Yogurt is now served in various reusable dishes from bulk containers. The hotel uses approximately 80 kilos of yogurt per week, saving the hotel $46 072 a year.

Fairmont Hotels & Resorts has won many provincial, national, and international environmental awards including the 1996 Green Hotelier of the Year award presented by the International Hotel Association, and at the Fairmont Royal York, the Recycling Council of Ontario's 1996 Waste Minimization Silver Award.

WTTC HUMAN RESOURCE CENTRE COMMENT

Fairmont Hotels & Resorts carefully surveyed employees to determine their support for a national environment program. Encouraging employee responsibility and involvement through in-house environmental committees developed a sense of ownership and loyalty. The program has resulted in both national and international environmental awards, which recognize and applaud employee commitment to sound environmental practices. The program continues to encourage participation and new initiatives keep employees interested and committed to providing better environmental stewardship.

KEY TERMS

benchmark	environmental stewardship
evaluation	environmental management systems
survey	conservation
motivation	standardization
incentive program	best practices

 **www.fairmont.com**

DISCUSSION QUESTIONS

1. In this model, how does Fairmont Hotels & Resorts incorporate employee, guest, and executive suggestions into its overall environmental planning?

2. As an employee, what would you suggest be done to expand this program, and thus make properties even more environmentally friendly?

3. What other kinds of motivational programs can you think of to keep employees interested in practising good on-site conservation initiatives?

United States
Marriott International

Submitted by: Fred Kramer

ENHANCING SELF-SUFFICIENCY THROUGH EMPLOYMENT OPPORTUNITIES

… A proven, reality-based training program that has helped thousands of disadvantaged individuals develop the skills for full-time employment and careers with Marriott and other hospitality industry employers.

LEARNING OUTCOMES

1. Identify skills which a welfare recipient returning to the workforce needs in order to successfully obtain and hold a job.
2. List the factors that make a corporate-sponsored employment and training program a success.
3. Learn to recognize a program delivery format which fosters personal development through clear communication and a positive working environment.

> *"Why do I work on the Pathways program? I find the program to be very rewarding, especially when I see what it means to the participants and their families. I'll never forget the day a graduate of the program told me her children were proud that she was working. Now that's proof that this program really works. It not only works for Marriott, but also for the people we help."*
>
> *Fred Kramer, Director*
> *Marriott's Community Employment and Training Programs*

OVERVIEW

Marriott's Pathways to Independence: A Training-for-Jobs Program has trained more than 2 700 people in 45 cities for employee positions in hotels, senior living services, and reservation centres. What makes this program different is that it teaches participants the skills necessary to obtain and hold a job. The program addresses factors that may be standing in the way of an individual holding onto a job. These obstacles include poor communication skills, low self-esteem, inappropriate behaviour, underdeveloped work ethic, tardiness, and absenteeism, as well as personal challenges such as finding reliable transportation and child care.

Considered a national model, Pathways to Independence is a large-scale, corporate-sponsored training and employment effort within the United States. It was designed to move welfare recipients to a work setting. Participants who successfully complete the program are offered full-time employment, with benefits, at a Marriott business or with another hospitality employer. The program is a win-win situation for both the participants and for Marriott.

IMPLEMENTATION

Marriott Community Employment and Training Programs created Pathways to Independence in 1990 to address the company's need for developing and retaining qualified employees for Marriott's diverse hospitality businesses. The community employment and training department at Marriott International administers the program from Washington, DC.

The program provides trainees with valuable job skills necessary to gain entry-level positions and build successful careers within the hospitality industry. This training goes beyond job-specific skills to include practical skills (outlined below) that will serve participants well at any job and in their personal lives.

Job acquisition skills
Completing job applications and preparing résumés, developing job interview skills, and exploring career opportunities within the hospitality industry.

Skills for retaining a job
Building skills and attitudes critical for success in entry-level positions and in career development, such as:

- committing to long-term employment;
- developing a positive attitude;
- being dependable and reliable;
- contributing as a team member;
- serving customers and handling complaints successfully;
- communicating effectively with customers (face-to-face and on the telephone);
- accepting and offering constructive criticism;
- appreciating and working effectively with diverse groups of people; and
- adhering to grooming and hygiene policies.

Basic safety
Preventing workplace accidents and food-borne illnesses, using basic first aid, and applying the Heimlich maneuver.

Personal life issues

Building confidence and self-esteem, managing and coping with stress, setting and achieving goals, and balancing work and personal life.

Skills for personal financial management

Formulating a personal budget, meeting expenses with entry-level wages, establishing and managing credit, opening and managing a chequing account, and differentiating between necessities and luxuries.

Pathways to Independence is an intensive, six-week, pre-employment program that typically trains eight to eighteen participants.

Written and designed by experienced Marriott managers, the Pathways to Independence curriculum assists individuals in overcoming barriers to employment before they are hired. Other goals of the Pathways to Independence program include:

- providing graduates with full-time positions in the hospitality industry;
- increasing Marriott's pool of qualified applicants for entry-level positions;
- ensuring that individuals are fully qualified and possess basic life skills;
- contributing to the economic development of communities where Marriott does business;
- providing participants with a transition from public assistance programs to full-time careers;
- creating direct links between organizations that support individuals in need of job training and businesses in need of qualified employees;
- establishing partnerships with funding sources and other agencies to share training costs; and
- customizing and updating the curriculum to meet the needs of both participants and the hospitality industry.

In addition to 60 hours of classroom instruction, participants undergo 120 hours of occupational training. Actual Marriott managers and supervisors conduct this training on site at designated Marriott businesses. The occupational training component features worksite activities such as job shadowing (working one-on-one with existing Marriott employees) and hands-on practice in all work settings. Pathways to Independence trainees wear Marriott uniforms and build effective communication skills by working directly with Marriott guests, co-workers, managers, and supervisors. This ensures that the training is reality-based and current with the needs of the hospitality industry.

Pathways to Independence is a bona fide training program. Depending on the structure of the training contract, some training programs are paid while others are unpaid. Trainees do not displace any current Marriott employees, nor do they cause a reduction in employee work hours. Experienced Marriott human resources and management professionals evaluate, test, and counsel participants. Once participants successfully complete the program, they are offered full-time positions, with benefits, at a Marriott business. To help them onto a successful career path, program participants continue to receive appropriate training and counselling.

A strength of the Pathways to Independence program is its flexibility. The program can be tailored to accommodate individuals with disabilities, public assistance recipients, and those who have little or no work experience. Because Marriott continues to update and enhance Pathways to Independence, the company ensures that the program continues to meet the needs of participants and the hospitality industry.

RESULTS

Pathways to Independence has received numerous awards. These awards reflect the program's ability to prepare individuals for the world of work in general, and, more specifically, entry-level jobs that lead to a career in the hospitality industry.

- Marriott was awarded a $3.5 million (US) competitive grant by the United States Department of Labour to train and employ another 1 000 people through Pathways to Independence.
- Marriott also received the first annual Welfare to Work Partnership Award for the Pathways to Independence program.
- On average, the Pathways to Independence program has an 80 percent graduation rate and a 55 percent retention rate.

Because many of the skills taught in the program are applicable to all work situations, other companies have expressed interest in hiring graduates of the program. In addition, many businesses outside the hospitality industry have approached Marriott for assistance in developing their own training-for-jobs programs.

The vested interest of both participants and instructors is another reason the program has been successful. Participants understand that their potential employer is training them. Managers and supervisors know that they are training individuals who may become their employees. With the enactment of welfare reform legislation, programs such as Pathways to Independence are in great demand throughout the United States. To meet this need, Marriott is interested in expanding the program to other cities and exploring partnership opportunities with funding sources and community-based organizations.

WTTC Human Resource Centre COMMENT

The reasons why Pathways to Independence is a proven success are numerous: lower cost per placement (by eliminating the expense of using separate training institutions and outside job placement services); guarantee of full-time job offer; job retention; high quality, reality-based training; and innovation. Marriott, in turn, is in a better position to meet the challenges of developing a qualified workforce by assuming responsibility for training individuals who are not otherwise qualified. This good practice is a model for businesses outside the hospitality industry and an example of a program that will remain viable, as it is flexible and easily adaptable to the specific needs of the partner agencies and the participants.

KEY TERMS

occupational skills training

welfare reform

sponsored training

entry-level job skills

self-sufficiency

practical life skills

job shadowing

 **www.marriott.com**

DISCUSSION QUESTIONS

1. Explain how Marriott has created an environment where program participants are readily accepted at their training workplace.

2. Expand on the win-win situation that the Pathways to Independence program offers to both program participants and Marriott. List the benefits for both.

3. Choose a tourism sector (other than hospitality) and explain how a program concept such as this might be applied.

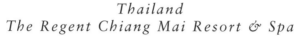

Thailand
The Regent Chiang Mai Resort & Spa

Submitted by: Pattra Jonqcharoemkulchai

MOBILE ENGLISH CLASSES

. . . A uniquely flexible and employee-friendly English language program takes learning to the workplace environment through its mobile classroom program.

LEARNING OUTCOMES

1. Explain how management created a flexible on-site training program and how progress is monitored.

2. Discuss how an English language training program can be customized and modified to suit the needs of the audience.

3. Relate why employees feel comfortable and gain proficiency in mobile English language skills training workshops.

OVERVIEW

The Regent Chiang Mai Resort & Spa (Regent Resort) is located in the beautiful Mae Rim Valley, just a quick hour's flight north of bustling Bangkok, Thailand. This Four Seasons Hotel attracts an international clientele seeking a world-class spa and Thai culture. Guests of the resort live in Lanna-style pavilions decorated with rich Thai materials and fabrics, each overlooking gardens, terraced rice paddies, and mountain views. There are also 13 residential suites complete with a Mae Baan (live-in housekeeper) and accompanying guest and children's bedrooms.

Amidst such luxury, guest expectations are high. Among many other necessary job skills, the Regent Resort's 240-plus staff is required to speak English. As nearly all staff is of Thai background, management provides training in English language skills and encourages language practice throughout the workday.

During high occupancy season, management was faced with the challenge of not only finding the space and time to run English language training sessions, but also identifying how to encourage staff to attend classes. To provide staff with continuous training while at the same time encourage attendance, the Regent Resort developed a new format for language instruction.

IMPLEMENTATION

The Regent Resort established English language training classes that were "mobile." This meant instruction could take place anywhere within the resort. Mobile English Class was a unique new training format which provided a platform for year-round staff training, regardless of resort occupancy level and staff workload.

Instruction takes place during short sessions (generally 40 minutes to one hour) during midday, when morning and afternoon shifts overlap. Teaching is conducted in appropriate department areas, such as in the restaurant between mealtimes for servers and in vacant guestrooms or gardens for housekeeping staff. Class size averages five to 12 persons depending on the department, and session content is predominantly conversational, focussing on real work situations.

Participating departments include:

- engineering (electricians, technicians, mechanics, and head gardener)
- housekeeping (supervisors)
- food and beverage (supervisors, captains, and servers)
- Tennis & Health Club employees.

Language instruction is also provided for contracted limousine chauffeurs who work in direct contact with resort guests.

One session per day is offered in each work area, two or three times per week. Due to the large number of employees in housekeeping and food and beverage, these departments offer additional sessions to room attendants, restaurant servers, and captains.

In terms of conducting the English language sessions, in-house trainers include the on-site training manager, the director of the Tennis & Health Club, and the director of public relations. All on-site language instructors are certified in language proficiency, hold a master's degree, and have three to five years working experience within the resort.

Class training techniques include role-playing, paired work activities, games, and the use of authentic props when appropriate. For example, a session for room attendants might occur in a vacant guestroom, the topic concentrating on "items frequently requested by guests," with props consisting of towels, a bathrobe, and bottled water. Other teaching tools include flash cards (vocabulary and/or pictures), handouts, cassette tape drills, and listening practice. The session objective is to make learning fun, quick, and, most importantly, relevant.

Employees are "tested" informally by role-playing their comprehension of session topics. Employees with perfect class attendance receive a small award, such as an English book, and are photographed with the resort's general manager for display on the staff notice board. Additional assistance is offered to employees through the resort's Self Access Centre (a resource centre where employees may pursue further study). Employees at all levels are encouraged to practice skills by using the hotel's self-study package.

Bringing class instruction to employee workstations—instead of relying on staff to visit the resort's Self Access Centre—brought many advantages:

- The familiar work area in which classes are held helps staff better understand the topics covered. This environment also helps employees to remember particular situations, and encourages discussion.

- Area props, such as tools or products normally used in a workday, are easily available during class.

- During their shifts, employees are able to join classes easily, without losing time in walking to formal classrooms or waiting for full attendance.

- It is convenient for managers and supervisors to attend and witness employee interaction first-hand, thereby encouraging practice throughout the workday.

- The short duration of classes encourages participants to be attentive and happy to learn, even during peak occupancy.

In early 2000, the resort introduced the luxurious Lanna Spa, which offers specially designed treatments to guests. While the spa receptionists speak excellent English, the therapists were hired based on their massage skills. Training in English language was critical for therapists to communicate with guests. The Mobile English Class delivery method was extremely practical for this department in that it could be carried out simultaneously with other training. While working in the spa, some trainers were lucky enough to double as the "subjects" of massage technique training while overseeing English classes!

RESULTS

A formal written English test is used during the hiring process at the Regent Resort. This test serves to verify individual English proficiency levels and is used to determine appropriate self-study language materials for use by each new employee.

Although no formal test has been constructed to measure English language improvement specific to the Mobile English Class program, class participation has increased from between 10 and 20 percent to 100 percent since the introduction of the program in May 1996. Management feels that this increase is largely due to the renewed class design, making it easy and fun for staff to attend, even during busy resort periods. Staff members enjoy attending class and feel it is important to maintain proficiency levels equal to those of their peers.

The next challenge for the Regent Chiang Mai Resort & Spa is to expand mobile classes to include Japanese language training. Currently, Japanese is taught at various properties in a classroom-style format.

WTTC HUMAN RESOURCE CENTRE COMMENT

Building essential English skills in a workplace setting, rather than a classroom setting, provides front line, supervisory, and management employees with accessible training windows during their workday. The structuring of the program allows language learning to take place in settings where English-speaking guests are most likely to be encountered. Through group instruction, employees are challenged to "keep up" with the current level of teaching. This encouraged regular participation in the mobile workshops, which were also considered by many to be enjoyable and worthwhile.

KEY TERMS

proficiency
customer service
mobile delivery

self-study
English language training

 **www.fourseasons.com**

DISCUSSION QUESTIONS

1. Thinking as an instructor, outline an on-the-job English language mini-session.
2. What other kinds of training might benefit from delivery in a mobile format?
3. How does this approach improve the working conditions for the predominately Thai workforce?

Canada
British Columbia Chefs' Association

Submitted by: Julius Pokomandy

THE EVOLUTION OF THE BRITISH COLUMBIA CHEFS' ASSOCIATION

… Explore the formation of British Columbia's professional chefs' association as it evolves from a small group of men into a gender equality trade association promoting professional behaviour through a code of ethics and mentorship for its junior members.

LEARNING OUTCOMES

1. Explain why culinary competitions help apprentices attain higher skill levels.
2. Interpret the role a trade association can play in increasing the career opportunities of a professional trade.
3. Describe why it is important for a professional trade association to have Junior Chapter members as part of its membership.

OVERVIEW

As North America's premier gateway to the Pacific Rim, Vancouver has developed a range of fine restaurants rivalling many world culinary establishments. As the hospitality industry has matured across Canada, Canadians have discovered that distinctiveness and diversity exist here at home. Regional foods coupled with locally produced wines have created an identifiable, original Canadian culinary style, reflecting the land, the people, and the foods produced across the country.

In British Columbia's (BC's) pioneer days, employment opportunities for a cook or baker were few and generally transient. With some exceptions, such as in the larger cities of Victoria and Vancouver, professional jobs in cooking and baking were perceived as domestic servant positions. British Columbia's early chefs did not receive the same prestige that their counterparts did in Europe or even central and eastern Canada. Between 1900 and 1960, social attitudes and values changed with the growth of BC's primary industries such as forestry, agriculture, and fisheries. BC's economy prospered, its population grew, and people in society became wealthier.

During this time, there were only a few notable hotels and restaurants in BC. These included the Empress and Strathcona hotels located in Victoria, the Georgia Hotel, the Ritz Hotel, the Devonshire, and Hotel Vancouver in downtown Vancouver, as well as both Love's and Scott's restaurants. Initially, skilled labour was imported. The Canadian Pacific Corporation sponsored trained journeyman cooks and bakers from Europe to be employed in their world-class kitchens and bakeshops. Other food service establishments did the same, creating a steady influx of food-trades people arriving from Germany, France, Switzerland, and Italy.

As the province's hospitality sector was developing, local training was needed to meet market demands. Little formalized trade training existed in the province until the late 1940s. Vancouver Community College (then the Vancouver Vocational Institute) opened its doors in 1949, offering trades training in baking, cooking, plumbing, barbering, carpentry, and power sewing.

In July 1958, a handful of chefs gathered to discuss the formation of a chefs' association. Nine men, all originally from Europe, wanted to create an organization much like the associations in their home countries. These associations were trade guilds, often with compulsory membership, a stern eligibility criterion, and firm internal discipline. Retired chef Xavier Hetzman, today seventy-eight-years-old, is the last remaining member of the founding fathers of what is now called the British Columbia Chefs' Association. While working at the Georgia Hotel, Hetzman was the first chef to demand and receive gender equality in wages for his staff. A man of strong humanitarian convictions, and a consummate culinarian, he formally arranged the first cook apprentice contract with Vancouver Community College (VCC) and the BC Ministry of Labour.

IMPLEMENTATION

As Hetzman recalls, "We wanted to establish an assemblage we were familiar with. Our aim was to create better working conditions through awareness, the education of young cooks, and just socializing with each other."

Originally named the Association of Chefs' de Cuisine of British Columbia, the organization was granted a non-profit association charter on February 27, 1959. For the first 20 years, the association focussed on building and maintaining membership. By 1960, chef membership totalled 30 and there were 15 associate members. Associate members were industry representatives and sales people, as well as importers and processors of specialty food items. Mutual respect and collegial interaction between the "active chefs" and the "associates" was established early on and today remains crucial to the success of the organization.

In June 1967, during the presidency of Chef Eugene Veronneau, the association's name was changed to the British Columbia Chefs' Association. An established code of ethics was developed, placing emphasis on membership discipline and responsibility: "I will endeavour to conduct myself in a professional manner at all times. I shall place the honour and the standing of our profession before personal advantage."

Culinary Competitions

Chef member Karl Shier joined the association in 1978. He encouraged registered apprentices to attain higher skill levels. Through his efforts, the association launched the Karl

Shier Apprentice Competition. This hot food competition has been held in cooperation with VCC for over 13 years. Industry financial and "in kind" sponsors provide awards and monetary prizes to the successful competitors. The event continues to gain in popularity: the first competition hosted five apprentices, while in 2001, 16 young cooks participated.

> *"The young cooks needed an opportunity to compete at their skill level for professional achievement and recognition. Noted chefs in the industry judge their performance. This occasion provides the apprentices with a clear aim and goal to work towards, to measure their achievement against the skills of their peers. More than a hundred young culinarians have participated in this event since 1987. A fine success."*
>
> *Chef Karl Shier*
> *BC Chefs' Association*

Since the 1980s, Canadian chefs have achieved renowned success in international culinary competitions. The Culinary Olympics in Frankfurt, held every four years, are the most prestigious competitive platform in the world. Canadian chefs placed first in the world in 1996, and fifth in 2000.

Youth Training

Culinary training was introduced into BC secondary schools in 1965, when the new Carson Graham Secondary School in North Vancouver included commercial cooking—cafeteria courses—for graduating students. Many BC public schools followed this example. To date, 75 such programs are offered in secondary schools throughout the province. These students receive a sound and realistic introduction to the trade of cooking and to the hospitality industry in general. Teachers are professional chefs with solid industry and trade experience, and many are members of the BC Chefs' Association.

Since 1979, the association has awarded thousands of dollars in scholarships to students entering post-secondary cooking and baking programs throughout the province. Annual fundraising events (such as the Bavarian Night Dine and Dance held at VCC) and corporate donations provide additional resources for funding young students. The retention rate for students receiving scholarships is over 50 percent and many past scholarship recipients are now active chef members of the association.

Junior Membership

In 1993, the BC Chefs' Association considered a proposal to expand association memberships to recognize apprentices and student cooks attending post-secondary institutions. Chef member Bruno Marti, one of the most accomplished and decorated culinarians in Canada, was a strong promoter of this initiative. According to Marti, "Our profession depends on those we can motivate to continue what we have started in the culinary arts. I believe that there is tremendous greatness and respect still to be achieved in this profession and our young people, if they are enthusiastic and passionate about what they do, will find it."

Junior membership status gives young cooks the opportunity to approach professional chefs socially as well as in the workplace. The association was prepared to modify its constitution and bylaws to create a parallel organization under the umbrella of the BC Chefs' Association. In 1995, the Junior Chapter of the BC Chefs' Association was formed with a simple eligibility requirement: those wishing to join had to be working in the trade, studying under a qualified chef, or attending an accredited trade school. The chapter welcomed its junior industry members. Upon acquiring their Trades Qualification Certificate (known as the TQ), junior members were then eligible to become active chef members. To date, Junior Chapter membership comprises 40 percent of the total association membership.

Both females and males are equally represented in the Junior Chapter, reflective of what is happening in the food and beverage industry. This was unheard of 25 years ago. Gender equality in commercial kitchens is also improving and future labour predictions support continued movement in this direction.

Current activities for Junior Chapter members include monthly meetings, where respected chefs and industry professionals demonstrate their specialities. Members attending these events have the opportunity to learn new techniques, acquire career-specific information, and network with influential industry professionals. Recently, a mentor program was implemented, matching experienced chef members with younger junior members.

Two real-life student examples illustrate the success of this program. Reza Pourdana joined the Junior Chapter in October 2000. He completed the Baking Program at VCC in 1996, and he is presently enrolled in the Cooking Program, with a graduation date of July 2001. Fluent in English, Farci, and Turkish, he is a young parent committed to working hard for a rewarding career in the food service industry. He works as a kitchen chef at the Bamboo Café in Vancouver, while attending school every day. "The members push me towards becoming a better chef. I also have the chance to meet other accomplished chefs and learn from them. I obtain information and news I cannot get anywhere else," says Pourdana. "I can learn what is going on in BC and develop networking for my future."

In the upscale Whistler ski resort, just north of Vancouver, Natalie Syssoloff, twenty-two years old, is working solidly to complete her required hours on the job towards her certification. She is a graduate of Lord Tweedsmuir Secondary School's cooking program in Surrey. She has been working at Fairmont Chateau Whistler since July 1996, two weeks after her high school graduation. She commenced her apprenticeship program in September 1997 and completed the requirements in March 2000. Syssoloff has been a Junior Chapter member since 1996. "I enjoy meeting people to learn about opportunities and [like to] enter the Junior Chapter's hot competition. I felt welcome as a new member, and I try to attend as many meetings as I can."

RESULTS

The British Columbia Chefs' Association began with the inspirations of its founding fathers. Within a short time, it evolved into an organization focussed on improving the future of the industry and aiding the professional development of those working within it. The association's growth and success are cemented by its dynamic membership base and strong focus on values. The association's code of ethics summarizes the basic focus of its existence: "I will endeavour to conduct myself in a professional manner at all times. I shall place the honour and the standing of our profession before personal advantage."

WTTC HUMAN RESOURCE CENTRE COMMENT

Canada has increased its reputation as a tourism destination through hosting international events such as the 1967 Montreal Expo, the 1976 Olympic Games, and Expo 86. Local training of those working as cooks, apprentices, and students in the food and beverage industry has helped Canada prepare for the increase in market demands. The press coverage and television exposure of culinary competitions and similar events has increased the profile of the cooking and baking profession, making it a more attractive trade option for young people.

KEY TERMS

apprenticeship   culinarian
mentor   gender equality
prestige   associate members
trade association   code of ethics
journeyman

www.bcchefs.com

www.cfcc.ca

DISCUSSION QUESTIONS

1. Recommend other ways a trade professional association can encourage young people to consider a career in its trade.
2. What other ways can you think of that would give junior members the opportunity to approach professional peers socially, as well as in the workplace?
3. List five reasons why it is of mutual benefit for the professional and associate members to mentor Junior Chapter members.

chapter three

Recognizing and Rewarding Your Team: Team Building, Morale Boosting, Incentives, and Compensation

The Bahamas
Sheraton Grand Resort Paradise Island

Submitted by: Morgan Graham

Sheraton Grand
R E S O R T
PARADISE ISLAND, BAHAMAS

MOTIVATING STAFF THROUGH AWARD RECOGNITION

… A franchise hotel motivates staff, both individually and as a winning team, by promoting participation in a local government tourism competition.

LEARNING OUTCOMES

1. Identify why it is important for a company to ensure that all employees understand the importance of customer service.

2. Explain why a corporation would want its training programs designed and delivered with consistency at all its properties worldwide.

3. Identify the advantages of having general customer service training sessions that include a cross-section of employees from all departments.

"The success of the Sheraton Grand in recent years can be directly linked to the Cacique Awards and the number of staff members who have been winners or finalists."

Herman Ross, Director of Operations
Sheraton Grand Resort Paradise Island

OVERVIEW

The Sheraton Grand Resort (Sheraton Grand) is situated on a beach of white sand on Paradise Island, three kilometres from downtown Nassau, the Bahamas. Built in 1982, all 340 rooms carry the Sheraton Grand "ocean view guarantee," ensuring that every visitor enjoys a private balcony view of the crystal clear waters of the Atlantic Ocean. The resort has a warm and relaxed atmosphere and caters to a variety of clientele, including families, couples wanting to get married on the island, and honeymooners.

With almost 800 square metres of meeting space and a 650-square-metre ballroom, the resort hosts numerous functions, training seminars, and receptions for both local and international clientele. The resort also caters to incentive business. The property's world-class chef works to ensure that the Sheraton Grand continues to be the most popular food and beverage venue in the area. Because many couples want to get married in the Bahamas, the resort employs two certified wedding planners.

Realizing the importance of customer satisfaction, all 250 employees are trained to put customer needs first.

IMPLEMENTATION

Customer Service Training Program

Customer service training at the Sheraton Grand has always been a key component of employee training. As a Sheraton property, the Sheraton Grand has benefited from the corporation's Sheraton Guest Satisfaction System (SGSS), developed in the 1980s. Sheraton training programs are consistently designed and delivered at all Sheraton properties to ensure quality customer service worldwide.

In 1995, the Sheraton Grand became a Radisson franchise, during which time employees benefited from learning additional customer service skills from Radisson's Yes I Can training program. When the hotel reverted back to a Sheraton franchise in October 1998, an updated version of SGSS training was reinstated. Transitions between the training programs were smooth as the systems complemented each other. Both programs focussed on one common goal—pleasing the guest.

Sheraton Grand management felt that the local tourism ministry awards program also complemented its in-house training programs. The national Cacique Awards thus became another tool used to motivate staff to meet and exceed customer expectations. Management agrees that increasing customer satisfaction increases repeat visitor business, to the resort and to the Bahamas. For this reason, employees from all hotel departments attend regular customer service training sessions. Employees from the heart of the hotel (back-of-the-house) affect the service of front line employees. Thus, all employees must understand the importance of customer service. Training sessions are delivered during work hours and held in resort meeting rooms in a classroom-style format. Attendance is mandatory, so employees are paid regular wages during session hours, whether training is scheduled on a workday or on days off.

General customer-service-training session topics include:

- how to win customers with service;
- service standards and principles;
- turning negative situations into positive situations;
- how to recover from a potentially disastrous situation;
- delivering quality guest service;
- communication and motivation;
- telephone skills; and
- teamwork.

A dining experience at the Sheraton Grand Resort in the Bahamas.

Sheraton Grand Resort Paradise Island

The hotel's director of human resources leads general sessions, with assistance from the front office manager. These sessions are based on actual examples involving the hotel and its guests. Consequently, sessions are based on "real life" learning to meet customer demands. General discussions consistently focus on customer satisfaction and are in line with the company's goal of generating repeat business and a good reputation. Department heads and/or department trainers then continue with department-specific training, such as front-office-quality service, quality guest room maintenance, food and beverage suggestive-selling techniques, and guest room cleaning.

Training sessions average one day in duration, with 20 participants in each session. By attending two sessions per week, it takes each employee six weeks to complete the entire training program. General session classes include a cross-section of all departments. This format allows for: the sharing of a variety of experiences; a better understanding of colleagues from different departments, and of each department's specific challenges and victories; and the fostering of teamwork. Training tools include workbooks, audio cassettes, and video cassettes, which are designed and distributed by Sheraton's head office.

Customer service training is ongoing. Although Sheraton modifies the training program every two to four years, the overall content and goals remain the same. Occasionally, supplementary programs are offered. Attending a variety of customer service training sessions throughout the year promotes staff unity, increases job performance, and provides ongoing motivation to please the guest.

Details for the hotel's Employee of the Month and Employee of the Year competitions are presented during the in-house customer service training sessions. In this way, employees are kept abreast on the standards of excellence required to qualify for award recognition, and all employees are given an equal chance to apply for the awards. On average, department supervisors and managers nominate five employees each month. Generally, two winners are selected monthly—one for front-of-the-house and one for "heart-of-the-house." Employees of the Month are eligible for the Employee of the Year award. On average, approximately 24 to 28 persons are finalists for the Sheraton Grand's Employee of the Year award.

The Bahamas Ministry of Tourism Cacique Awards

Tourism is the number one industry in the Bahamas today. In 1995, the Bahamas Ministry of Tourism introduced the Cacique Awards—the highest honour bestowed upon those employed in the Bahamian tourism industry. The award recognizes those who have distinguished themselves by making valuable contributions to the national growth and development of tourism. Hotel-specific awards include:

- Employee of the Year
- Supervisor of the Year
- Hotel Manager of the Year
- Hotelier of the Year
- Chef of the Year
- Sales Executive of the Year
- Casino Executive of the Year
- Human Resource Director of the Year.

To encourage employee participation in the awards program, each year the Sheraton Grand's human resource department distributes a memorandum outlining the criteria for the Cacique Awards. It is the Bahamas Hotel Association (BHA) that sets the award criteria. Each fall, all employees are invited to nominate co-workers whom they feel have met the award's qualifications and criteria.

To qualify for any of the award categories, nominees must have been employed within the Bahamas hotel industry for a minimum of five years. Each hotel may only submit one nominee in each category. The nomination form requires a minimum of three—and a maximum of seven—letters of recommendation. Of the letters, one must be from the employing hotel, one from a work colleague, and one from a guest.

At the Sheraton Grand Resort, nominated employees are often those who have previously won the hotel's Employee of the Month award. The hotel's executive committee either selects a finalist from this set of nominees, or chooses an employee whom it feels to be most deserving. Upon choosing the best candidate for each category, the hotel's human resource director and the human resource manager complete nomination details.

A committee representing the BHA selects three finalists in each category and then forwards the short list to the Ministry of Tourism. In early December of each year, the hotel finalists are announced at a luncheon hosted by the BHA and American Express. Winners are announced at the Cacique Awards ceremony held in January of the following year.

The categories on which the Hotelier of the Year and the Manager of the Year award criteria are based include:

JUDGING CATEGORY	JUDGING CRITERIA
1. Activities	achievements in management of hotel operations
2. Food and beverage management	effective cost control, menu planning, use of Bahamian food products, restaurant décor, theme planning, etc.
3. Marketing	sales promotion, advertising, public relations, printed material, etc.
4. Building and grounds	innovation in improving visual appeal of property and facilities, maintenance, innovation of facilities, etc.
5. Staff training and motivation	procedures and programs undertaken to improve level of staff professionalism, incentive training, etc.
6. National	commitment to national affairs and participation in BHA activities
7. Background	education and employment history
8. Memberships	in civic, fraternal, or professional organizations as well as allied industry associations
9. Interests	hobbies and leisure activities

Criteria for all other categories in the hotel field include:

JUDGING CATEGORY	JUDGING CRITERIA
1. Guest response	employee's position, interaction, and professional performance with guests
2. Manager's response	manager's opinion of why the employee should be considered for the award
3. Professional	individual's professional service record
4. Community	individual's community service record
5. Background	employment and past employment history
6. Education	principal academic qualifications
7. Interests	individual's hobbies and leisure activities

As a sidenote, to apply for the Human Resource Director of the Year award (which is not a hotel-specific award) the nomination package is submitted directly to the Ministry of Tourism. A committee selects three finalists for this award and a blue ribbon committee chooses the winner.

RESULTS

Since implementing the revised SGSS customer service training program, Sheraton Grand has a competitive and winning spirit to be "number one." This makes it easy to encourage staff to strive individually and collectively towards achieving a Cacique Award. Between 1995 and 1998, Sheraton Grand employees have received a total of 11 awards. Each year, the hotel has had an increase in the number of finalists and winners in the varying categories of the Cacique Awards. More and more employees are motivated to win the award each year, so much so that the Sheraton Grand has become known as the hotel to beat!

Return visitors are made aware of employee accomplishments through conversations and the local news media. In one unprecedented move, the director of human resources was invited to a guest room so they might share their praises for a room attendant who had worked for the resort for 17 years and received the Cacique Award for Employee of the Year. Award recognition is circulated in the Bahamas and internationally through various media and through the *Sheraton Newsletter*.

WTTC HUMAN RESOURCE CENTRE COMMENT

Using nationally recognized awards helps the industry promote expertise in a given profession, from front line to management level. This can help stimulate both pride and national recognition among one's peers. Human resource training and development is a key component in training and educational policies throughout the Bahamas. Committed to improving the customer service of the Bahamian tourism industry, the government recognizes both individual and group accomplishments through the Cacique Awards. The Sheraton Grand case study illustrates how the hotel has assisted staff and management participation in the national awards and promoted the yearly competition in a positive manner, thereby motivating staff to provide customer satisfaction.

KEY TERMS

franchise

employee incentives

customer service training

national awards program

employee motivation

incentive business

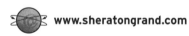 **www.sheratongrand.com**

DISCUSSION QUESTIONS

1. Explain how the Cacique Awards (recognition) program complements the existing training program at the Sheraton Grand hotel.

2. Describe the benefits of the awards program in terms of community recognition for the hotel.

3. What benefits do national awards programs have on the profile, image, and credibility of the area's hotel tourism industry?

Canada
Sheraton Suites Calgary Eau Claire

Submitted by: Greg Hayward

Sheraton
Suites Calgary
EAU CLAIRE

BUILDING A HOTEL CULTURE

... A Calgary hotel conducted seminars to identify ways of boosting employee morale and uncovered ways to develop the company's individual culture.

LEARNING OUTCOMES

1. Describe the benefits of cataloguing employee's workplace concerns.
2. Recognize how a training facilitator succeeded in getting employees to report on workplace concerns.
3. Explain how the management created an employee incentive program that was a win-win situation for both the property and the employee.

OVERVIEW

In November 1998, the Sheraton Suites Calgary Eau Claire opened as the most recent all-suite hotel to enter the Calgary, Alberta, market in close to 20 years. The hotel had a soft opening to accommodate the eager pre-booked banquet business. With only two of its 14 floors open, and only 11 of its guest rooms ready for use, the hotel opened its doors with warm western hospitality.

Prior to the soft opening, recruitment and employee orientation was done in rented office space. Full training began in October 1998 in the hotel's finished—but still unfurnished—administrative office area. (In the beginning, everyone had to wear hard hats and steel-toe boots to enter the finished office area, as the rest of the hotel was still a construction zone.) Front office employees were split into teams, which were identified by a colour. Numbers and letters were not used as team identifiers so that teams would not feel pre-graded.

The front office manager, assistant front office manager, and a team of three assistant managers conducted training modules on a variety of subjects, from hotel etiquette to empowerment. A trainer from the property management system also trained employees in the concepts of check-in, check-out, blocking, etc. Each module included role-playing exercises and a method of testing to ensure that everyone grasped the basic concepts.

All the service training modules were created by the combined expertise of each departmental management team and their assistants. Sheraton does not provide franchises with structured service standards or policies, just product standards. Sheraton uses a JD Powers Survey, the Guest Satisfaction Index (GSI), to benchmark and grade the quality of products and services in all North American properties. As of 2001, part of Sheraton's annual inspection has a graded service element. This will now be available to new properties to help benchmark service training expectations.

Training sessions lasted eight hours a day, and incorporated morale-building games, meals, and field trips. For larger mixed groups, trainers would start with a fun icebreaker. For example, they might go on a full walking tour of downtown Calgary to ensure everyone was familiar with the various services and products within the hotel's geographic area. Local restaurants offered either free or substantially reduced meals to give exposure to their product, for possible future recommendation.

As new employees joined the team, management and assistants based their training on their specific area of employment. Much of the housekeeping training, for example, was done while actually assembling the soft goods in the guest rooms. All hiring continued to take place, based on a critical path set out by each department and by turnover of floors from the construction company. This helped spread the training out, once the original opening team was in place.

Prior to the grand opening, every area conducted a trial run on employees. This included employees staying overnight in the hotel to test guest room services. To this day, Sheraton Suites Calgary Eau Claire still offers this benefit to each and every hotel employee, to ensure they are familiar with the hotel's products and services.

By February 1999, all 323 suites were ready for the hotel's official grand opening. The Sheraton Suites Calgary Eau Claire promised to provide "casual elegance delivered with vibrant style." More than 500 VIP guests were treated to a spectacular show of music, costumes, and food from around the world. Tours were conducted throughout the hotel. Guests experienced the look and feel of the restaurants, function space, Health Club, fifteenth-floor Club Lounge, and numerous guest suites—including the hotel's Premier and Imperial suites, complete with a butler's pantry, hardwood maple flooring in the living room and dining room, two gas fireplaces, and a whirlpool tub.

From the beginning, the franchise owner mandated a hiring practice of first selecting individuals with a positive attitude. Company philosophy is based on the premise that if you treat your employees with respect and fairness, the employees will do the same for the external customers of the hotel.

IMPLEMENTATION

Because the hotel was newly opened, staff at the Sheraton Suites Calgary Eau Claire underwent a transition stage, from the pre-opening stage to when the hotel became fully operational. During this time, employee expectations were impacted, and management suspected there was an underlying sense of turmoil as the hotel had lost some key people in several departments. Being proactive, the hotel's general manager and team of department heads agreed to offer a confidential employee satisfaction survey to all of its 221 staff members, not including those employed in the property's two food outlets, as they were operated independently.

The survey was conducted in March 2000, just after the hotel was a year old. An outside company, specializing in this type of survey, provided the general manager and human resource department with a list of questions for consideration. Together they determined which questions would be most beneficial to gauge the current morale of the employee base. Ten of the questions were slightly modified to dig deeper into specific issues. The general manager designed a separate set of questions specifically to assess department heads and their immediate assistants. Prior to finalizing the survey, the questions were circulated to management for feedback. The survey was conducted in-house by the human resource department.

Confidential Employee Survey

By conducting an in-depth examination of its workplace culture, hotel management wanted to hear the staff's opinions and learn what was working well, and what issues needed to be addressed. Survey results noted areas requiring improvement, from the quality of food in the staff cafeteria to the need for a broad-based incentive program for all employees, and many things in between.

The survey was translated into the first language of many of Sheraton Suites Calgary Eau Claire's employees. Employees did not sign the surveys and placed the completed survey through a small slot in a pre-sealed shipping box. The company initially hired to produce the survey was located in California, so the pre-sealed boxes of surveys were then shipped off to be examined, tabulated, and formatted into multiple reports. The handwritten comments were typed out and also randomly included in the report. The actual employee surveys were then destroyed in California, and only their findings were sent back to the hotel.

The survey was conducted over three days in one of the hotel's break rooms. Employees were invited to come and fill in the survey while on shift. The department managers staffed accordingly, to ensure that service would not be impacted, nor would the employees have to return to their jobs and feel they had to make up for the time lost while filling out the survey.

Employees were eager to have their voices heard—or at least read! The questions were all done on a graded scale. There was a section at the end of the survey that offered employees a chance to write down their comments. The average survey took approximately 20 minutes to complete, with some staff taking up to 30 minutes to supply additional written comments.

The management team was expecting the survey to identify areas of opportunity. Some managers may have been surprised by some of the findings, but none were truly overwhelmed by the survey results. To ensure that all concern areas were identified, it was decided that a consultant could best achieve this goal. Fortunately for the hotel, it had an established relationship with a professional facilitator. Having proved effective in helping to build the hotel's management team strength, the facilitator was the obvious choice for this task.

Motivational Seminars

For more than seven months, the Sheraton Suites Calgary Eau Claire worked with an outside consultant who specialized in facilitating seminars. The consultant conducted 11 intensive seminars on-site, to uncover workplace obstacles and problems and identify what steps could be taken to boost morale. The seminars focussed on cultural transformations (the culture of the organization), including employee feelings. Employees who naturally feared that they might lose their job, or a promotion, overcame their hesitation to speak up in seminars because of the neutral and confidential approach used. Once employees were comfortable, the obstacles were easily identified and the employees freely listed everything down on paper.

To encourage employee feedback on such sensitive topics, prior to the project's outset, it was explained to staff that no personal feedback would be given to the general manager from the facilitator. Also, at any time, any individual could be asked to leave the room in order for the rest of the group to discuss topics of a sensitive nature. The group themselves would be the ones presenting the information back to the general manager, not the facilitator. He was there to help them identify the issues that required action.

Staff attendance was mandatory at each of the three-hour sessions. Management felt it was necessary for everyone to be involved, so no one would be left without a voice and no one person could be singled out as a non-participant. Where possible, entire departments were kept together. In large departments such as housekeeping, banquets, and front office, some of the sessions were repeated with different groups of people until everyone had attended. Seminars ran with a minimum of five persons, and were attended by as many as 15 to 20 people.

As always when dealing with the entire employee base, much planning was done to ensure that employee's shifts were set up so that they could attend, or if they chose to come in on their own time, they were paid for their attendance. In one month, all staff had completed the 11 seminars.

The seminars were fully interactive. They involved a basic process of identifying what issues were moving each particular team forward, and which ones were holding them back. During the session, the actual survey results were handed out and reviewed to ensure that all items had been identified. Following that, it was determined what could be resolved at a line level, what required a supervisor or manager, and what required the input or assistance of the general manger. To deal with department-specific issues, a team of volunteers from each group prepared a presentation for a private session with the general manager. With management's full support, the facilitator was able to establish a certain degree of trust.

After the 11 seminars were completed, the management had a report cataloguing employee concerns. In total, 61 points were identified as needing the attention of the general manager. Approximately three times this amount of concerns were brought up for the department managers and supervisors to specifically discuss with their employees. The discussions could be used as a springboard for implementing solutions. These lists were the result of the initial survey and the several evaluations that took place during the seminars. As the facilitator noted: "The seminar evaluations revealed [that] the underlying assumptions were found to be the same for half of the workers."

At a leadership forum in Banff, Alberta, the same facilitator used the same methods for the department heads and hotel executives to brainstorm and formulate answers to the numerous questions that the employees brought forward to the general manager. He also addressed the executives' issues. The result was a resolution of many issues holding the team back and a code of conduct for future behaviour. Once a resolution was agreed upon, the information was presented at a number of general staff meetings to inform the employees that their words had not fallen on deaf ears. From an operational standpoint, the senior management team realized that the employees themselves could rectify many of their own concerns.

Issues from the management side of the business were addressed, mostly relating to communication. Company processes and policies were changed or modified as necessary, with explanations provided. In areas of company-wide concern, such as the lack of employee incentives, new programs were created and implemented. All along, progress reports, given on large-scale projects at general staff meetings, helped keep employees in the loop. Following the meetings, the actual lists were posted on the two main employee bulletin boards for their personal review.

Incentive Program

When addressing the issue of an employee incentive program, management felt it was important to create a win-win situation for both the property and the employee. The overall incentives themselves were items that exemplified the qualities of hotel employees. Perfect attendance, good grooming, a clean workspace, and a positive attitude were just a few of the items that these "star" performers embodied.

The "Star Bucks" employee incentive program was born of these and other good work practices. Each and every hotel employee is able to earn Star Bucks each month. They can then turn in or save these points to purchase items that they themselves chose in a brainstorming session during the conception of the program. Employees can purchase a number of things, including but not limited to:

- underground parking privileges for a day, week, or month
- half and full days off with pay
- additional vacation time
- movie passes
- limousine rides
- tickets to sporting events
- cakes and pastries from the hotel pastry chef
- brunch, lunch, or dinner in hotel food outlets
- passes to the YMCA.

The hotel is also working on a line of Sheraton Suites Calgary Eau Claire keepsake items—from key-chains to clothing—all with the hotel logo.

In September 2000, the human resource department issued a memo looking for interested individuals to attend an information meeting on developing an employee incentive program. After establishing a good cross-section of employee input, a brainstorming session ensued. The group discussed items that they felt would be fair to judge all employees on. During the next session, the group discussed possible rewards. Department heads and executives discussed the two lists generated through the employee brainstorming sessions, and agreed upon a base.

To enhance the program, department or position-specific performance elements were added to the base, while still maintaining an equal availability of points to each employee. Each department established performance benchmarks specific to their department's needs, or the specific needs of a certain position. These benchmarks, or values, are what department heads would like their specific employees to meet. A point value was assigned to each of these values as a further incentive, and as a way for employees to earn more Star Bucks.

Some of the tasks or behaviours that are graded for Star Bucks include:

- perfect attendance
- excellent grooming (must meet 10 guidelines set out in employee handbook)
- clean work space (must meet agreed upon criteria to qualify)
- positive attitude (must use proper hospitality greeting/make eye contact/smile, etc.)
- the giving and receiving of "Shining Stars." (This is another level of internal employee recognition. An employee can identify a specific good deed of another employee by submitting a Shining Star form to the human resource office. The employee nominated for a Shining Star receives a personal thank you letter from the general manager. A copy of the letter is placed in the employee's file. Shining Star awards are also given for guest recognition of superior service.)

The program, which is unique to Sheraton Suites Calgary Eau Claire, is generating more enthusiasm among employees as staff perceive the program as a fun activity or process in which to participate.

> *"What it did was bring us together and brought trust and understanding into the team atmosphere."*
>
> *Randy Zupanski, General Manager*
> *Sheraton Suites Calgary Eau Claire*

RESULTS

Management admits that this was a slow means for the executive team to achieve its goals; however, guest satisfaction was immediately impacted. As for the hotel's human resource department, they gladly admit that the entire process transformed employee morale and the change in company atmosphere was incredible.

Continuing its philosophy of treating the employees as number one, the Sheraton Suites Calgary Eau Claire conducts regular performance evaluations, which are mandated to be a positive experience. It is their responsibility as leaders to deal with any issues of discipline in an appropriate and timely manner. The evaluation process is not a forum for discipline, but a tool for management to give positive feedback and direction, and to set goals for employees to achieve personal success for themselves. This ensures continued success for the property as a whole.

Combining its five-star product with successful employee practices has helped the Sheraton Suites Calgary Eau Claire to continually rank as one of the top three Sheraton hotels in North America. Guest satisfaction feedback rated the hotel the best out of 210 in North America, from January to June 2000. As of December 2000, the hotel had been awarded the prestigious Hotel of the Quarter award three times by parent company Starwood.

Sheraton Suites Calgary Eau Claire is also pleased to report it is leading in the areas of market share, average rate, and occupancy for the past year, as compared to its competitors. It has cut year-to-date turnover exactly in half as of the same month last year. In January 2000, turnover was 44 percent (including full- and part-time employees). In January 2001, turnover was only at 22 percent for the year to date (including full- and part-time employees). A second survey is scheduled for March 2001.

WTTC Human Resource Centre COMMENT

Essentials of business are the same in any country. Worldwide, businesses strive to obtain the same thing—all staff members working together to achieve a common goal. The Sheraton Suites Calgary Eau Claire chose an outside facilitator to provide company seminars to boost employee morale. With management's full cooperation and support, the facilitator gained employee trust, and in turn enabled the employees themselves to identify their workplace concerns and present these issues directly to the general manager. Given the same facilitation, management was able to resolve many issues holding the team back, and develop a code of conduct for future behaviour. By effectively communicating with staff, new company policies and changes were better understood and thereby made easier to implement, departmental teamwork was improved, staff felt empowered to rectify many of their own concerns, and the culture of the organization became firmly entrenched.

KEY TERMS

morale
employee satisfaction
cultural transformations
corporate culture

recognition and incentive programs
product and service standards
soft opening
facilitator

 **www.sheratonsuites.com**

DISCUSSION QUESTIONS

1. Imagine that a facilitator is hired by your employer to uncover employee concerns. What would convince you that you could trust this individual as someone to whom you could voice legitimate workplace issues? How could the individual gain your confidence?

2. You are appointed as the staff representative at your company's monthly board meetings. How would you gather staff opinion to ensure you represent the issues of your fellow colleagues?

3. As a hotel employee, you are asked to develop a staff incentive program. How would you acquire staff input?

Aruba
Costa Linda Beach Resort

Submitted by: Marlyn Geerman

CREATING A VISION OF QUALITY

. . . The Costa Linda Beach Resort has taken the principles behind total quality management and modified them to maintain the basic habits and values of Aruba's inhabitants.

LEARNING OUTCOMES

1. Describe how a resort is able to quickly create a core set of in-house trainers.
2. Explain the function of incentives and monetary rewards in a quality improvement strategy.
3. Explain the uses of feedback gathered from suggestion boxes for both employees and guests.

OVERVIEW

The shutdown of the Exxon oil refinery in 1984 made the Aruba government focus on its developing tourism industry. Together, the government, the local tourist board, and private businesses worked to increase hotel room capacity and to create a marketing strategy which would generate more inbound tourism.

Native Arubans are known for being very courteous, hospitable, warm, and extremely polite to visitors. Because the island's tourism industry developed rapidly, the government was forced to open its doors to foreign labourers. Many feared the locals' authentic characteristics would be lost.

Inspired partly by challenges surrounding the issue of authenticity, the Aruba Quality Foundation (AQF) was established. The foundation's vision was to make the quality of life in Aruba better for future generations by bringing a caring attitude to everyone. The goal would be achieved by working together as a nation, using knowledge, innovation, and lessons learned to create a model society. The AQF developed a national program built around four strategies that all businesses, including tourism, could work towards.

The program was modelled after the American Malcolm Baldrige Quality Award, which emphasized total quality management. The AQF's program incorporated the basic habits and values of the island's inhabitants while setting industry performance standards for service. Leaders from all sectors of the community attended several island-wide retreats to further define total quality management and to apply it to the program's objectives. By joining forces, Aruban business leaders created the mission, vision, and values of this new venture, and founded, for Aruba, a model of quality.

One island business that successfully developed an upscale timeshare resort based on the above principles is the Costa Linda Beach Resort. Committed to training Arubans to be quality-conscious, customer-service oriented, and highly skilled, the resort is noted for providing quality service and for creating future leaders in the industry.

IMPLEMENTATION

To reach its goal as an industry leader, the Costa Linda Beach Resort developed a flow chart plan called Creating a Vision of Quality (CAVOQ). The chart incorporated the resort's corporate vision and adapted the AQF's program criteria to create a nine-step training module on total quality management.

The company's corporate quality trainer worked with management for three weeks, providing training in the following areas:

- leadership
- gracious hospitality
- coaching and counselling
- customer focus and responsiveness
- strategic planning
- benchmarking.

All instruction and training for management was done in-house. Training sessions were held five days a week for four hours at a time. The instruction was based on the quality control and improvement techniques of W. Edward Deming. These techniques emphasize an employee's involvement within and across all departments.

After management training was complete, 20 staff members with high performance records were chosen from various departments. For a three-week period these 20 employees participated in training, using the nine modules of CAVOQ. At the end of the training period, the 20 employees became in-house trainers and began working with supervisors, other employees, contractors, outsourced security, kitchen utility services, and concessionaires throughout the resort. All trainers followed the nine-step training module.

Orientation programs for new employees were also improved by incorporating the company's vision, mission, and values into course content. Resort employees learned methods to improve the quality of business and customer service by understanding the reasons for improvement. All employees are encouraged to further their knowledge, skills, and abilities through educational opportunities outside the organization. As part of the company's human resource development program, the company pays all costs involved.

Building upon the resort's quality improvement strategy, employees created a program called Coin Your Idea to improve their own—and other—departments. Employees are encouraged to provide written suggestions targeting ways to improve the resort. Completed forms are placed in suggestion boxes located throughout the resort. Suggestions are reviewed weekly at the general departmental-heads' meeting, where ideas which may be implemented are discussed. Selected ideas are honoured through a reward system. Prizes include monetary compensation or a dinner for two, along with a thank you letter signed by the general manager.

Similarly, Aim for the Stars is an incentive program that rewards employees' personal achievements. At the time of check-in, every guest room has a welcome package with a red

Superstar Award card and a blue Brilliant Star Award card. Guests can also read about this incentive program in the information package located in their room. A resort guest fills out a card noting an employee who has delivered extraordinary quality service. Each card has a value of one point. When twenty or more points are achieved, an employee can redeem the points for gift items.

In addition, each month every department selects a candidate to the general department-head meeting for the "Costa Quality" Star of the Month election. A secret ballot is held and a cocktail party is organized for the elected quality Employee of the Month. The employee gets an award, monetary compensation, and a dinner for two.

Management, too, has incentives. On a quarterly basis, a supervisor is honoured for high performance of excellence. Rewards include monetary compensation and a dinner for two.

Informal feedback from employees is also important. To improve this line of communication, the yearly performance evaluation system was changed to biyearly evaluation reviews. Management wanted a system that properly addressed employee performance, and set practices for improvement. A compensation and recognition program was also structured into the biyearly review.

To monitor guest feedback, customers' suggestions are gathered through comment cards presented to guests upon check-in or check-out. Like the red and blue Star Award cards, guest comment cards are also located in each room as part of the guest's information guide. Various techniques are used to measure the quality of service, and to inventory recommendations for improvement.

Additional practices which complement total quality management include:

- welcoming and using the talents and intelligence of all employees;
- recognizing and rewarding results;
- establishing recognition and reward programs with the assistance of managers and employees; and
- incorporating quality factors into hiring and selection processes.

RESULTS

Throughout its nine-year existence, Costa Linda Beach Resort has received a bronze award from the Aruba Quality Foundation. The resort also won the Gold Crown Award from Resort Condominium International, which honours ten consecutive years of excellence in customer service. Among its other achievements, the resort has:

- achieved several awards from the Freeman Inspection as the most popular timeshare resort on the island;
- hosted the Dutch royal family and entourage, and, twice, His Royal Highness Crown Prince of the Netherlands, Prince William Alexander;
- hosted several celebrities including Nestor Torres, Ana Gabriel, La India, Kenny G, and Sinbad;
- received the 1999 American Express/Caribbean Hotel Association Achievement Award for first place in the large hotel category; and
- received the Green Globe Award after being assessed, and currently registered, as meeting the requirements of the Green Globe 21 Standard.

WTTC HUMAN RESOURCE CENTRE COMMENT

The Costa Linda Beach Resort has taken solid principles in human resources and applied them to its situation with appropriate cultural modifications. In this good practice, the use of recognition and reward programs has proven successful; however, both the employees and employer were involved in their development, so employee buy-in was easily achieved.

KEY TERMS

total quality management	incentive
train-the-trainer	feedback
customer service	staff assessment
awards	benchmarking
authenticity	industry performance standards

 www.costalinda-aruba.com

DISCUSSION QUESTIONS

1. Describe, in your own words, why the Aruba Quality Foundation was needed, and interpret its mission. As a tourism industry professional, what kinds of local values would you want to incorporate into this country's model?

2. How were employees at the Costa Linda Beach Resort brought into the total quality management circle?

3. How did this hotel achieve employee buy-in to its new company goals and visions?

Canada
UNIGLOBE Travel (International)

Submitted by: Brian Dahl

EVALUATING TRAVEL AGENCY PERSONNEL

… Evaluation programs, which include rewards, recognition, and both personal and professional development, result in improved employee performance, enhanced customer service, and increased company profits.

LEARNING OUTCOMES

1. Explain how a head office works with a task force of agency owners, managers, and counsellors to develop a franchise training program.

2. Describe a multinational approach to competency development for front line employees, founded on industry-wide criteria.

3. Explain the rationale for establishing standards higher than the industry norm for travel counsellors.

> *"The Counsellor Excellence Program has been beneficial to us when hiring new employees. Particularly, it helps pinpoint and define characteristics that UNIGLOBE looks for in employees—professionalism, dependability, and a high focus on customer service."*
>
> UNIGLOBE Western Canada Region

OVERVIEW

UNIGLOBE Travel (International) is the world's largest single brand travel franchise organization, with 1 100 locations in more than 20 countries. Operating under a well-recognized brand name, UNIGLOBE travel agencies specialize in providing travel services to small-to-medium-sized corporate accounts and to leisure travellers.

Since its inception in 1979, UNIGLOBE has worked to set travel industry standards by providing support, education, and a company code of ethics for UNIGLOBE family members. UNIGLOBE's mission is to become the largest and most profitable travel organization in the world, and to set the standards in professionalism and reliability.

To accurately evaluate its own travel agency personnel, UNIGLOBE's program development department worked with a task force of agency owners, managers, and counsellors to develop the Counsellor Excellence Program. Program design was completed in 1995, and a similar structure for managers was developed two years later. Both programs are updated (as appropriate) annually.

These comprehensive programs are based on a set of industry-wide criteria and performance levels, which took two years to develop. One year was dedicated to research and development, and another year was needed to test the pilot program. The goals of the program are to:

- enhance customer service levels;
- improve performance and productivity;
- assist with personnel recruitment;
- increase personnel retention;
- encourage personal and professional growth; and
- recognize performance excellence among staff.

Upon completing the program, managers and travel counsellors alike are evaluated against the defined criteria. UNIGLOBE head office verifies which counsellors and managers have met the requirements to earn an Award for Excellence designation. For counsellors, there are three levels of designations, identified by a bronze, silver, or gold pin. Managers receive a platinum pin with a precious sapphire stone for their achievement.

IMPLEMENTATION

Pilot-tested in 1995 on 85 travel agencies throughout the UNIGLOBE Western Canada region, the Counsellor Excellence Program was extended worldwide in 1996 to all UNIGLOBE agencies, in 20 countries. The first Award for Excellence was presented later that year.

The Counsellor Excellence Program evolved as follows:

Standards developed

UNIGLOBE outlined performance standards based on industry benchmarks. Company benchmarks and expectations were also considered. From this point, universal standards and evaluation criteria were built.

Ratings defined

For travel counsellors, three levels of ratings were established: bronze, silver, and gold. A counsellor must perform at higher than industry average levels to achieve even the bronze designation. To ensure the UNIGLOBE designation retains a high value, requirements are challenging and evaluations are done annually for consistency.

Promotion prior to program launch

Regional staff announced the start of the Counsellor Excellence Program to all agencies at the regional fall conferences held prior to the launch of the program. Throughout the year, regional promotions continued and training was offered to individual agency owners and managers, in hopes of generating excitement and participation by the different offices.

Staff were enthusiastic, as this was the type of program they had been asking for. Therefore, buy-in was easily obtained. The program offered staff clear goals to strive for and to achieve. Although it is up to each agency to decide whether it will partake in the program, UNIGLOBE's head office strongly recommended participation. Of eligible managers (those that have been with UNIGLOBE for at least one year and are in compliance with system standards), 75 to 80 percent participated in the program.

Public relations efforts

General promotions were handled by UNIGLOBE's communications office, in order to market the program globally. Press releases announcing the program were also distributed to national and local media in each region, thereby increasing public awareness.

Training for managers

At one-day training workshops, UNIGLOBE training specialists instructed agency owners and managers on how to implement the Counsellor Excellence Program. Because of the structure of the company, the agency manager would typically oversee the program at each individual agency. Training methods included discussion groups, workbooks, role-playing, scripting, and group exercises. Participants received a comprehensive program guide for follow-up support.

Training tools developed

Program start-up guides, instructor training guides, class workbooks, and individual evaluation booklets were prepared and distributed to all UNIGLOBE regions. All staff received the evaluation booklets. Each participating staff member received a workbook and took part in both group and one-on-one training. Training was held during and after work hours, on-site, and in classroom settings.

Final implementation

At the 1996 regional fall conferences, the first 100 pilot travel counsellors were recognized for the UNIGLOBE Counsellor Excellence Awards in the bronze, silver, and gold categories.

All counsellors who participate in the program have evaluation booklets, used to rate their performance against the defined criteria. The booklets are submitted to regional personnel who collect, compile, and verify the information to determine which counsellors achieved the set requirements to earn an Award for Excellence designation. Award designations are presented each year at similar ceremonies.

Each region provides UNIGLOBE's head office with the names of the counsellors who achieved the highest number of points in their respective regions. In 1996, 18 counsellors were nominated for the first system-wide International Counsellor Excellence Award for the top-performing travel counsellor. This person was announced at the UNIGLOBE international convention in New Orleans in June 1997. The process continues and is highly anticipated as an integral part of UNIGLOBE's convention. UNIGLOBE also has a program for managers who work to achieve the platinum manager pin.

After the pilot test, a survey evaluated the Counsellor Excellence Program. Based on the feedback, some of the program's criteria were changed to better reflect UNIGLOBE's expectations. Revisions and/or updates are still made annually. When introducing the program globally to remaining UNIGLOBE offices, the same process was used. Some of the criteria were adapted to reflect and accommodate specific countries.

Continued publicity

Press releases about the Counsellor Excellence Program are distributed to the travel industry, to all UNIGLOBE agencies, and to customers. The names of award achievers continue to be printed in all regional communications, including UNIGLOBE's intranet site.

Ongoing activities

Performance and compensation are based on achieving and surpassing bronze, silver, and gold standards of achievements. Continuous feedback from regions and agencies is requested to ensure that the program is regularly updated and improved. UNIGLOBE strives to maintain the program's objectives, while, at the same time, rewarding personnel who achieve the *Award for Excellence*—and thus challenge others to attain the designation.

RESULTS

In less than two years, a system-wide program was introduced, tested, and implemented. Over 100 awards for bronze, silver, or gold achievement levels have been awarded. The company considers these to be excellent results, since the program has rigorous standards and performance levels.

UNIGLOBE's Counsellor Excellence Program is an effective win-win program. Benefits are easily identified for everyone involved, and the customer receives better service. Counsellors and managers have a clear understanding of which skills, knowledge, and expertise they must demonstrate to excel in the program and obtain performance bonuses. Individual agency management has a well-defined tool for staff training and evaluation. The company as a whole benefits from the improved productivity, performance, and heightened morale that flow from on-the-job success and satisfaction.

The program continues to be successful, with numerous counsellors and managers gaining recognition. UNIGLOBE's annual system-wide sales volume is nearly $3 billion, and the company has been voted the number one franchise by *Entrepreneur Magazine* for 11 years.

Since the program's development, other travel agencies have asked to purchase UNIGLOBE's Counsellor Excellence Program. The program is presently not for sale; however, this may be reviewed in the future.

WTTC HUMAN RESOURCE CENTRE COMMENT

Although this successful UNIGLOBE system was designed by a large international corporation, the small operator can still benefit by applying the same four steps: communication; buy-in; needs assessment and education; and systematic monitoring on a small-scale basis. Education and needs assessment are readily available through local tourism/business institutions, and the other three steps can be implemented internally by even the smallest organizations.

KEY TERMS

travel trade

evaluation

travel counsellors

award recognition

performance levels

customer service

benchmarking

industry standards

franchise

designation

 **www.uniglobetravel.com**

DISCUSSION QUESTIONS

1. UNIGLOBE has offices of all sizes around the world. How does this travel franchise organization use training programs to a) maintain its corporate image, and b) maintain competitiveness?

2. How would you ensure that evaluation criteria, already higher than industry norms, retain their value and remain challenging?

3. How has UNIGLOBE provided value to its franchisees through this program?

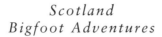

Scotland
Bigfoot Adventures

Submitted by: Mahri Prince

EMPLOYEE LOYALTY AND MORALE IMPROVED THROUGH TRAINING AND ASSESSMENT

… A dynamic and growing company looks for outside help to better define and document its operational structure and to improve communication.

LEARNING OUTCOMES

1. Describe the benefits that outside assistance can provide a company in identifying areas of its operation which need improvement.

2. Explain how a company philosophy may be imbedded in business and human resource planning.

3. Recognize the value of aligning with industry performance standards in building capacity for business growth.

> *"Access For All."*
>
> *Mission Statement*
> *Bigfoot Adventures*

OVERVIEW

Bigfoot Adventures began in 1991 as a mobile outdoor activities company offering a range of outdoor pursuits to tourists, schools, and companies. Three years later the company purchased a former Drovers Inn in the remote Highland Glen area of Boultenstone in Aberdeenshire, northeastern Scotland. After renovating the inn, Bigfoot Adventures opened the Boultenstone Outdoor Centre four months later.

With a permanent facility, Bigfoot Adventures could expand its services. As a result, the company offered outdoor activity packages with comfortable accommodation. Other features in its packages were a licensed bar and restaurant, noted for its wholesome home-cooked meals. The purchase of another seven acres in 2000 further expanded Bigfoot Adventures' facilities and the activities it offered.

Activities are customized to meet a client's needs. Groups and individuals experience a variety of activities in a safe and controlled manner in the great outdoors. Also available are single-day events, taking place off-site at hotels and other activity areas throughout the country. Mobile activities include climbing towers, mountain bikes, archery, and themed team-building activities such as treasure hunts and games.

Bigfoot Adventures currently operates with a staff of 11. There are six full-time and five part-time/seasonal employees. Upon opening the Boultenstone Outdoor Centre, an internal company review determined that although staff was loyal and motivated, operational procedures needed to be more clearly defined and better documented to provide consistent support and communication. After careful research, management chose the Investors In People (IIP) program to help restructure the organization. It was important to find a program that complemented the "people-led" business culture of Bigfoot Adventures.

IMPLEMENTATION

Investors In People is a national-standard program in the United Kingdom designed to help businesses work with and get the best from their employees. Following IIP guidelines, companies are able to create a solid foundation for growth and development. Bigfoot Adventures committed to working with IIP for six months to design a formal structure for the day-to-day running of the centre.

> *"Working towards and achieving IIP recognition has been a valuable and worthwhile exercise. The business is on a clearer path, with management and staff fully aware of roles, responsibilities, and future developments."*
>
> *Mahri Prince, Manager*
> *Bigfoot Adventures*

To set up a formal business structure, the company needed to:

- document staff induction (selection and orientation) procedures;
- design and administer a staff training and appraisal plan;

Bigfoot Adventures

Staff pose outside of Bigfoot Adventures' Boultenstone Outdoor Centre in Aberdeenshire, Scotland.

- design a formal company training plan; and
- create a new budgeting model.

Costs to incorporate the above procedures were covered by the local enterprise company (a government funded body set up to promote growth in the local economy by promoting different sectors). The enterprise company also provided specialist assistance in training issues, business advice, fund sourcing, direct funding, feasibility studies, etc.

Induction Program

During Bigfoot Adventures' induction program, new staff learn about "Bigfoot Culture." The orientation process uses both formal and informal training and covers such topics as:

- company structure
- company culture
- employee roles and responsibilities
- health and safety procedures
- area information
- training
- appraisal details, including evaluation formats and scheduling.

> *"A complete understanding of the company culture is considered to be the most important selling point in this people-led business, a philosophy that is supported by customer feedback sheets."*
>
> *Bigfoot Adventures*

Staff Appraisal

All staff participate in a regular company appraisal system. The purpose of the appraisal system is to make staff aware of ongoing company planning, business goals, developments, and their own role within the company. Appraisal forms are distributed one week prior to appraisal sessions, giving employees the opportunity to complete a personal review on the quality of their performance. The forms note staff strengths, weaknesses, opportunities, and concerns. All comments documented are confidential and considered key to the appraisal process. To formalize staff appraisals, training and development plans are revisited and evaluated so they continue to be in line with the business plan.

Company owners are involved in the appraisal sessions. To ensure that evaluations are objective and fair, individual training plans, previous assessments, and the company business plan are used as reference points. Full-time staff is appraised every six months. Seasonal staff is appraised every three months.

Staff Training

Bigfoot Adventures uses national governing bodies to train staff in the necessary outdoor qualifications. In-house trainers qualified in many of the outdoor disciplines perform instructor training. Staff receive outside assessments and exposure to different training methods when they undergo training at different areas within the United Kingdom. Outside assessments are conducted when staff fulfil the pre-entry requirement criteria, which are outlined in national governing-body awards. All national governing-body courses are conducted by approved, governing-body personnel.

Budgeting Model

Bigfoot Adventures also worked with a specialist to create a simple budgeting model. The model was designed around business income streams, business expenses, growth and development expenses, and borrowing options.

After working with IIP for six months, Bigfoot Adventures received Investor In People status in March 1996. Bigfoot Adventures continues to work with IIP, which provides ongoing support and reassessments. To retain IIP status, the company must perform the reassessment process every three years and is scheduled for its next reassessment in March 2002.

RESULTS

Since the opening of the Boultenstone Outdoor Centre, Bigfoot Adventure sales have increased 107 percent. Being part of the restructuring process, staff feel they contribute to the success of the business. The refined business structure has succeeded in improving customer service, while increasing staff morale.

Noteworthy results related to Bigfoot Adventure's business restructuring are:

- increased efficiency;
- better staff morale;
- accountable and measurable structured practices;
- clearer business goals and targets that are better understood by staff;
- measurable staff growth and development;
- higher levels of satisfaction noted in critique sheets and feedback letters; and
- other industry standards and licenses are met with ease.

WTTC Human Resource Centre COMMENT

Bigfoot Adventures restructured its company by incorporating systems and programs, which helped to define business goals and to better manage staff. A comprehensive employee induction process strengthened the corporate culture of Boultenstone Outdoor Centre and provided staff with continuous feedback and growth opportunities. A better-organized internal structure improved both operating efficiency and customer service. Finally, the use of outside trainers ensured that national outdoor leadership standards were maintained. This small tourism company took steps to utilize outside help in designing and following a simple restructuring program, which is helping to ensure continued growth and success.

KEY TERMS

team building	assessment
mobile delivery	communication
morale	staff training
Investors In People	company culture
staff appraisal	operational procedures
business plan	staff induction

 **www.bigfootadventures.com**

DISCUSSION QUESTIONS

1. What steps did this company take in its restructuring process?
2. What key decisions were made that have allowed for sustainable growth in the company?
3. What key customer service issues were addressed by using national outdoor leadership standards and a strengthened corporate culture?

chapter four

Building a Performance Culture: Improving Performance Service, Evaluations, Appraisals, Monitoring, and Accountability

United Kingdom
Little Chef & Travelodge

Submitted by: Phil Turner

CUSTOMER JOURNEY

... Generating consistently high-quality service in a nationwide restaurant chain while building employee productivity and morale.

LEARNING OUTCOMES

1. Recognize the importance of incorporating brand consistency throughout an organization.
2. Identify the factors that prevent a customer evaluation program from becoming stagnated.
3. Explain how an evaluation program increases staff morale.

> *"The Customer Journey is a journey that never ends as we constantly review and update the process to ensure that customers consistently receive excellent service."*
>
> *Management*
> *Little Chef*

OVERVIEW

Little Chef is the largest and leading roadside family-style restaurant chain in the United Kingdom (UK), with a full menu selection ranging from all-day breakfast to traditional foods and desserts. Little Chef has grown from a single property in 1958 to a chain of over 430 restaurants, found on most main roads throughout the UK. Despite impressive nation-wide growth, Little Chef has lacked brand consistency.

Little Chef management built a five-year action plan to improve customer service, using a new induction and training approach with an internal customer service auditing system. The action plan involved every employee and manager in the organization. Brand consistency emerged as a core value of the company, and a program called Customer Journey was born. Customer Journey involved every aspect of the customer's experience in a Little Chef restaurant, from driving into the car park to dining and departure.

IMPLEMENTATION

Customer Journey was launched nationally in spring 1997 through a series of countrywide road shows, led by a team of managers and trainers. Immediately following the road shows, each Little Chef property received a starter pack containing support material for implementing the Customer Journey program. This included an employee induction pack, a poster to display in the staff room, and a computer-based training package.

Head office management—in cooperation with restaurant managers—developed the computer-based training package. Designed for staff, the training package is an integral part of Little Chef's brand consistency training and covers all the theoretical elements of Customer Journey. Staff can retake the program until a passing grade is secured.

Twelve months after its introduction to all sites, Customer Journey was reviewed and updated by a Standards Committee (consisting of company managers, field managers, and staff). During the review process, management identified that the method of site evaluation could be improved. During the first year of the program, external companies were hired to dine incognito at Little Chef restaurants. However, feedback from the assessors was typically slow, and the assessors did not seem to know enough about the restaurant business to provide quality information.

Following the review, an in-house evaluation procedure was developed. The evaluation mirrored the objectives of the Customer Journey program. It was decided that the company's trainee managers were best suited to perform site evaluations. The second version of the program was introduced, and the entire evaluation process grew more efficient, focussing on the most accurate and relevant information.

To launch the auditing process, 10 restaurant manager designates were trained as auditors and instructed to work undercover for one month. Using a company car and payment vouchers, each auditor was instructed to visit certain sites within a two-week period, completing an unannounced Customer Journey audit. Results from each audit were immediately sent to a central base. There, the score was recorded and feedback was sent to the property within 24 hours.

After one month, participating auditors, company directors, and a selection of field management attended a debriefing session. The experiences of over 900 restaurant visits were detailed in up-to-the-minute feedback. The debriefing session focussed on the following topics:

- best visit

- worst visit

- flagship sites (large turnover sites)

- common issues (i.e., food quality and service standards)

- Travelodge issues (i.e., reception check-in process, cleanliness of room, and room standard). Because many Travelodge hotels had a Little Chef restaurant on premises, evaluations of Travelodge issues were included in the Customer Journey audit.

A synopsis of the results, together with action points, was sent to all restaurants. Each restaurant also received detailed information about its own site, together with general data for the region and the restaurant franchise as a whole.

After the first 10 restaurant-manager designates completed four weeks of undercover audits, another group repeated the procedure. Characteristically, the returning trainee managers came back to their place of work highly motivated to deliver quality service, having experienced both good and poor service from the perspective of the customer. As an invaluable motivational tool, this auditing process is now a core element of the fast-track development program for trainee managers.

After 120 restaurant-manager designates had completed undercover visits, the program was again revised. Changes this time included:

Weekly commentary
Weekly audit scores were distributed to field management, providing up-to-date feedback regarding customer service. Restaurants that had performed poorly were required to provide head office with an outline of action points within the week.

Audit records
To assist individual restaurants in tracking their audit findings, a "write-up poster board" was placed in each restaurant staff room. The poster board was updated after feedback was received and acknowledged by staff signatures. Some of the topic areas recorded were:

- areas "we" did well in

- areas of concern

- action points

- last two audit scores.

Hardware upgrading
New tills were placed in all Little Chef restaurants.

Business reviews
Periodical business reviews are based on a firm measurement process. Over the years, the company has set higher benchmark standards to improve evaluations. For the past year, scores have been rewarded in four new formats.

- **Fun fund**—Each site receives a "fun fund" statement every month, informing it how much is in its account so that employees can enjoy a night out together. The fun fund is increased by improved sales compared to the previous year and/or if the site is listed in the top 20 sites from Customer Journey audits.

- **Customer satisfaction index**—This is a quarterly award based on the average audit score. The audit score is a combination of customer feedback (this includes verbal and written compliments and complaints) as well as Customer Journey scores. The award is split into three categories based on turnover so each type of site has a chance of winning up to £2 500 (GBP).

- **Heroes**—Individual employees who are identified by the auditors as delivering excellent service receive a letter of thanks plus a voucher for £10 (GBP).

- **League tables**—Results are ranked in league format. For example, if a restaurant's average is 88 percent it is in the premier league. If the average is 75 to 87 percent, the restaurant is in the first division. If the restaurant average is below 75 percent, it is ranked in the second division—Little Chef's worst performers.

RESULTS

With regular audits received bimonthly, the drive to monitor and deliver consistently good service has resulted in measurable changes.

The average audit scores for the entire company have increased over 8 percent since the audits commenced. Service-related complaints have declined on average 20 percent, while compliments have increased over 50 percent against last year. The number of customer visits has increased for the first time in several years.

> *"Excellent standards of service."*
> *"A pleasure to visit the branch."*
> *"All staff set out to succeed."*
>
> *Recent customer quotes at Little Chef Restaurants*

Statistics from the audits have shown which day of the week and what time of day "best and worst service" is experienced. In the light of these data, changes have been made to provide more consistent service throughout the week. For example, weekend service problems were resolved by introducing more flexible contracts across the workforce. The lull in service during shift hand-over times was another challenge resolved by assigning shift accountability to the outgoing duty manager and incorporating a shift hand-over section into daily shift plans. The day shift (7 a.m. to 3 p.m.) is handed over to the night shift (3 p.m. to 10 a.m.).

From the employee's perspective, customer service is now a number one priority. Employees recognize that they are constantly measured and rewarded for the service they provide. Customer Journey has become a positive buzzword for all employees.

Recently, Little Chef has been accredited with a Definitive Standard for Customer Service Excellence by Hospitality Assured. This is a national scheme for service excellence set up by the Hotel & Catering International Management Association and the British Hospitality Association. Little Chef was the first national restaurant chain to achieve the award, and it attributes its success to the Customer Journey program.

In 1998 and 1999 Little Chef restaurants also received the Tommy Campaign Award for the "Best Family Restaurant in the UK." More recently, the British Hotel Guest Survey named the company the "Most Improved Brand of the Year" in 1999.

Travelodge was initially included in the Customer Journey program because many hotels have a Little Chef on the premises. The same team of trainee restaurant managers carried out the audits, but the restaurant audit did not suit the accommodation properties. Instead, the program has been adapted and relaunched as Travelodge Rest Assured. Program results are not known at this time.

Simultaneously, Customer Journey addressed two essential company needs. The program integrated a stand-alone training package with a motivational corporate philosophy. Particularly successful aspects of the program include:

- Monetary and non-monetary incentives motivate employees intrinsically and extrinsically.
- The program avoids stagnation by being updated regularly.
- Trainee managers return to their place of work highly motivated and well prepared to anticipate and understand customers' needs. (By investing the time to train these employees as Customer Journey auditors, trainee managers pass on to their staff the core values that ensure vigorous growth and profitability in a competitive and demanding environment.)

WTTC HUMAN RESOURCE CENTRE COMMENT

Customer Journey developed through the input and support of front line staff, field management, and head office employees. Management updated the training program to prevent stagnation, and provided both financial and prestige rewards and incentives to encourage participation. Forward thinking by Little Chef management is demonstrated in their selection of restaurant manager designates as the regularly scheduled auditors of Customer Journey. As noted, these "managers-in-training" returned to their workplace motivated and, possibly, better equipped to conduct training from the "bottom up."

KEY TERMS

customer service

mystery shopper

brand consistency

site evaluation

auditing system

computer-based training

incentive

intrinsic

extrinsic

assessor

www.little-chef.co.uk

www.travelodge.co.uk

DISCUSSION QUESTIONS

1. As an auditor visiting a Little Chef restaurant in the role of a mystery shopper, create a 10-point checklist to evaluate the staff and the restaurant.

2. Explain how Little Chef made its evaluation process more efficient and accurate.

3. What other kinds of incentive programs can you think of to support the friendly competition between Little Chef restaurants?

South Africa
The Blue Train

Submitted by: Ntahli Borotho and André van Rooyen

TRAINING TRAINS

… A proud South African national monument builds a powerful reputation in the international luxury train market, adding competitive advantage through service excellence training.

LEARNING OUTCOMES

1. Identify how a consultant may structure a training program to meet a client's specific needs.

2. Describe how a product may be successfully relaunched through product upgrading, staff retraining, and market repositioning.

3. Explain how a company may retrain and upgrade employees in a productive, non-threatening way.

OVERVIEW

The Blue Train is one of South Africa's most successful travel and tourism products—often referred to as a national monument. Originally called the Union Limited, people referred to the train as "*those Blue Trains*" because of its distinctive sapphire blue carriages. In 1946 the train was officially named The Blue Train.

In operation for over half a century, the train originally shuttled South Africa's president and his entourage between the Parliament in Cape Town and the administrative capital of Pretoria. In 1972 the train embarked on a new career and was recommissioned as an exciting and unique international luxury tourism product.

The train ran as a successful tourism service for 22 years. In 1994, the management of Spoornet (a division of Transnet Ltd., a South African public company which is in charge of South Africa's railway lines) realized the train cars needed updating to compete in the international luxury train market.

By 1997 two entire trains were rebuilt at a cost of 70 million rand—surpassing all existing international standards for luxury train travel. Design details include Italian birch panelling throughout the train, suites with individually controlled air-conditioning and closed-circuit television, Italian marble ensuite bathrooms, and personal CD players and video recorders. Having two identical carriage sets (twin Blue Trains) enabled one of the two Blue Trains to be refitted for the inaugural journey on September 26, 1997.

Demand has grown remarkably since the refit. The two trains now travel between Pretoria and Cape Town thrice weekly. To provide diversity and to court repeat business, they also embark on a monthly return journey to Victoria Falls, Zimbabwe. In 1999, The Blue Train opened additional new runs between Cape Town and Port Elizabeth (Garden Route) and between Pretoria and Hoedspruit (Valley of the Olifants), both once a month.

With such a unique top-end product, it's not surprising that 90 percent of Blue Train patrons are international visitors. Guests spend one to two nights on board the train, depending on the journey, travelling in cars that reach a speed of 110 kilometres (68 miles) per hour. A total of 82 passengers are accommodated in the first renovated Blue Train, while the second carries 74 patrons in 10 guest coaches.

Each Blue Train has a complement of 30 hospitality staff including the train manager, executive chef, sous chef, cook, three kitchen assistants, restaurant manager, two rooms-division managers, 10 rooms-division butlers, and 10 food and beverage butlers. There is a first-aid worker on board and a contingency medical plan should an emergency arise. Doctors are on standby en route.

The Blue Train has a significant on-board staff-to-guest ratio, because its service rivals that of five-star hotels, exclusive holiday luxury resorts, game parks, luxury cruises, and other luxury trains. The Blue Train's service standards need to be of the highest quality and match those of a first-class hotel, with memorable scenery and luxurious cabin comfort.

IMPLEMENTATION

While designing service standards, management recognized that a large percentage of staff had years of experience on the "old" Blue Train, but would need specific retraining to update their skills to match the new, higher international service standards. In contrast, new recruits would have different training needs, as they would require training from scratch.

A service concept called Superior Personalized Service was developed to achieve the professional standards of service one would expect in a superb hotel. Every detail surrounding on-board service was examined and improved upon. Management responded by designing a strategy to create appropriate service standards, and to build a monitoring method to ensure that standards were maintained.

A training company was hired to design and implement the required program. Over two months, operational standards, service standards, skill-set requirements, and guest-orientation training programs were created according to management's specifications. A system for monitoring these new standards was also established.

Every employee received a manual detailing the international expectations of deluxe service. These expectations were applied to all jobs on board the train. Diagrams and sketches were developed for maximum clarity. The manuals served as the framework for the training courses.

The skills-training courses reviewed the product, built service confidence among staff, improved staff's people-handling skills in providing professional service, helped in understanding guest needs, and explained how to deal effectively in different situations. The training company's instructors taught employees the Service Excellence theory at training venues off-site.

Each employee received 72 hours of preparation prior to the launch of the new Blue Train, much of it on board the train itself. Ongoing instruction has since averaged 16 hours per employee. Coaching has been delivered in three key styles:

- **Off-the-job skills training**—The training techniques used for butler service, food, drink, wine, and bar service aspects included a combination of classroom sessions, role-playing, and group exercises.

- **Developing staff confidence and morale**—This component was considered controversial as it did not deal with specific situations but focussed on developing self-esteem, service confidence, and a thorough understanding of how attitudes and moods affect interaction with guests from different cultures. These concepts were then applied to the working environment aboard the train. Having completed this training component, staff reported an increase in confidence as well as a better understanding of their roles within the service program.

- **Corrective on-the-job training**—Each month, trainers travel on both Blue Trains to review staff performance against service standards and to provide coaching and guidance to address deficiencies.

All staff members are interviewed on the train at least twice a year by both management and trainers. Throughout the year, staff members have the opportunity to take courses that develop a specific career path, skill requirement, or service competency. Various companies, including Spoornet, offer these courses at diverse venues. A management development program is also available off-site for employees who have demonstrated the potential to be future supervisors or managers.

Staff in 20 different jobs rotate positions over a three-month period. Job rotation helps employees remain stimulated, develops a shared understanding of all service positions, and provides a multi-skilled staff pool that can cover positions as necessary.

The Blue Train management and human resource trainers periodically stay aboard the train for a month at a time to measure staff performance against service standards, to provide feedback, and, if necessary, to modify standards while in direct communication with staff.

Because of the exceptionally high guest expectations, a monthly mystery guest program has been implemented, wherein an individual is hired to act as a patron. Prior to the journey, the mystery guest is asked to telephone The Blue Train with an enquiry. The remaining part of the evaluation concentrates on station lounges and the standards on board the train. The areas of service evaluated include:

- telephone standards
- arrival and boarding procedures
- compartment standards
- service and standards in all public areas, the club, lounge, and observation cars
- afternoon tea standards and service
- breakfast, lunch, and dinner service as well as standards (presentations and taste of meals)
- souvenir and memorabilia standards
- exceptional or unacceptable service experienced. (The guest is requested to mention names.)

The mystery guest expects 100 percent compliance while evaluating all departments, and, on the detailed form provided, rates all services with yes and no answers. On a monthly basis, staff members are given the exact guest feedback and receive recognition for exceptional service experiences. A summary of areas for improvement is also discussed with staff.

RESULTS

The "new" Blue Train has now been "on the rails" for approximately three years. The Blue Train won the prestigious international award of "World's Leading Luxury Train" in 1998, 1999, and 2000—in other words, for three consecutive years after the relaunch!

Feedback from guests during September to April of 1999 has been positive, with many guests expressing their delight in dealing with capable staff who maintain their South African charm. Guests frequently comment on staff confidence and the obvious pride they take in their work.

Staff turnover is negligible. Promotions are predominantly from within the company and staff teamwork initiative and work commitment is extraordinary in comparison with other local companies.

WTTC Human Resource Centre COMMENT

The Blue Train was relaunched with a commitment to a legendary vision of luxury and service excellence. A three-phase program was developed that first defined and established service and performance standards, rebuilt staff confidence and morale, and finally monitored and guided service on board The Blue Train. Multi-skilling and job rotation support service consistency, and staff development programs contribute to commitment and internal prospects for promotion. On a luxury train, employees are under intense scrutiny from demanding guests. The strategic approach to organizational change has created a learning culture on the train that continually measures performance against service standards—which are themselves continually revisited.

KEY TERMS

on-board service

service excellence

monitoring

job rotation

staff-to-guest ratio

mystery shopper

competitive advantage

luxury train

staff performance

 **www.bluetrain.co.za**

DISCUSSION QUESTIONS

1. Describe the key steps taken to reposition The Blue Train in the marketplace.

2. Explain the use of the mystery guest program to help maintain exceptionally high levels of service.

3. What are the characteristics of the target market The Blue Train is trying to attract? List five products that could be considered to present direct competition to The Blue Train.

Canada
CorporaTel

Submitted by: Susan Tilley-Russell

A MEMBER OF THE CCL GROUP

BUILDING A CONTACT CENTRE'S QUALITY MANAGEMENT PROGRAM

. . . A client-driven program provides customers with exceptional service through incorporating industry standards and establishing in-house policies, by monitoring procedures, and by using coaching as a staff training tool.

LEARNING OUTCOMES

1. Recognize how CorporaTel's total quality management program improved its average quality rating of contacts, as well as the corporation's morale, teamwork, and professionalism.
2. Explain the purpose of coaching staff, and why customer-service representatives and team leaders view coaching positively.
3. Describe the importance of monitoring in total quality management at the call centre.

> *"The Internet has changed everything. And it will continue to change almost daily. A traditional in-house call centre isn't enough any more. Today, you need the technology and expertise required to keep up with the latest changes. Investing the resources to manage this in-house can divert companies' attention away from their core business. Selecting an outside expert whose business is customer contact in all areas makes financial sense."*
>
> *CorporaTel*

OVERVIEW

CorporaTel currently employs over 400 staff at any given time of the year, with locations in three Canadian cities (Halifax, Saint John, and Vancouver). One of the company's key areas of expertise is tourism reservation and information systems. Having started as one of Canada's leading call centres serving clients countrywide, CorporaTel has evolved into a multi-channel contact centre with clients throughout North America. Key clients include provincial tourism departments, financial institutions, and FORTUNE 500 companies.

A call centre is an organization where representatives accept calls for the purpose of providing customer service for inquiries, reservations, and mailing information. The nature of the industry, however, has changed dramatically over the past few years. Today, companies are devoting significant resources to customer relationship management strategies. These strategies depend on being able to interact with customers through several points of contact.

Recognizing this shift in customer behaviour, CorporaTel offers fully Web-enabled customer interaction solutions—combining customer contacts over the telephone, Web self-service, e-mail, and text chat. However, the human factor, and the need to have consistent quality delivery of every contact remain vital components of this new customer interaction.

> *"Agents in a contact centre not only talk on the phone, making and receiving calls—they also work to personalize the online experience. For example, if a customer is browsing a Web site and has a question, with the click of a button they can connect to a live agent. Using integrated contact tools on a knowledge-based platform, the agent can interface with this customer any way the customer chooses. Every screen the customer has clicked through during the session has been tracked and stored. The agent can then have a text chat online (both parties type messages back and forth to each other in an online conversation), or speak (using voice-over IP technology) online, or even co-browse and 'push' screens of information down to appear on the customer's screen."*
>
> Susan Tilley-Russell, Vice President
> Corporatel

The type of service CorporaTel chooses to provide is client-driven—that is, based on client needs. However, the high level of service that CorporaTel expects from each of its three centres is the responsibility of the company. For this reason, CorporaTel has developed a standardized practice to be used by all staff throughout the nation. To achieve quality contacts, new and improved monitoring and coaching processes were developed. Many were established after reviewing best practices.

IMPLEMENTATION

Dedicated to excellence in customer service and professionalism, CorporaTel developed a national strategy to improve its service quality management. The strategy is to:

- determine the client's needs;
- set standards for the types of contacts per client;
- implement a total quality management program; and
- monitor and improve the program as needed.

To satisfy the needs of both the client and the customer, CorporaTel decided that its total quality management program should be applied to all types of contacts (telephone, Web site, e-mail, etc.) and to all CorporaTel clients. At the same time, CorporaTel wanted to improve the average quality rating of contacts and the corporation's morale, teamwork, and professionalism.

It was decided that a total quality management program would not be achieved unless the program was implemented throughout all CorporaTel offices, and continuously evaluated for improvement. The program was staged in different phases in order to monitor progress and to ensure that each step was properly carried out. Full program set-up took between 12 to 18 months, with monitoring steps put into place to continually measure the program's effectiveness.

Training Quality Listeners and Effective Coaches

All CorporaTel offices selected team leaders, who were each responsible for nine to ten customer-service representatives. Team leaders became the role models for customer-service representatives by portraying all the characteristics of quality customer-service representatives, and providing training and feedback to their team. There are 20 team leaders in the Halifax and Vancouver offices and 14 in the Saint John office.

Each team leader completed an intense one-week training process to become a quality listener and an effective coach. This intensive course instructed the team leader in strategies to monitor calls and outlined CorporaTel's standards in quality service. Next, team leaders were trained to list the strengths and weaknesses of individual customer-service representatives in terms of their quality of contact. The following are some of the features used to evaluate a customer-service representative's contact quality:

- voice quality and tone
- professionalism
- handling of difficult calls
- listening skills
- typing ability
- cross-selling and up-selling
- ability to close the sale
- ability to effectively direct/service a customer over the Web.

Team leaders were then able to determine the areas in which each customer-service representative required further training.

Monitoring

CorporaTel's monitoring program was developed and based on the national standards for reservation sales agents, developed by the Canadian Tourism Human Resource Council (CTHRC). Through the provincial arm of CTHRC—the Tourism Association of Nova Scotia's Human Resource Council—CorporaTel has supported the certification of its agents, thus ensuring industry standards are met at all times.

> *"CorporaTel is a leader in supporting the use of national standards and certification. The professional development of their people is an inherent part of their business plan, and as a result they have supported more staff through national certification than any other Nova Scotia business."*
>
> *Darlene Grant Fiander, Director*
> *TIANS Human Resource Council*

Twice a month, each customer-service representative is counselled by their team leader, who monitors at least 10 of his or her calls. During this period, the team leaders analyze monitored calls/contacts to identify each representative's mastery of the required skills. For example, one may have "excellent" voice quality, compared to the standard, whereas another customer-service representative may have "good" voice quality. In this example, the team leader will identify the "good" and work with the customer-service representative to improve the service to "excellent." CorporaTel's performance reward program for all customer-service representatives measures productivity and quality equally. After commencement of this program, agent performance improved in both areas.

Coaching

Coaching sessions are designed as a forum through which team leaders are able to communicate areas in which a customer-service representative excels, and areas where improvement is required. Coaching sessions last approximately 30 to 45 minutes, and occur every two weeks for each customer-service representative. This process is very important for ensuring quality and has proven effective. Customer-service representatives and team leaders view coaching positively, as each session is goal-oriented and non-threatening.

Reinforcement/Retraining Sessions

In the final phase of CorporaTel's quality call-management program, self-paced training tools (such as video and audiotapes) are used to help train customer-service representatives. Most of the training tools were purchased through the local telephone company and were specifically designed for call centres. Other tools were developed in-house, particularly those that focus on the skills used by agents working in the multi-channel environment (Web and phone). The average time to use any of these training tools is approximately one hour.

CorporaTel has several monitoring and coaching rooms, as well as a training facility within the centre where customer-service representatives are able to access the self-paced training tools. Employees are paid extra if they are required to work longer hours to complete the training. Depending on the time of year and day of the week, customer-service representatives may or may not train during their regular schedule shifts. They may come in early or stay late to complete training.

CorporaTel views training as an essential investment. The total cost for implementing the quality contact management program was within budget, and the training tools required are reusable after the initial purchase. The majority of training was completed in-house, with additional assistance from quality training consultants.

RESULTS

This new approach to total quality management has improved staff morale, teamwork, and professionalism. Once implementation began, team leaders had more opportunity to discuss these issues with each customer-service representative. Customer-service representatives claimed they were happier 95 percent of the time as a result of this program, largely because it made them feel part of CorporaTel's team.

As CorporaTel continuously evaluates every customer-service representative over a two-week period, each team supervisor is able to monitor progress in all areas. There has been a marked improvement in teamwork between all members of the team. Monitoring and coaching processes are directly attributed to improving the quality of calls. The average mark for a quality contact improved by 25 percent. Quality calls/contacts are critical to ensuring satisfied customers, satisfied clients, and an increased quality of work.

WTTC HUMAN RESOURCE CENTRE COMMENT

The telephone is a powerful and often underused tool in supporting friendly, efficient, and effective communication with both customers and business relations. With the spread of Web-based services, human contact is still a vital component of contact service centres. In the tourism business, customer-service representatives have a crucial role as the first contact between the customer and services. Given the nature of tourism, small-, medium-, and large-scale businesses— which rely on inquiries, reservations, mailing information, and market research— can learn from CorporaTel. Using a national strategy, focussed on improving the performance of their customer-service representatives, CorporaTel meets its client's needs and provides continuity throughout the organization.

KEY TERMS

call centre
integrated contact centre
Web-enabled
Web self-service
e-mail
text chat
customer-service representatives

monitoring
coaching processes
total quality management
reservation and information systems
national standards
certification

 **www.corporatel.ca**

DISCUSSION QUESTIONS

1. When employees feel that they are contributing to the company's success, their morale, teamwork, and productivity improve. What can employers do to make employees feel they are a vital component of a business?

2. Having calls monitored can be intimidating for the customer-service representative. What can the company do to alleviate the employee's apprehension? What systems should the company have in place to explain why monitoring is positive?

3. What five employee characteristics are needed to succeed in this demanding job?

Scotland
Scottish Borders Tourist Board

Submitted by: Riddle Graham

LINKING TRAINING TO BUSINESS GOALS

… The Scottish Borders Tourist Board transformed its corporate culture with the help of Investors In People—revitalizing its leadership role in its tourist region.

LEARNING OUTCOMES

1. Recognize the importance of linking training and development activity to the business plan.

2. Describe the elements and processes involved in a major corporate restructuring initiative.

3. Define the function of employee empowerment in designing and implementing corporate reorganization strategies.

> *"The Scottish Borders—Scotland's leading short-break destination."*
>
> *Scottish Borders Tourist Board*

OVERVIEW

Covering about 4 600 square kilometres, the Scottish Borders stretches from the rolling hills and moorland in the west, through valleys of rich agricultural plains in the east, and on to the rocky Berwickshire coastline with its secluded coves and picturesque fishing villages. For a traveller visiting the area, the tourist board's local tourist information centres are mines of valuable information.

The Scottish Borders Tourist Board was first established in 1982 as the Scottish Borders tourism authority. It is one of 14 area tourist boards in Scotland that provide visitors with a variety of travel services and products. A 12-person Board of Directors governs the tourist board. Board representatives include individuals from the local tourism industry, the local council, and the local enterprise company (a public agency funded by central government, but operating at a local level and responsible for economic development and training). Also on the Board of Directors are representatives from the national tourist authority—the Scottish Tourist Board.

During the financial year 2000/01, the Scottish Borders Tourist Board employed 58 people (14 full-time and 44 seasonal/part-time positions) with an operating budget in excess of £2.6 million (GBP). Its corporate objectives are to:

- encourage holiday and business visits to the area;
- provide a comprehensive information service for visitors; and
- develop partnerships with public and private sectors to encourage improvements in the quality of local tourism services and facilities.

The Scottish Borders Tourist Board recognizes that its employees are key to achieving corporate objectives. It also realizes that training and staff development are essential components of staying in business, improving business, and managing change. This philosophy is a factor in the organization's past successes, and is responsible for positioning the organization to meet the changing needs of its diverse customer base.

In 1994, the Scottish Borders Tourist Board began working with Investors In People (IIP), under the United Kingdom's national "people standard." With IIP assistance, businesses can improve employee relations and better link staff training development with business goals. IIP is the national standard that sets a level of good practice for improving an organization's performance through its people. Through self-assessment, the Scottish Borders Tourist Board learned its business objectives were not being achieved, as staff training was not linked to its objectives.

IMPLEMENTATION

Prior to working with IIP, the Scottish Borders Tourist Board had a business plan containing clear aims, objectives, targets, and an efficient staff training program. The Scottish Borders Tourist Board began the IIP process by evaluating itself. First it worked though IIP's self-assessment process. The process has the organization match its internal performance against IIP's 23 standard indicators. These standard performance levels are divided into four key activity areas: commitment, planning, action, and evaluation.

The process determined that while the Scottish Borders Tourist Board had numerous human resource systems and business processes in place (and the paperwork to prove it), it

Scottish Borders Tourist Board

Scottish Borders Tourist Board staff are ready to set sail!

needed to better link training and development activity with the working business plan, and to improve evaluation procedures.

Though initially sceptical and concerned about the amount of paperwork, extra meetings, and challenges in reorganizing an entire organization, the Scottish Borders Tourist Board reviewed the benefits of achieving IIP status. The tourist board quickly realized that by achieving IIP status it would improve its communication. By improving communication it would increase staff motivation, reduce ineffective training, and create clearer goals and objectives. The Scottish Borders Tourist Board committed itself to the process.

An in-house team of five to seven persons—consisting of management and staff from all levels of the organization—met on a regular basis to chart the organization's progress. The goal was to move the Scottish Borders Tourist Board towards final assessment. The team was empowered to deliver in the decision-making process. The chief executive chaired the team and outside consultants were hired when necessary.

After 18 months, the Scottish Borders Tourist Board completely transformed the way it approached planning and implemented business and human resource activities. During the final assessment process, the Scottish Borders Tourist Board prepared a report summarizing how it felt now that it had met each of the IIP standards. Included within the report were supporting documents, such as the organization's business plan, training plan, and staff development review paperwork. The portfolio also included samples of completed pre-/post-training and development-assessment forms, examples of evaluation and feedback forms, evidence of internal and external communication of IIP issues, individual job descriptions, induction training programs, and training records.

> *"We continue to realize that IIP is a continuous process which probably never had a real 'end.'"*
>
> *Management*
> *Scottish Borders Tourist Board*

The written documentation also went through a thorough analysis. There was a day-long visit by an external IIP assessor, who interviewed 12 staff (selected at random) from all levels of the organization, and compared what was written with what was observed.

In February 1996, Investors In People recognized the Scottish Borders Tourist Board with an award. This was the first area tourist board to achieve such status at the time, and one of only a handful of tourism businesses in Scotland with the award.

RESULTS

Since first gaining IIP recognition, the Scottish Borders Tourist Board has successfully completed a three-year reassessment in 1999 and a further one-year assessment in 2000. The Board is now reassessed annually to maintain IIP accreditation. The accreditation symbolizes a commitment to policies and good practice, and has been instrumental in achieving such benefits as:

- improved level and quality of communication;
- enhanced staff morale;
- improved employee skills and knowledge;
- better performance measured in terms of increased revenue, increased efficiency; better use of resources, and positive customer feedback on service;
- increased staff awareness of the importance of training, development, and the associated costs and benefits;
- improved Board management;
- training and development outputs linked to national certificate standards (Scottish Vocational Qualifications, or SVQs);
- enhanced organizational status; and
- continuous review and change management.

As of April 1996, the organization operates with an updated staffing structure, revised job descriptions, new staff terms and conditions of employment, and a people-oriented business plan. But most of all, the Scottish Borders Tourist Board has a total commitment to IIP principles. It continually updates and challenges its business and human resource systems and processes.

Linked to the IIP award, the Scottish Borders Tourist Board revised its staff induction program, implemented quarterly review meetings to discuss the evolving business plan, and structured continuous reviews for both progress and evaluation. To its honour, the Scottish Borders Tourist Board was awarded the prestigious Scottish Tourism Thistle Award for "Training in Small Business" in November 1996.

In the two years following, the Scottish Borders Tourist Board introduced a range of staff initiatives to improve communication, evaluation, and staff involvement in decision-making and planning processes. Two examples implemented to improve direct communication include a staff newsletter and e-mail.

Employees are more conscious of how their particular roles affect the "business future" of the Scottish Borders Tourist Board. Management reinforces this concept by regularly reviewing business goals and training needs to match the changing environment in which the organization operates. Job-specific, technical, and personal development opportunities for all staff complement training and development. Formal systems are in place to facilitate this process and to measure the results in the areas of:

- business planning
- induction
- job descriptions
- staff development reviews
- objective setting and review
- team meetings
- external network meetings
- Board of Director meetings.

As part of management's ongoing commitment to review and change, the Board produced a new customer-focussed business plan during the year 2000. It is also in the process of reorganizing the staffing structure. The new structure will match the newly identified customer-base needs, namely visitors and funding partners. Implementation will take place in 2001 and it is expected that the new structure will be more customer-focussed than the previous structure.

WTTC Human Resource Centre COMMENT

The Scottish Borders Tourist Board successfully restructured its organization by linking enhanced staff training to its business plan. Accreditation of the organization helps ensure sustainability of the changes, and supports a renewed culture of business achievement and employee development. This transformation takes a great deal of effort and perseverance, but this case study demonstrates the rewards of systematic efforts towards the development of a corporate training culture.

KEY TERMS

information centre
tourist board
business planning
staff training
employee relations

self-assessment
communication
Investors In People
staff induction program

 **www.scot-borders.co.uk**

DISCUSSION QUESTIONS

1. Discuss the possible impact that a major reorganization of a tourist board could have in encouraging improvements in the quality of local tourism services and facilities.
2. What important changes in business practice—occurring as a result of new training and staff development—are illustrated in this case study?
3. In your own words, explain the role of Investors In People.

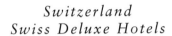
Switzerland
Swiss Deluxe Hotels

Submitted by: Inge Steiger

Swiss Deluxe Hotels

IMPROVING SERVICE ATTITUDES

… Building better attitudes through mystery guest evaluations and interactive training.

LEARNING OUTCOMES

1. Explain the mystery guests' role in the evaluation system.
2. Describe how the methods used in the interactive training program helped management train and coach all hotel property employees consistently.
3. Identify on-site evaluation procedures and outcomes.

OVERVIEW

In 1993, Swiss Deluxe Hotels made a commitment to survey all 36 of its hotels to identify strengths and weaknesses in their delivery of customer service. Swiss Deluxe Hotels joined forces with the Ecole Hôtelière de Lausanne (the world's first hotel school, located in Lausanne, Switzerland) which provided direction in designing and administering an evaluation system appropriate to the needs of the hotel group.

The evaluation system was conducted through the use of mystery guests. All mystery guests were qualified inspectors. These inspectors stayed for two to three days at hotels participating in the evaluation program, quietly observing the service and behaviour of employees.

For each hotel evaluated, the inspectors completed a 40-page questionnaire. Written or photographic records were kept to document areas of concern. Services identified as below standard were tested numerous times to determine if the incident was simply an isolated lapse, or a serious problem. Performance was assessed against a list of over 1 500 criteria.

Overall, results of the evaluation program identified a need for attitude training throughout the hotel group. Swiss Deluxe Hotels developed the Service Excellence Training Program as a training tool to consistently train and coach all hotel property employees.

IMPLEMENTATION

The Service Excellence Training Program uses a lighthearted approach to raise staff awareness about quality service. The primary goal of the program is not so much to boost participants' "knowledge" as to bring about changes in "attitude." The objective is to stimulate a friendlier and more helpful attitude in staff, and to increase awareness of hygiene standards.

The course can vary in length but generally takes two hours to complete. Results are noticeable within a short period of time, as there is an immediate improvement in the hotel's service culture. The program can be used for one-on-one training using a CD-ROM, or for training groups of 10 to 15 using a system which projects the program onto a larger screen. The program is available for purchase in CD-ROM and interactive CD-ROM in six languages.

To begin the program, the user loads the CD-ROM. Their "service journey" begins with an invitation to register at the Dolce Vita Hotel, an (imaginary) elegant establishment that is currently going through a major crisis. At the Dolce (Italian, meaning sweet) Vita Hotel, staff have been resting on their laurels, are satisfied with being merely average, and have lost the ability to feel good about what they are doing. As a consequence, the hotel (which was once a model of excellence) has slid downhill and is now more like the Triste (French from Latin *tristis* meaning sad, melancholy) Vita Hotel.

While engaging in the game, the user quickly becomes aware that what is needed is not renovations, but a change in staff attitude. The program highlights two guests—Mr. Feelgood and Mrs. Hacker—who demonstrate positive and negative behaviour as a result of staff actions. The program user wins points each time a mistake is recognized and a problem is solved.

The interactive training approach allows the user to follow the program chronologically, or to choose specific topics of interest and work through the related exercises.

RESULTS

The inspectors' reports clearly distinguished areas of strength and areas of weakness within each hotel. After completing an evaluation, inspectors identified themselves to management and continued with an on-the-spot review of the hotel's standards of excellence. Instant feedback was considered highly beneficial by hoteliers because it was specific and immediate.

Sceptical initially, individual hoteliers within the Swiss Deluxe Hotel group acknowledged the value of on-site evaluation as a tool for identifying problems within each hotel. Where staff attitude was identified as an area needing improvement, the Service Excellence Training Program could be used.

It took 12 months to evaluate all 36 Swiss Deluxe Hotel properties. Results highlighted both strengths and weaknesses in service delivery. Some significant outcomes are listed below:

- Swiss Deluxe Hotels holds the worldwide record for the shortest interval between arrival at the hotel and luggage in room: nine minutes.
- The company holds the same top ranking for hotel departures.
- On average, breakfast served in the room arrives within 13 minutes.
- Housekeeping and laundry services received an above-average rating.
- Standards of friendliness at reception and in restaurants showed room for improvement.
- The highest-scoring departments were laundry (94.9 percent), health and beauty (93.9 percent), and restaurants (92.1 percent).

Swiss Deluxe Hotels is pleased with the results of the Service Excellence Training Program, but realizes there is a continued need for customer-care training in specific areas of the hotel's operations.

WTTC HUMAN RESOURCE CENTRE COMMENT

Collaboration with a local training institution, as demonstrated by Swiss Deluxe Hotels and the Ecole Hôtelière in Lausanne, is another example of a partnership benefiting the tourism industry. Once initial scepticism was overcome, management buy-in paved the way for Swiss Deluxe Hotels to consistently train and coach all hotel property employees. Choosing an interactive training program that is capable of being used in self-study and in groups provides flexible training options to suit employees and trainers alike. Having the program available for sale in six languages brings this attitudinal training within reach of smaller establishments.

KEY TERMS

on-site evaluation	attitude training
interactive training	mystery guest
quality standards	hotel school
assessment	service culture

 **www.swissdeluxe.com**

DISCUSSION QUESTIONS

1. What can management do to encourage staff to voluntarily use the Service Excellence Training Program? List five ways to encourage staff to repeatedly review the material.

2. When presenting the on-site evaluation, in what ways can the inspector positively inform the hotel manager of areas needing improvement, while reinforcing the value of the entire evaluation process?

3. List the ways in which the silent shopper program provided a basis for service improvement throughout the system.

Canada
Delta Hotels

Submitted by: William Pallett

EMPLOYEE SERVICE GUARANTEES

. . . As a leader and innovator in the Canadian hospitality industry, Delta Hotels offers employee service guarantees, reinforcing management's commitment to employees.

LEARNING OUTCOMES

1. Judge how financial penalties may be used to protect guarantees to employees.

2. Describe how to implement and run an efficient employee-assessment system that is guaranteed by the company.

3. Describe how a human resource department maintains consistency by implementing a strategic employee performance-review system.

> *"We strive to be the preferred employer of choice in the hospitality industry—a good place to work, providing everyone with the opportunity for development and growth."*
>
> *Delta Hotels*

OVERVIEW

Delta Hotels is the largest first-class hotel company in Canada. Headquartered in Toronto, Ontario, Delta Hotels is a wholly owned subsidiary of Canadian Pacific Hotels & Resorts. The company manages and franchises 39 hotels and resorts throughout Canada, and oversees a workforce of approximately 8 000 employees. Delta Hotels' diverse portfolio of city-centre, airport, and resort properties caters to business and leisure travellers.

Known for its aggressive marketing strategies and innovative delivery of products and services, Delta Hotels introduced the One-Minute Check-In Service Guarantee for its Delta Privilege customers, and Great Meetings Guaranteed incentive for business travellers. These were both firsts in the Canadian marketplace. Delta Hotels went on to introduce service guarantees for its employees in 1995.

Employee service guarantees are Delta Hotels' overall commitment to excellence. Delta Hotels places a strong emphasis on training, development, and continuous learning. When beginning a career at Delta Hotels, you become part of a service-oriented team of professionals. "We believe that people who enjoy a good working relationship with their company project a positive attitude and personality towards our guests and fellow team members." Standing behind its words, Delta Hotels promises all employees timely training and performance reviews.

IMPLEMENTATION

Delta Hotels' human resource development team introduced the first employee service guarantee in 1995. Employee focus groups provided input and direction throughout program development. The program was launched and promoted through a series of departmental meetings, posters, paycheque "stuffers," and headline news articles in the hotel's employee newspaper.

> **Employee Service Guarantee #1:** *We promise to give you feedback on how you are doing and to give you a chance to tell us how we are doing ... on a regular basis. This means you will have an Employee/Management Development Review within 30 days of your anniversary date. If we do not keep this promise, we will give you one week's pay.*

The first guarantee simply states that all employees will receive their annual performance review within 30 days of their anniversary employment date. If the employee's manager (the company) does not adhere, the staff member will receive one week's additional pay on their next paycheque.

To help monitor the program logistics, Delta Hotels' human resource department notifies department managers of upcoming employee anniversary dates. Department managers and human resource associates are responsible for performing reviews and tracking results.

> **Employee Service Guarantee #2:** *As a new member of our team, we promise that you will complete a thorough training program within the first two months of your employment. For our currently employed team members, you will receive a minimum of 12 hours of job-related training per year. If we do not keep this promise, we will give you one week's pay.*

In 1997, a second employee service guarantee was introduced. This commitment guaranteed new employees the opportunity to take part in Delta's online training program, within two months of their employment date. Online training is job-specific and conducted in individual departments. Failure to receive the promised training results in an additional week's pay for new employees.

Existing employees are also included in Delta's second employee service guarantee. These employees are guaranteed a minimum of eight hours of job-related training per year, or they are eligible for an additional week's pay. This training commitment supports initial and recurrent training for all employees and is an essential building block for an organization committed to providing quality service.

Payments to employees are deducted from the operating budget of the department they work in. This links accountability for the guarantee directly to the manager responsible for delivering the promise. At the end of each year, the number of guarantee payouts per department are reviewed and compared with predetermined departmental performance objectives. The department manager's performance bonus is then adjusted according to the number of payouts.

RESULTS

Both employee service guarantees provide Delta's human resource departments with the assurance that minimum management standards of performance are implemented, measurable, and provided with linkages between desired behaviours and performance management.

These guarantees have also contributed to Delta Hotels' commitment to ensuring quality standards at all levels within the company. In the fall of 2000, Delta Hotels received the Canada Awards for Excellence from the National Quality Institute. This is the first time a hotel company has won the award (which is the equivalent of the Malcolm Baldridge Award in the United States). In January 2001, Canada's leading business magazine, *Report on Business Magazine*, named Delta Hotels as one of the "35 Best Companies to Work for in Canada."

WTTC HUMAN RESOURCE CENTRE COMMENT

Delta Hotels uses financial incentives and sanctions to ensure management is accountable for corporate promises to staff. The hotel not only provides training, feedback, and coaching required for employees to deliver quality service to guests, but directly links its corporate vision on training and feedback to assessment of management performance. Employees' personal growth is supported through continuous feedback, career advancement opportunities, and reward and recognition programs.

KEY TERMS

service guarantee
commitment
accountability
performance

performance standards
employee assessment
incentive

 **www.deltahotels.com**

DISCUSSION QUESTIONS

1. Discuss the pros and cons of this system, as an employee and as a manager.

2. How does this performance review system correlate with the obvious successes in customer service that Delta Hotels has achieved?

3. Explain how Delta's commitment to staff is reflected in its employee assessment program.

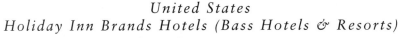

United States
Holiday Inn Brands Hotels (Bass Hotels & Resorts)

Submitted by: Tom Ruby

HOSPITALITY TRAINING NETWORK

… A new platform for training delivery is created to improve the quality, service, and revenue of Holiday Inn brands hotels.

LEARNING OUTCOMES

1. Describe the system designed for tracking professional development throughout Holiday Inn brands hotels.

2. Identify change in the delivery format of a management training program to meet the needs of a growing company.

3. Identify the importance of recertification after initial training has occurred.

OVERVIEW

In 1990, Bass Hotels & Resorts (the world's most international hotel company, directing the growth of some of the strongest and most recognized brands in the industry) purchased Holiday Inns. Although operating under new ownership, many of the in-place training programs—which contributed to the success of Holiday Inn brands hotels—continue to be supported. A number of the hotel's operational strategies and tactics have formed the basis for developing similar service excellence principles under the new leadership. An example of this is the Holiday Inn brands training platform.

Since the 1960s, all new Holiday Inn brand managers received certification training through the company. In the "old days," general managers, front office managers, and food and beverage managers were trained in a single location in Olive Branch, Mississippi. Today, management training has shifted from its central location to a network of training sites around North America. The new platform for training delivery supports Holiday Inn brands hotels in its mission of "Building the World's Preferred Places to Meet, Relax, and Dream."

A Hospitality Training Network, consisting of 80 North American hotel area managers and quality consultants, evolved as the new training platform. Through training workshops, managers are trained in the skills, techniques, and processes deemed necessary to improve the quality, service, and revenue of Holiday Inn brands hotels. Striving to be the best it can be in a highly competitive marketplace, Holiday Inn brands hotels redefined management's yearly retraining requirements by introducing a credit system.

IMPLEMENTATION

While developing the Hospitality Training Network, management wanted to ensure the training platform positively impacted the company's service culture. The training workshops were considered with the following points in mind:

- management commitment
- targeted "need-based" training programs
- a focussed delivery mechanism
- agreed-upon standards
- inspection for compliance
- credit for participation
- incremental increases in expectation levels
- constant communication
- zero tolerance for slacking.

Approximately 80 corporate consultants (hotel area managers, quality consultants, and area revenue managers) make up the Hospitality Training Network (HTN). All Holiday Inn and Holiday Inn Express hotels are part of this network of over 2 500 potential training locations. The HTN first redefined the yearly training requirements for qualifying management positions. A credit or "scoring" system was structured for each position. Managers must meet annual training expectations and achieve certification. Two types of certification are required by Holiday Inn brands standards:

A typical training workshop for management of Holiday Inn brands hotels.

Initial Certification

- Newly hired general managers, guest service managers, and sales managers of all Holiday Inn brands hotels must attend either the General Manager Program, Front Office Operations Training Program, or Sales Program within 180 days of assuming the position.
- Food and beverage managers must attain one training credit within 180 days of assuming the position.
- Executive housekeepers must attend INNspected for Cleanliness within 180 days of assuming the position.
- Maintenance engineers must attend the Holi-Kare workshop within 180 days of assuming the position.
- In the next calendar year, after this initial requirement is achieved, the manager must attain a specified number of credits or risk failing corporate inspection.

Ongoing Yearly Certification

Recertification applies to the year(s) following the achievement of initial certification.

- General managers of Holiday Inn brands hotels must complete a minimum of four recertification credits each year.
- Guest service managers, food and beverage directors, and sales directors/managers must attain two recertification credits each year.
- Executive housekeepers and maintenance engineers must attain one recertification training credit each year.

A series of workshops was developed to satisfy the above certification requirements. Recertification credits are earned by attending an approved workshop conducted by area managers, or quality consultants. The workshop is extensive and includes topics such as:

- Holidex—Back to Basics
- Building a Service Attitude
- Building a Service Plan
- Continuous Service Improvement
- Building a Revenue Plan
- Group Management Systems and Strategies
- RESults Training (reservations)
- Loss Prevention
- Best-4-Breakfast Skills & Standards.

Participation in workshops is mandatory. Following the workshop, each hotel manager is required to develop and implement a customer service plan in his or her own department. This plan is reviewed, on-site, by the quality evaluator and by the area manager. (An area manager is the equivalent of a personal trainer/consultant for each Holiday Inn brands hotel.) The plan is continuously critiqued and revised. All plans must contain the following: a graph poster in each department communicating two guest service goals and related "activities" and two service attitude standards; a service training log for each associate; and two service enhancements, coinciding with the hotel's market or clientele.

To monitor annual recertification, managers earn credits upon completing training workshops. Credit tracking helps the corporation ensure that managers continue to meet corporate standards while keeping service and operational skills up-to-date. By requiring managers to implement their own customer service plans, the company is guaranteed that current systems and processes are continuously utilized at a property.

The credit system can be looked upon as a reward system, but Holiday Inn brands hotels sees it as a PRIDE system—that is, each of its managers has a Personal Responsibility in Developing Excellence.

Bass Hotels & Resorts' managers on the new Hospitality Training Network initiatives:

"I found the I LEAD portion to be a good train-the-trainer tool. Since attending this workshop, we have begun to chart our progress and have scheduled more training classes within the hotel."

"...[I]t was just the best training event ever! I was able to apply the skills as soon as I got back to the hotel."

"The results class was an exceptional training tool for the front office staff. Their professionalism and reservation conversion rate has increased dramatically."

RESULTS

In 1999, 4 989 managers participated in HTN workshops. In Bass Hotels & Resorts' fiscal year ending September 2000, all previous records were broken for the number of training events offered and the number of hotel management staff trained.

Based upon feedback received, attendees returned to their hotels with new tools, strategies, and systems to enhance service and build loyalty. Participants also expressed a desire to drive performance and create new goals for themselves and their departments.

According to the brand RevPAR (revenue per available room), which measures operational performance, Holiday Inn brands outpaced other hotel brands such as Marriott, Hilton, Ramada, Hampton Inns, etc., in both the lower and the mid-scale segments. The hotel's internal service measurement indicator also improved.

WTTC HUMAN RESOURCE CENTRE COMMENT

Bass Hotels & Resorts has made a strong commitment to building its hospitality presence with the acquisition of Holiday Inns. Striving to be the best it can be in a competitive marketplace, Holiday Inn brands hotels has created a system where managers receive training at a network of venues, and from a variety of different sources. This format reduces stagnation and allows for different philosophies and styles to enter the training realm. A credit system allows the corporation to easily track individual managers' training needs, and offers participants a way to feel good about their professional development. By offering a year-round system of training delivery, management is able to advance its skills with flexibility and control.

KEY TERMS

manager training
service culture
motivation
standards

credit system
recertification
branding
evaluator

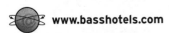 **www.basshotels.com**

DISCUSSION QUESTIONS

1. List the advantages of shifting management training from a central location to a network of training sites around North America.
2. Your hotel chain has just been bought out and the new owners want to change the existing credit-tracking system that ensures managers meet corporate standards. What reasons would you cite to convince the new owners that they should keep the existing training program?
3. How could you tie the management credit system into an incentive program? Give an example.

Leading Change for Tourism Organizations: Communication, Partnerships, Organizational Leadership, Decision Making, and Empowerment

Canada
Canadian Tourism Commission

Submitted by: Terry Ohman

PRODUCT CLUBS LEAD THE WAY

… Canada is experiencing unprecedented success with its tourism development program. This article explores the concept of product clubs and the impact of the Canadian Tourism Commission's leadership role as it encourages members to seek out like businesses—often in other regions—and to communicate goals, share visions, and exchange information on research and educational opportunities.

LEARNING OUTCOMES

1. Explain why tourists are attracted to clusters of tourism services.
2. Explain the steps involved in making a tourism product market-ready.
3. Analyze why the Canadian Tourism Commission's product clubs are willing to share ideas with other clusters even though they could be viewed as competitors.

"Canada's tourism industry will deliver world-class cultural and leisure experiences year-round, while preserving and sharing Canada's clean, safe, and natural environments. The industry will be guided by the values of respect, integrity, and empathy."

Mission Statement
Canadian Tourism Commission (CTC)

OVERVIEW

For years, academic publications have talked about the benefits of "clustering." Clustering is the term used to describe tourist interest in a particular area due to a main attraction. The attraction could be man-made (gambling in Las Vegas, USA), geographically influenced (Ayers Rock, Australia), or perhaps climate-based (like skiing in Whistler, Canada). It is the cluster of services surrounding the main attraction that benefits financially from tourists flocking to the area. These services include businesses providing transportation services, accommodation, food services, and other nearby attractions.

The Canadian Tourism Commission's (CTC) product club program has modified the concept of clustering. Instead of marketing the many services which enjoy the spin-off benefits of tourist spending, this program focusses on product development, i.e., developing more main attractions.

Canada's product club program is made up of partnerships. To date, there are 31 different product clubs in action. It is estimated that over 5 000 small- and medium-sized Canadian enterprises benefit from the CTC product club program. Each of the 31 clubs is made up of members who share a passion for their particular tourism product or niche.

The 31 product clubs to date are:

- Aboriginal Tourism Product Club
- Aboriginal Waterways Product Club
- Acadian Tourism Product Club
- Adventure, Outdoor and Ecotourism Product Club
- Arts in the City Product Club
- Atlantic ECONOMUSEUM Network Product Club
- Bay of Fundy Product Club
- Canadian Golf Tourism Alliance Product Club
- Canadian Sport Tourism Alliance Product Club
- Conservation Lands Product Club
- Country Roads Agri-Tourism Product Club
- Cross-Country Ski Product Club
- Cuisine, Wine & Culture in Canada Product Club
- Eco-Tourism Product Club
- Festival Network Product Club
- Garden & Bloom Tours of Canada Product Club
- GreekTown Product Club
- Health/Wellness Tourism Product Club
- Heritage Product Club
- Hostels Canada Product Club
- Independent Innkeepers Product Club
- Lighthouse Product Club
- Northern Wilderness Adventure Product Club
- Product Club for Tourists with Special Needs
- Ontario East Adventure Product Club

- Québec Maritime Product Club
- Saskatchewan River Basin Product Club
- Ski & Snowboard Industry Product Club
- The Great Canadian Fossil Trail Product Club
- Trail of the Great Bear Product Club
- Trans Canada Trail Product Club

The CTC works with each of the different product club niches in a leadership role. It brings members together through the clubs and then works to facilitate the business side of operations, by helping tourism operators get their product "market-ready." The CTC is not directly involved in this process, but instead works as a facilitator. Specifically, the CTC's role within the product club program is to:

- encourage industry communication;
- stimulate industry education; and
- support the product club as it undertakes and distributes targeted research.

Canadian Tourism Commission (CTC)

The CTC was created in 1995 to promote Canadian tourism as an industry-led and market-driven organization. It supports the growth and profitability of the Canadian tourism industry by marketing Canada as a desirable travel destination and distributing research and information throughout Canada's tourism industry.

The CTC recognizes that knowledge and expertise about Canada's tourism industry is found in the industry. Tourism people know about tourism! For this reason, the CTC designs, delivers, and funds market-research initiatives by partnering with "players" in tourism. Partners include provincial and regional tourism associations, government agencies, hoteliers, tour operators, airlines, and managers of tourism attractions.

Since the CTC is funded both publicly and through private sector partnerships, the Government of Canada contributes $75 million each year to the CTC, and private sector partners match or exceed this contribution. CTC partners include representatives from the transportation, accommodation, tour wholesaler/retailer, attractions, and food services sectors. Members also represent non-tourism industries such as financial services and manufacturing. These entities are encouraged to share in the CTC's vision. Since its inception in 1995, the CTC's marketing budget has risen to $165 million. This has allowed Canada to seriously compete for global tourist dollars.

IMPLEMENTATION

Creating a Product Chain

Product clubs are unique. Business ideas and strategies are shared, and members must be willing to exchange both challenges and success stories in developing and building their tourism products. The CTC's leadership role is very important in encouraging members to seek out like businesses, often in other regions, and to communicate goals, share visions, and exchange information on research and educational opportunities. In this way, like products throughout Canada can support each other and enhance the image of the product as a whole. This creates a well-established "product chain."

Creating a Product Club

CTC's product club program began in 1996 under the direction of the CTC's industry-led Board of Directors. Its objectives are to:

- take an under developed industry sector and to facilitate its transition to market-readiness
- improve the quality of existing product
- create new tourism product
- add diversity to the range of tourism product available in Canada
- address the issues of seasonality by encouraging year-round product delivery
- increase Canada's global competitiveness.

The CTC chooses to form new product clubs according to market demand. Guided by a committee comprised of members from the tourism industry, the CTC surveys the industry through a "marketing needs analysis." This research helps in determining where there is tourism demand and which areas are likely to support more products due to high tourism interest.

Research information is published and a "call-for-proposals" is then put out. The call-for-proposals is a way to let an industry know there is a need to develop a new product club. This process also tests the interest level in the product niche being discussed. Those interested in working together to develop and promote the highlighted product (e.g., lighthouses) must submit a five-year business plan. If accepted, the partnership is included as one of the product clubs in the product club program.

As part of entry requirements, each product club's five-year business plan must include a strategy outlining how the partnership can become self-sufficient after three years. On approval, the CTC becomes one of the partners of the industry-led plan and provides financial support for the first three years. After this time, no financial support is given, but the CTC remains involved through ongoing research, cross-sectoral training, and providing networking opportunities.

There is always the chance that businesses within each product club will compete against each other. In this sense, it is true that members of each product club are supporting their own competition. The CTC holds firm that there will be "more to go around" for all of industry as the club grows. Take the example of the Canadian Sport Tourism Alliance Product Club. Both big and small Canadian cities bid to attract sporting events to Canada. Whether the Olympics or a junior soccer championship, these international events draw both athletes and spectators. All are tourists. Members of the Canadian Sport Tourism Alliance Product Club are representatives from convention and visitors' bureaus across Canada. The Alliance believes that by educating all members on how to submit a first-class bid, Canada's overall success rate at attracting international events will increase. As one of the newer product clubs, it is still too early to tell how well the Alliance will succeed; however, the CTC is betting that this wager will pay off handsomely in the years to come.

RESULTS

Many of the CTC's active product clubs have similar success stories. Brief profiles of two clubs follow, as examples:

Conservation Lands Product Club

The Conservation Lands Product Club is made up of more than 70 partners who pay a yearly membership fee. Members come from a range of backgrounds and include canoe outfitters, llama trek operators, country inn operators, and Niagara wineries. The club has since extended its reach to tap into the area's growing incentive travel market. In doing so, members were able to attract corporate clients—such as conference attendees—to sample the region's wide variety of recreational activities.

Along with a brochure and marketing video, the club has produced two popular hiking trail guides, and also markets its own brand of bottled water. The club reinvests a percentage of membership fees and retail sales profits towards environmental conservation projects.[1] By working together and sharing best practices, the Conservation Lands group has improved its own bottom line and has added value to Canada's tourism industry.

It is interesting to note that common business interests are not the only reason for bringing a product club together; similar circumstances can also act as the catalyst. In 1997, many of southern Ontario's 40 conservation authorities—government-funded bodies, whose main purpose is to protect the region's vital watershed areas—found traditional revenue sources were running out. In response, four conservation authorities formed an alliance called the Conservation Lands of Ontario. This alliance facilitated the creation of the Conservation Lands Product Club to financially support its ecotourism goals and objectives by bringing together tourism industry partners which now provide and market sustainable ecotourism experiences in the urban fringe.

Lighthouse Product Club

Tourism associations in Atlantic Canada discovered that they had a common asset—lighthouses. With the advent of new technology, lighthouses are being used less frequently as navigational aids. For those who believe these buildings still hold value in our society, alternative uses are being found in tourism.

A group of local communities formed the regional Atlantic Lighthouse Council and successfully became a product club. With an absolute passion for lighthouse tourism, the council organized Canada's first ever international conference on lighthouse tourism. Held at White Point, Nova Scotia in May 2000, this event attracted participants from Europe, Australia, both the Pacific and Atlantic coasts of the United States, and from seven Canadian provinces. After the successful event, organizers expanded their Board of Directors to include representation from provinces outside of the Atlantic region.

Unlike the Canadian Sport Tourism Alliance Product Club—whose vision does not have a single geographic point of reference (a cluster characteristic)—the Lighthouse Product Club's success began locally but has since become a regional initiative. This club, in particular, illustrates how the product club program can develop a good idea locally and then encourage it to expand regionally and even nationally.

What about the Future?

With 31 clubs representing nearly every region of Canada, the product club program has evolved at a healthy pace. Participants within individual product clubs are encouraged to share information, exchange best practice ideas, and work together as a group to the benefit of the product niche they represent. Networking and communication are considered requirements for success. CTC is now seeing a new level of cooperation within the clubs. Information and exchange is occurring not only "within" the product clubs, but also "between" the different clubs.

For example:

- The Cuisine, Wine & Culture in Canada Product Club is finding much in common with the Country Roads Agri-Tourism Product Club, which focusses on farm vacation experiences.
- The national Garden & Bloom Tours of Canada Product Club draws many of its members from the visitor and convention bureaus, which also support the Sport Tourism Alliance Product Club.
- The Yukon-based Northern Wilderness Adventure Product Club has much in common with the Adventure, Outdoor and Ecotourism Product Club based in Québec.

The level of information exchange has exceeded the initial expectations of the program and requires CTC to monitor the development and implementation of ideas at a faster pace. Many factors have contributed to Canada's move up from ninth to seventh position in international tourist arrivals in recent years. Product clubs are one of them.

WTTC Human Resource Centre COMMENT

A club is a group of people united in a relationship and having some interest, activity, or purpose in common. Building on the CTC's mission to promote Canadian tourism, product clubs are also capitalizing on one of the fastest-growing international industries—tourism! The success of the product clubs is a reflection on the CTC's leadership role as a good facilitator of people and ideas. By recognizing that tourism people know about tourism, the CTC developed strategic partnerships with provincial and regional tourism associations, government agencies, hoteliers, tour operators, airlines, and managers of tourism attractions. Focussing on product development, Canada has more main attractions to market.

KEY TERMS

leadership

facilitator

small- and medium-sized enterprises (SMEs)

clustering

product club

product development

networking

market-ready

needs analysis

tourism demand

call-for-proposals

product niche

best practices

---

1 From the CTC publication "Product Clubs—Building Canada's Tourism Industry." The publication is downloadable on the CTC Web site. Access the product club Web site in English at **www.canadatourism.com/productclubs** (or in French at **www.canadatourisme.com/clubsproduit**). The publication is listed as "Product Club Partnerships Booklet."

www.canadatourism.com/productclubs
www.canadatourisme.com/clubsdeproduits

DISCUSSION QUESTIONS

1. Why do you think the conference put on by the regional Atlantic Lighthouse Council Product Club attracted individuals from as far away as Europe?

2. Think of four product clubs characteristic of a country's tourism industry. For each product club, provide an example of an outside group in another region that may share the same vision.

3. List five tourism clusters, at a regional, national, or international level.

Belgium
Bass Hotels & Resorts

Submitted by: Anne Robinson

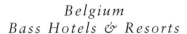

TRAINING IMPLICATIONS OF THE EURO

. . . Preparing staff, management, and franchisees for the introduction of the new European currency—the euro.

LEARNING OUTCOMES

1. Outline a corporate strategy to respond to a major business environment change.

2. Devise a method to assess employee awareness and comfort in undertaking a change management strategy.

3. Recognize the importance of timelines in the implementation of a multinational change management program.

OVERVIEW

The euro is the single currency of the European Monetary Union, which was adopted by 12 member states starting January 1, 1999. The 12 member states are Belgium, Germany, Spain, France, Ireland, Italy, Luxembourg, the Netherlands, Austria, Portugal, Finland, and

Greece. The currency name "euro" was chosen by the European Heads of State, i.e., the EU government, at the Madrid European Council meeting in December 1995.

On January 1, 2002, the transition period established for the introduction of the European Monetary Union—the euro—comes to an end. On this date, the existing currencies in 12 European countries will be completely replaced by new euro notes and coins.

With more than 3 000 hotels and 480 000 rooms located in over 95 countries, Bass Hotels & Resorts was concerned about maintaining guest satisfaction with the introduction of a new currency. Bass Hotels & Resorts is the world's most global hotel company, directing the growth of some of the strongest and most recognized brands in the industry. As an arm of Bass plc, Bass Hotels & Resorts owns and operates the Inter-Continental, Crowne Plaza, Holiday Inn, Holiday Inn Express, and Staybridge Suites brands.

With the help of an in-house multi-functional steering committee, Bass Hotels & Resorts began preparing for the changeover of currency. Based in Brussels, Belgium, at the company's Europe, Middle East, and Africa (EMEA) division offices, the committee is made up of individuals from many different areas of the hotel, including operations, information technology, legal, accounting and reporting, human resources, training, and communications. The purpose of the committee was to identify the key brand and business issues affected by the introduction of the euro.

The committee also determined how to resolve operational challenges that will occur with the new currency, in areas such as technology, banking, and accounting. It was soon determined that the biggest challenge would be in preparing and training staff to handle the change in currency.

IMPLEMENTATION

Bass Hotels & Resorts own over 30 percent of 300-plus branded hotels directly affected by the change in currency. In other words, during 2002, more than one million Europeans will experience Bass Hotels & Resorts service in one of the 12 countries—perhaps as much as 5 percent of the affected populations! Understanding the implications, Bass Hotels & Resorts focussed on securing the trust of the franchisee—and, more importantly, that of the guest and customer—during this transitional period.

Back in 1997, the steering committee presented the Board of Bass Hotels & Resorts with a strategy for handling the euro conversion. This strategy became phase one of the company's two-part euro conversion program. Phase one focussed on the transition period for the new currency which began on January 1, 1999.

Phase one stressed the importance of maintaining the confidence of guests in Bass Hotels & Resorts branded hotels during the transition period. The committee agreed that the transition period also offered other opportunities. Bass Hotels & Resorts viewed this time of change as a chance to establish industry leadership and reinforce the respect of its franchisees and other industry partners. Furthermore, all research showed that if the transition could be handled quickly, the business could deliver improved profits to shareholders.

Systems

While reviewing the major corporate accounts, the committee concluded that most clients intended to move their back office accounting to the euro at an early stage in the transition.

These clients would thus prefer to use hotel chains that could deliver invoices in both "legacy currency" (old currency) and the euro. Establishing dual pricing and dual accounting became Bass Hotels & Resorts' early objective.

To ensure consistency, contacts were made with the owners of the key property management systems and back office accounting systems, so that technical specifications could be agreed upon. Sulcus (the owner of the LANMark PMS, used widely in the EMEA hotels by Bass Hotels & Resorts) took the lead by adapting its products to meet the software specifications required by Bass Hotels & Resorts.

With a major investment in software development underway, attention turned to marketing. Both the accounting and software departments worked together to ensure that all corporate programs were dual priced for summer 1998. Holidex—the proprietary reservation system owned by Bass Hotels & Resorts and its GDS links—had to handle dual currency as specified by the European Commission.

Early 1998 was the moment of truth. If the technological, banking, and accounting solutions were in place, what was required of management and staff when customers and guests started using the euro and demanding dual currency menus, price lists, and invoices?

Training

Bass Hotels & Resorts hired a Belgium-based consultancy group to handle staff training. The company was experienced in European training issues and hotel marketing.

To assist in developing a realistic training program, the committee prepared a series of interviews to help determine the company's readiness for change. Interviews involving both management and staff were conducted at various Bass Hotels & Resorts. Management and staff at the European central reservation office, major franchisees, and corporate management were also interviewed. The interviews were supplemented by the responses from a questionnaire addressed to all employees that simply asked: "What do you need to know about the euro to do your job?" The questionnaire was made available on the company's intranet.

From the interview results, it was possible to customize training programs according to the needs of different groups. Several categories of staff were identified, each with different training needs. Groups included:

- corporate executives
- sales and marketing executives
- procurement executives
- guest contact staff
- call centre staff
- the entire employee population, in terms of payroll issues.

The questionnaire generated more than 100 questions, which were examined by a subcommittee of the steering committee. This exercise enabled the committee to:

- get a feel for the degree of readiness throughout the organization;
- identify common issues among groups; and
- determine issues within specific groups.

The research suggested that staff had a low level of understanding about the changeover. This was not surprising, as there had been few awareness campaigns created by governments or other organizations. The exercise uncovered exactly the information Bass Hotels & Resorts needed to develop a training program.

The steering committee developed the hotel's policy statement, summarizing planned strategies and tactics. This policy statement became the benchmark for designing training programs. The policy detailed Bass's intentions in changing salary structures, pension schemes, and other aspects of compensation—from local to euro-denominated currency—throughout Europe. The policy was shared with work councils throughout Europe. All restructuring is due to the new currency.

A training company was retained to design and develop tools necessary for delivering training to all owned, leased, and managed hotels. Training was to occur prior to December 1998. This ensured that staff at all the brand hotels would reach similar levels of readiness in a timely fashion. Training tools included a written manual and CD-ROM. Franchisees were offered the training program at cost. All development costs, including research, analysis of questions and answers, drafting of scripts, illustrations, and the creation and reproduction of the manual and CD-ROM were absorbed by the franchiser.

RESULTS

Phase one of the conversion program was successfully implemented. Bass Hotels & Resorts properties were fully functional in handling euro conversions and able to supply client accounts in euros beginning January 1, 1999. Bass Hotels & Resorts believes it has succeeded in achieving industry leadership in the eyes of the credit card companies, the PMS vendors, and particularly the franchisees. This was achieved through careful research and preparation.

The steering committee is now focussed on phase two of the conversion program to ensure the following objectives are met:

- the conversion of staff payroll to euros;
- the pilot and roll-out of final software conversions; and
- a comprehensive review of staff training requirements.

The steering committee is confident that careful planning of its conversion program will ensure a seamless transition, enabling guests to handle the transition with confidence and trust in Bass Hotels & Resorts.

Investing in staff training in both owned and managed properties has increased staff awareness about the currency conversion in general, and has created an understanding of the importance in customer service during the launch of the euro. Bass Hotels & Resorts anticipates positive results from phase two of the conversion program and will continue to provide supplementary training tailored to the launch of the notes and coins.

In acknowledgement of Bass Hotels & Resorts leadership in this area, the European Central Bank has invited the company to become an official partner in their "80 Million Euro" communications campaign which will be conducted in the final quarter of 2001.

WTTC HUMAN RESOURCE CENTRE COMMENT

Bass Hotels & Resorts responded to a major challenge by adapting technology, and by involving management and staff in the design of training programs. Benchmarking was possible due to the creation of a defined policy. Bass Hotels & Resorts anticipated the needs resulting from the change and responded expediently to give the company a good state of preparedness for the transition. This good practice illustrates how a multinational corporation—with operations spanning an entire continent—is able to structure its response to a major change in its business environment through the strength of its training culture.

KEY TERMS

euro	franchise
currency conversion	questionnaire
benchmarking	leadership
transitional period	shareholder
European Monetary Union	dual pricing
compensation	

 **www.basshotels.com**

DISCUSSION QUESTIONS

1. As the company's human resource director, other than preparing training seminars to teach staff how to handle the change in currency, what else could you do to prepare your workforce for the introduction of the euro?

2. List 10 criteria to use when selecting a training company to tackle a major, multinational change management problem.

3. Choose a front line job in the travel and tourism industry. If the currency in your country were going to change, how would this affect your job performance? What issues would you want your employer to address?

United States
Wilderness Aware Rafting

Submitted by: Joe Greiner

USING GUEST FEEDBACK TO CREATE A LEADER IN THE RAFTING INDUSTRY

... This river rafting company has developed a computerized evaluation process for guest feedback and reservations. The system has streamlined internal operations, improved efficiency, and provided a system for monitoring guide conduct and performance.

LEARNING OUTCOMES

1. Evaluate the considerations in designing and setting up a customer feedback system.
2. Describe how employee morale is improved through workplace design and consistent, reliable performance feedback.
3. Explain how effective management-staff communications impact customer service and safety.

OVERVIEW

Wilderness Aware Rafting is a river raft outfitting company that started as a hobby business in 1976. When purchased by a husband and wife team in 1985, the base operation was moved to its current location near the town of Buena Vista, Colorado, at the base of the 4 300-metre Collegiate Peaks mountain range in central Colorado, USA. The company sells river rafting adventures ranging from half-day trips to 10-day excursions on five different rivers throughout the Colorado Rockies. Excursions vary from guided-oar and paddle-powered raft trips on rivers with wildwater flood conditions, to mildwater conditions suitable for scenic family-float excursions.

Domestic travellers from Florida, California, Texas, and the Midwest states are the company's major markets. Families with children (as young as eight years old), corporate groups seeking team-building activities, recreational groups, church groups, and youth groups make up the company's clientele. Approximately 93 percent of reservations are made in advance by telephone, fax, and e-mail. The remaining 7 percent are last minute or walk-in reservations.

Since 1997, Wilderness Aware Rafting has operated with three full-time, year-round employees and 33 full-time, seasonal employees. In 1998, 38 seasonal staff members were hired and in 1999, 47 seasonal staff members were hired. In 2000 the company increased

Rafting with Wilderness Aware Rafting on a Colorado Rocky Mountain river.

its year-round staff from three to four, while structuring product marketing and pricing so as to maintain an approximate annual growth rate of no more than 5 percent to 10 percent. Due to the safety-sensitive nature of the business, Wilderness Aware Rafting considers higher annual growth rates difficult to maintain if quality is to be assured.

To improve business operations and increase guest satisfaction, Wilderness Aware Rafting created a computerized evaluation process for guest comment cards and developed a specialized computer reservation database. This, coupled with the construction of a state-of-the-art rafting facility, is credited with improving service efficiency. It is also the main reason why the company has been honoured as Colorado's "Company of the Year" in the Service and Recreation/Tourism categories.

IMPLEMENTATION

Customer Comment Cards

To measure its current level of customer service, Wilderness Aware Rafting designed guest comment cards to survey customers at every point of contact during their rafting experience. Recorded on the comment card is the name of the trip leader, name of the guide, trip date, and water conditions. Guides distribute the card questionnaires at the end of each trip, during the 30-minute bus ride back to the base facility. Each guest also receives a complimentary pencil, engraved with the company's toll-free number, to answer the questionnaire. On each card, guests may include their name and address to be automatically entered in a weekly draw to win a half-day rafting trip for two. All cards are collected prior to bus arrival at the base.

The customer comment card includes:

- four yes or no questions
- 21 scaled questions (A = Outstanding, B = Good, C = OK, D = Needs work, and E = We blew it!)
- five open-ended questions.

It takes 1.25 minutes to process each guest comment card, totalling approximately 135 labour hours per season. To streamline data entry, the database is designed on a spreadsheet with a layout closely matching that of the comment card, thus requiring little training for accurate and efficient data entry. Between customer service calls, reservation and front desk personnel enter comment card results.

Management spends 16 hours per month (64 hours per season) categorizing all open-ended questions into appropriate departments, sorting data, and developing reports. Prior to data entry, management reviews cards on a daily basis. Cards with particularly positive or negative comments are copied and distributed to appropriate managers for immediate discussion with the necessary personnel. Immediate feedback has proved to be helpful in handling complaints and improving customer service.

Comment card responses are sorted, charted, and graphed for specific reports. For example, office and transportation staff are provided with charts and graphs reviewing their progress as a team. Individual guides receive reports concerning personal data and customer comments directed to them specifically. Comment cards also help monitor guide conduct and performance in the field. The customer comment cards also deter inappropriate behaviour, as guides are aware that they are being evaluated constantly.

Guests have also commented on guides' boating skills, communication skills (including inappropriate language), and even personal hygiene. Positive feedback serves to reinforce positive actions and attitudes. Skills with children, cooking ability, conversational skills, professional appearance, boating ability, compassion for nervous or injured guests, and the use of humour have all been noted as staff strengths.

Individual guide reports are printed bimonthly and are included in paycheque envelopes. Reports provide guides with the open-ended guest comments referring to their trip performances during that pay period. Questions requiring numeric rating are averaged per guide and are reported for each question applying to a given guide. This score is reported as high, average, or low, reflecting the scores of all guides rated for that question during the same period. Yes and no questions are also reported in this format.

After each guide receives their paycheque envelope, management sets aside time for a one-on-one discussion with employees. During the meeting, management interprets the individual guide and trip leader reports. Employees are encouraged to voice personal concerns and issues during this informal meeting time.

Reservation, transportation, and food service personnel also receive bimonthly reports containing relevant open-ended comments in numerically scored categories. Management reviews these reports on a departmental level. Comments specific to an employee (driver or office personnel) are handled individually. General comments help identify what service levels are most important to guests and valid suggestions are incorporated into company training manuals.

As a result of the information collected from the guest comment cards, employee training, product design, and marketing materials have all been improved. The open-ended questions have proved to be most valuable for this purpose. For example, in 1999 the full-day raft excursion was changed to include an additional section of whitewater. This added 45 minutes to the overall trip time, as feedback indicated that trips were too short and that too much time was spent at lunch and on scenic hikes.

The rental equipment maintenance program was also altered in response to customer comments. A new nine-barrel washing system has replaced the three-barrel system, and a new drying room in the main facility has greatly reduced equipment odours and related guest comments. Complaints regarding small holes in rafting gear were also acknowledged. Although these defects did not affect equipment performance, guests perceived the equipment as faulty. Rental equipment is now removed from circulation more regularly, and is instead sold in the retail store. As a result, there are fewer rental equipment concerns.

Customer surveys are also useful as a basis for employee recognition. Employee rewards are presented on a semi-monthly basis to guides and trip leaders receiving the highest scores. Rewards include such items as gift certificates from local tourist-related facilities, which are often acquired by Wilderness Aware Rafting in exchange for free rafting trips.

In 1998, 9 500 guests took rafting trips with Wilderness Aware Rafting, and 5 400 completed a customer survey card. In 1999, the number of guests remained the same, but 800 more customers completed a survey, for a return rate of 65 percent. This increase is directly attributed to staff circulating comment cards at the beginning of the season, rather than three weeks after the start of the season in 1998.

Computerized Reservation System

In 1998 Wilderness Aware Rafting also incorporated a new computerized database reservation system from Microsoft Access, called Office Pro Reservation Assistant (OPRA). After working on program design part-time for nine months, management realized that developing the program would require full-time attention, in order to properly address the specific nature of the industry.

Initially, the program was based on how Wilderness Aware Rafting traditionally operated the company. However, it quickly evolved to include additional areas not yet considered by the company. Throughout the design process, information required conversion into a series of yes and no answers, to lists, and to a priority rating system, all of which could be interpreted by a computer. Other program elements were frequently added during this process. The program developer was eventually able to address the specific needs of Wilderness Aware Rafting, while creating a product compatible with the needs of virtually any outfitter in the river rafting industry.

In total, the project took approximately 5 000 hours of programming at a cost of $150 000 (US). The developer is attempting to recoup this expenditure through additional sales to other rafting companies. In total, Wilderness Aware Rafting devoted 2 500 hours to designing and internalizing the program over a two-and-a-half-year period. According to Wilderness Aware Rafting, most of the time has already been recouped in saved labour.

To train staff in using the new system, a training CD-ROM provides an introduction in system use. Much of the reservation process is intuitive or has mouse rollover instructions on screen. Thus, initial training time required ranges from 10 to 15 hours per reservation staff person. Sales training sessions have been incorporated and management training has evolved naturally.

Wilderness Aware Rafting credits the new system for increasing revenue 22 percent during the first year of use. This increase is exceptional, as it was generated by means other than purchasing additional boats. The system provides for detailed information concerning customer personal data and customer reservation information, and automates the communications process within the company.

OPRA's reporting system has increased operation efficiency. Below is an example of staff efficiency and internal reporting generated through the system.

Staff efficiency

- Manifests are easily updated and printed for drivers, detailing shuttle pickups at local hotels.
- Guide schedules (for 30 guides) are generated for over 80 different trips.
- Guide river training qualifications and certification dates are automatically checked when scheduling trip guides.
- A report advises trip leaders which boats are available for individual trips, figures out optimum boat assignments for both guides and guests, and outlines access points for each trip. The report also assists reservations in identifying available boat space.
- Trip menus and equipment packing lists are generated for each trip.
- The state requires reports tracking each rafting trip, including guides, boats, passenger lists, and launch-point/ending-point information. Time needed to generate this report has decreased from four weeks to two days.

Internal reports

- Local lodging and attractions have a separate screen providing information and assistance in customer service.
- Accounts receivable can now generate a collection report in minutes rather than hours.
- Accounts payable can generate collection reports concerning commissions due to booking agents and access fees due to landowners.
- Payroll has reduced the amount of time it takes to track guide pay, from between 30 to 40 hours per month to less than 10. (Guides are paid by the trip.)

OPRA is being marketed nationwide and has been sold to most of the top commercial outfitters operating on the Arkansas River (America's most popular rafting river).

New Building

The company's new main building is immediately visible when approaching the Arkansas Valley from Denver or Colorado Springs, the main metropolitan areas in Colorado. The 670-square-metre facility is located on 17 acres adjacent to the Arkansas River. The location is credited with increasing walk-in business 5.4 times over. It is also responsible for increasing trip efficiency, in that trips can begin, end, or resupply (in the case of overnight trips) at the base. Guests frequently comment on the beauty and quality of the building, and employees marvel at how easily 50 personnel are able to work together efficiently.

Before designing the structure, the company owner and the operations manager visited over 30 successful rafting facilities located on the United States East Coast. The East Coast rafting industry is far more mature than the Colorado industry, offering advanced infrastructure design elements for this specialized industry. During a 10-day business trip, Wilderness Aware Rafting conducted interviews with property managers, and photographed and measured various facilities.

Based on the input of customers, staff, and the above research, management generated a list of the operational functions which the building would need to accommodate. Management wanted a building where guests, guides, drivers, office employees, and managers could all work efficiently. Considering all operational areas, the key layout areas needed to include:

- **Administrative**—three management offices, a computer/electronics room, a reservation room, and an employee break room.

- **Trip specific**—guide packing area, guide changing area, commercial kitchen, rental gear and equipment washing area, wetsuit drying/storage/distribution area, lifejacket drying/storage/distribution area, equipment and boat storage space, and an equipment repair room.

- **Customer specific**—retail/check-in/drink bars, retail storage, customer changing-room/toilets, and ample overnight parking.

Although most staff training is hands-on and occurs "in the field," multiple private rooms were necessary for group meeting space and quiet study and testing. The reservations area encompasses five workstations, provides ample space for computer training, and has been leased on occasion for software sales seminars.

RESULTS

Twice, Wilderness Aware Rafting has been honoured with Colorado's Company of the Year award. In 1996 Wilderness Aware Rafting won the recreation and tourism category, and in 1999 the company was awarded the service category from the *ColoradoBiz* magazine competition. The company has also been featured in *Entrepreneur* magazine with a feature article on the topic of business start-up success stories.

During the year following the introduction of the OPRA system, the company experienced the following:

- an increase in utilized boat capacity from 54.1 to 60.2 percent;
- an increase in Colorado market share from 3.4 to 3.6 percent; and
- an increase in guest booking per incoming telephone call from 1.21 to 1.39 percent.

Comment cards have inspired a number of operational changes. Overall scores on reports (in the 21 areas identified) average between 4.5 and 4.9 on a scale of 1.0 to 5.0. This places comments between "good" and "outstanding." Each year, the lowest score averages are targeted as areas to improve.

Staff morale has also improved since the introduction of OPRA and the move to the new building. Employee exit interviews are conducted at season end, in which each employee is asked to report on their experiences and offer suggestions for improvements within the company. At the end of the 1999 season, interviews indicated that the improved facility greatly reduced stress levels and that the improved communications supported by OPRA has increased job efficiency.

WTTC HUMAN RESOURCE COUNCIL COMMENT

River rafting, whether in mild or wildwater conditions, legally requires professionally trained guides to ensure consumer safety. Without internal evaluation measures in place, however, company owners are often unaware of tour conduct. Poor tour conduct will decrease repeat business and result in negative word-of-mouth advertising. By charting all the elements of guest feedback, from reservation to departure, and by using technology to analyze this information, Wilderness Aware Rafting has illustrated the advantages to company productivity, efficiency, and staff morale. Apart from the on-site research of existing businesses on the East Coast river rafting industry, guest survey data heavily influenced the design of Wilderness Aware Rafting's new building. Owners attribute increased staff productivity, better quality service, and positive attitudes to the new building. This case study highlights both the need for on-site research and the benefits resulting from the effective use of technology to learn from customer feedback.

KEY TERMS

customer service
business operations
data collection
performance feedback

technology
computerized evaluation
guest comment card

 **www.inaraft.com**

DISCUSSION QUESTIONS

1. Consumers of adventure products have specific concerns about safety. How has this company managed to reduce concerns?

2. In what ways has this company made changes acknowledging employee needs?

3. How has this company's competitive position been improved by the investment in integrated computer systems planning?

Hong Kong
Island Shangri-La, Hong Kong

Submitted by: Fiona Szeto

TRAINING TO MEET BUSINESS GOALS

… This hotel uses measurable business goals to tailor its training programs.

LEARNING OUTCOMES

1. Indicate how human resource department goals are tied to the overall strategy of the company.
2. Analyze methods of supporting employee empowerment through delegating authority.
3. Explain how human resource activities support the well-being of hotel employees.

OVERVIEW

Island Shangri-La, Hong Kong is situated atop Pacific Place, a prestigious shopping and entertainment complex in Hong Kong. This five-star hotel has 784 employees and features the largest number of guest rooms on Hong Kong Island. Hotel amenities include spacious rooms with spectacular views, award winning restaurants, and a complete range of leisure facilities.

At the Island Shangri-La, the goal is to be the market leader for deluxe hotels in Hong Kong. The hotel's mission statement is threefold:

- Deliver maximum shareholder profit.
- Maintain a reputation of being a preferred employer.
- Be a highly respected company within the community.

To meet and maintain these objectives, hotel management realizes its human resource department plays a significant role in the company's operations, as it provides training to employees and support to management.

Each year, the human resource department reviews the hotel's business plan and strategic objectives. This process helps human resource personnel reaffirm company goals. This "refresher" takes place prior to designing or updating staff training and development programs. The review helps human resource personnel in making sure that employee training programs are geared to improved customer service (as defined in the business plan), while also providing individuals with opportunities to build and improve personal skill-sets. As an employer, Island Shangri-La's policy is to promote from within and to provide all employees with a competitive benefit package.

IMPLEMENTATION

Staff productivity and efficiency directly influence the hotel's ability to meet its business goals. Understanding this, management defined two key areas of focus for its human resource department:

- Maintain an employee retention rate of above 85 percent annually.
- Increase the hotel's market share by exceeding customer expectations.

To begin working towards these two objectives, the training department worked with outside consultants to design a series of management training programs. Throughout the training series, management received instruction in how to better coach employees to increase work performance. The courses also provided ways to design evaluation systems for use in evaluating employee performance quickly and fairly.

Management course topics included:

- interaction management
- communication
- leadership
- labour productivity
- crisis management
- multi-skill cross-training
- empowerment
- presentation skills
- team building.

The hotel also provided an empowerment workshop for all division and department heads. During the workshop, participants engaged in a series of activities that focussed on motivating and empowering employees. The workshop included topics focussing on:

- identifying areas appropriate for introducing empowerment departmentally;
- sharing scenarios common across departments;
- establishing staff guidelines;
- determining how to distribute and reinforce staff guidelines; and
- establishing a monitoring process whereby management could follow employees' progress.

While focussing on the issue of empowerment, the topic of decision making was discussed. Management at the Island Shangri-La agreed that a large part of employee empowerment rests in giving employees the "right" or "authority" to make decisions. It was decided that a guide was needed to outline commonly asked questions and challenges faced daily by employees. This guide provided the point of reference for staff to follow. Guidelines detailed those situations where front line staff were encouraged to handle decisions on their own, as well as areas where decision making should be referred to management. This "delegation of authority guide" was created to help reinforce the protocol for decision making within departments. The guide is reviewed and updated periodically. Management has noted that by providing a clear decision-making procedure, employees have the confidence to respond better to customers.

> *The creation of a delegation-of-authority guide has contributed to effec-*
> *tive empowerment at this deluxe hotel.*
>
> *Management*
> *Island Shangri-La, Hong Kong*

Island Shangri-La Hotel offers multi-skill cross-training in both departmental and divisional sections. Multi-skill training in both areas provides staff with an operational understanding of the hotel and the opportunity to broaden their career path. Only selected employees are trained under this program. Overall, the program has increased management's flexibility in shifting staff as needed.

> *"It's our mission to be the preferred employer by promoting empower-*
> *ment and providing motivation, training, and development programs to*
> *all staff so they may work towards exceeding customers' expectations*
> *while achieving personal and career goals."*
>
> *Island Shangri-La, Hong Kong*

Island Shangri-La Hotel believes that education and training support company goals and increase employee skills. Management training is also a priority. Numerous courses and workshops are offered throughout the year for this audience, including an interaction management workshop and supervisory skill program.

The supervisory skill program focusses on handling day-to-day interaction with employees and offers advice in enhancing employee self-esteem and improving employee performance. The program also tackles the difficult subject of disciplinary action. Suggestions on how to improve on-the-job performance, product knowledge, and practical skills training are generated during workshops and later distributed to individual departments. The participants evaluate all courses. Information gathered assists training personnel in targeting areas of interest and concern, and helps in constantly improving content and delivery.

Specialized workshops are also organized for specific audiences when deemed necessary. Many of these workshops are designed and delivered by outside training consultants. Examples are the hotel's language classes and personal grooming workshops. Language skills are important in order to improve communication internally, between employees, and with hotel guests. Personal grooming workshops have been successful in improving employees' self-image while supporting the hotel's grooming standards.

RESULTS

A staff opinion survey is conducted every two years. This survey helps in assessing how well human resource activities support the well-being of hotel employees. Survey feedback provides information crucial to developing detailed action plans focussing on improvement.

The human resource division regularly reviews staff turnover rate. This helps in determining the hotel's employee retention rate. In 2000, the employee retention rate was 87 percent—exceeding the company goal. Island Shangri-La, Hong Kong credits its low employee turnover, in part, to its compensation and benefits program, which is extremely competitive and highly regarded within the industry. Should employees choose to leave the property, exit interviews are conducted, which provide further feedback to human resource personnel.

Island Shangri-La, Hong Kong has designed additional programs to measure improvements in the area of customer service. A Performance Monitoring Program evaluates customer satisfaction on a daily basis. Guest comment cards and letters provide immediate feedback, and guest focus groups are periodically organized to address key customer concerns.

WTTC HUMAN RESOURCE CENTRE COMMENT

Island Shangri-La Hotel's commitment to fostering a balanced approach towards work, career, and personal growth has resulted in a low employee turnover rate and improved guest satisfaction. Management has committed to building employee confidence by reinforcing empowerment through education, discussion, and written guidelines. In this manner, employees are supported in their abilities to make decisions at the customer contact point. The approach is further grounded in Island Shangri-La's business plan, which sets measurable performance goals.

KEY TERMS

guest satisfaction

employee retention

empowerment

decision making

multi-skilling

cross-training

market leader

performance evaluation

 **www.shangri-la.com**

DISCUSSION QUESTIONS

1. What kinds of "commonly asked questions" or "challenges" do you think are in the guideline book discussed? List five challenges which might apply to front line staff working at the front desk, in food and beverage, and in housekeeping.

2. One of the goals of the Island Shangri-La's human resource department is to keep employee turnover at a minimum. As an employee of this hotel, what would entice you to stay?

3. Name three ways to exceed customer satisfaction that could increase the hotel's market share.

United States
Travel Montana

Submitted by: Victor Bjornberg

FUN ON THE FARM: MONTANA'S FARM AND RANCH RECREATION BUSINESS WORKSHOP PROGRAM

> … Montana's tourism, agriculture, and rural development agencies assist agricultural producers in deciding if farm and ranch recreation would provide economic and social benefits.

LEARNING OUTCOMES

1. Identify positive approaches to economic and social change in agricultural communities.
2. Outline workshop approaches which respond to rural community needs.
3. Describe how participants' needs affect the program's focus, design, pace, and development.

OVERVIEW

In the early 1990s, Montana's profile as a destination for visitors interested in experiencing the western ranch lifestyle got a boost from a number of mass media and public events. Montana's 1989 statehood centennial celebration was highlighted by an 80-kilometre cattle drive that attracted thousands of participants and media from around the world. The feature film *City Slickers* and the television movie series *Lonesome Dove* sparked the public's interest in experiencing the "cowboy way." Following these events, Travel Montana, along with the state Commerce Department's Tourism Promotion and Development Program and its tourism industry partners across the state, began receiving an increasing number of inquiries regarding Montana's guest ranch, cattle drive, and wagon-train opportunities.

During this same time period, Montana's economy was suffering from low agricultural product prices, drought, and structural changes in its other traditional natural resource industries. Tourism, which experienced double-digit percentage *growth* in the early 1990s, was the only bright spot in Montana's economy. For state ranches to survive, Montana's agriculture producers needed to diversify their operations.

In 1992, the Montana tourism industry began operating under a five-year strategic plan. This plan had many goals. One of these goals was to spread the benefits of tourism

The opportunity to participate in a cattle drive attracts visitors to Montana, USA.

more broadly across the state, and, in particular, into Montana's less-travelled areas. The less-travelled areas were generally the state's rural, agricultural regions, which were some distance from its two national parks, Glacier National Park and Yellowstone National Park.

In response to this situation, Montana's tourism development partners decided to test the interest of local farmers and ranchers. The state's tourism development partners included Montana State University Extension, Small Business Administration (SBA), and Resource Conservation & Development (RC&D) programs, along with the Montana Department of Agriculture, Travel Montana, the University of Montana's Institute for Tourism & Recreation Research, and the state's regional tourism organizations. The question for which state partners needed an answer was, "Would area farmers and ranchers consider tourism or recreation as a way of diversifying agricultural operations?"

To find the answer, a one-day workshop was developed and held in southwestern Montana. About 30 participants were expected, but over 100 people attended. In response to positive feedback, a feasibility study surveyed Montana farmers and ranchers not currently involved in a recreation business. The study concluded that there were good opportunities for producers to earn additional income without a major disruption of their regular operations.

Workshop Series

In response to the obvious interest and opportunity, the state's tourism development partners created the Montana Farm and Ranch Recreation Business Workshop series. The workshop series was designed to help Montana's agriculture producers assess whether the addition of a recreation component would provide economic and social benefits for their particular business. A recreation business was not presented as something farmers and ranchers "should" do, but as an "option" to consider. For those who felt it was compatible with, and complimentary to, their agricultural operations, the workshops provided planning tools that could increase their chance for success.

Between 1995 and 1998, 20 workshops were held in rural areas across Montana. About 1 000 Montana farm and ranch operators participated in the workshops. By the end of the decade, the state's farm and ranch recreation product increased by 50 percent. Much of this growth happened in the state's traditionally less-travelled areas.

The workshop program was put on hold in 1999. Now, with renewed interest from the agricultural community involved in planning for Montana's role in the upcoming Lewis and Clark Bicentennial Observance (2003–2006), the workshop program is being refreshed and prepared for another series, beginning in 2001.

IMPLEMENTATION

The Farm and Ranch Workshop series was designed by the Montana tourism development partners in planning sessions held throughout the spring, summer, and fall of 1994. An overriding theme in the development of the workshops was not to promote the creation of farm and ranch recreation businesses, but to provide agriculture producers with the tools to assess whether this was an appropriate business for them and their operations.

The design and planning duties of the workshop series were divided among the partners in the following manner:

MONTANA TOURISM DEVELOPMENT PARTNERS	DUTIES
Montana State University Extension, SBA, and RC&D	curriculum development and speaker selection
Travel Montana and tourism region partners	dates and locations
Travel Montana and SBA	brochure layout, printing, and distribution
Travel Montana, Montana State University Extension, SBA, and RC&D	publicity
All partners contribute, with publication coordinated by Travel Montana	producing a resource handbook for workshop sessions

During its first year, in 1995, the workshop series offered six day-long sessions in six different rural communities during the months of January and February. The locations were selected to provide participants from every region of the state convenient access to at least one of the workshops. The workshop dates selected also corresponded with Montana's agriculture producers' off-season. Given the high attendance, the workshops were offered each year during the same two months.

In 1995, the workshop was divided into morning and afternoon sessions. The morning was filled with an introduction to the topics of business planning, development, and marketing. The afternoon focussed on "real life" farm and ranch recreation-business experiences, along with current and future trends in Montana's recreation businesses. Four farm and ranch recreation-business operators—all of whom operated businesses in the workshop area—conducted the real-life presentations. All 24 presenters shared their successes and mistakes, and responded to questions from workshop participants.

> *"Visiting and networking with others in the recreation business was of great benefit to us at last year's Farm and Ranch Recreation Workshop."*
>
> Carol Greenwood, Doonan Gulch Outfitters and
> Oakwood Lodge B&B, Broadus, MT

The 1995 workshops attracted 413 participants, each of whom was surveyed to determine the quality of topics and presentations in that year's offering. The survey also asked for new topic ideas and approaches for future workshops. Survey results indicated an interest in learning more about insurance issues, financing, industry trends, and what other recreation-business operators were doing.

Given this information, the first segment of the day-long session at the 1996 workshops was designed to cover feasibility assessments, along with discussions on financing, business plan development, and insurance. The other segment featured trends in the international and domestic markets, marketing tools, and the real life experiences of farm and ranch recreation practitioners involved in these markets. As in the first year, six workshops were offered in six rural communities. In total, the 1996 workshops attracted 300 participants.

The 1997 workshop series followed the format of the previous sessions, but incorporated two video presentations, developed by Extension and Travel Montana, titled *Fun on the Farm: Starting a Farm and Ranch Recreation Business*. This is a 45-minute video, divided into three 15-minute presentations. The first 15-minute segment features six existing operators talking about the why, what, and how of their farm and ranch recreation business. The second and third segments use these same presenters—along with additional resources—to cover topics such as business and licensing considerations, facilities, and marketing. A second video featured a half-hour presentation on insurance issues.

In addition to the video presentations, the 1997 workshop sessions provided information about break-even and cash flow analysis, business planning assistance, consumer expectations, marketing and sales techniques, state marketing programs, and marketing partnership opportunities with the state tourism region. Approximately 170 participants took part in the six 1997 workshops.

After three years of offering introductory level information, the workshop planners decided to focus the 1998 workshop agenda on Montanans already involved in a farm and ranch recreation business. In other words, it was a "Farm & Ranch 201" course. More advanced presentations included in-depth discussions on industry trends, marketing, and pricing. Existing operators shared information on making the most of a farm or ranch's recreation resources, and two attorneys discussed legal issues. Two workshops were scheduled in the urban centres of eastern and western Montana.

The 1998 workshops attracted 120 attendees. Only half of the attendees were from the target audience. Many participants were newcomers interested in finding out about this type of business. The advanced presentations went beyond what they were seeking. Because of this, the 1998 workshops were not considered as successful as those held in previous years.

Workshop materials provided to participants during each year of the program included a *Farm & Ranch Recreation Resource Directory*, as well as handouts from various presenters not included in the directory. The contents of the directory varied from year to year, but generally included the workshop agenda, an outline of assistance programs provided by the planning partners, information on state building codes and health permits, business plan forms, speaker profiles, and other pertinent presentation materials. In 1996 and 1998, one workshop was videotaped in its entirety. These videos—along with the *Fun on the Farm* videos and the resource directory—were made available, at cost, to the public.

The planning team set the workshop fee at $35 (US) per person for pre-session registration, and $45 (US) at the door. This was deemed to be an affordable price for participants and enough to cover most of the workshop costs. The remaining costs were distributed among the planning partners.

Groups in other western states contacted the Montana workshop planners about creating similar programs in their areas. As a result, the Montana group led farm and ranch recreation business presentations in Arizona, Texas, New Mexico, California, and North Dakota. The increased interest in the farm and ranch workshops concerned the Montana planners. The planners worried about competition from other states, and whether supply would outstrip demand if more agricultural recreation businesses were created. It was also felt that interest in this topic had been saturated. For these reasons, the Montana program was put on hold in 1999.

For 2001, Montana's tourism development partners are reviving the program to respond to interest generated by the upcoming Lewis and Clark bicentennial observance. The bicentennial observance is expected to increase visits to Montana's rural areas, where much of the historic trail is located. The 2001 workshops will focus on helping Montana's agriculture community make the best use of this opportunity. This will be accomplished by adding a recreation business component to the workshop and developing programs to highlight land stewardship efforts and avoiding negative land access situations.

RESULTS

In October 1996, Montana's Farm and Ranch Recreation Business Workshop program was awarded the prestigious ODYSSEY Award from the United States Tourism Industry Association of America (TIA). The TIA award recognized the Montana workshops as the best tourism "education and training" program in the country.

The workshops' goal was to provide farmers and ranchers with the tools to assess the costs and benefits of adding a recreation business. The workshops would allow them to make informed decisions. The workshops did not promote the creation of such businesses. Because the success of the program was not dependent on whether a participant opened a recreation business, it is difficult to measure if the program was successful.

There are two ways to decipher the workshop results. First, one can examine the workshop participant evaluations. Secondly, one can look at the growth in Montana's farm and ranch recreation opportunities between 1994 and 2000. Although the latter cannot be directly linked to the program, the results are listed below.

The workshop participant evaluations were generally favourable. Most participants rated the presentations and materials useful. Some felt that too much information was presented in a short period of time, while others said certain topics should have been presented in more depth. These latter comments were used to improve workshops for the following year.

A review of Travel Montana's statewide *Montana Travel Planner* data from 1994 to 2000 shows the following farm and ranch recreation business listing changes:

- wagon train/cattle drive services—up 50 percent (14 to 21)
- bed and breakfasts with agriculture tie—stayed even at 23 statewide
- guest ranch opportunities—up 51 percent (81 to 123)
- guide services—declined 9 percent (605 to 550).

Since the *Montana Travel Planner* publication offers free statewide listings for travel service and product providers, it is thought to be the most complete listing of such services. The publication and its information database is part of the printed and electronic information which Travel Montana provides to potential visitors requesting state travel planning materials.

Looking at the geographic distribution of the farm and ranch recreation businesses in the planner, almost half of the increase in guest ranch services has been in the traditionally less-travelled agriculture areas of Montana. Two-thirds of Montana's wagon train/cattle drive operators are located in these same areas. While one cannot make a direct link between the workshop program and these developments, the outcome does satisfy the goal of spreading the opportunities and benefits of tourism more broadly as directed by the state's travel and tourism strategic plan.[1]

WTTC HUMAN RESOURCE CENTRE COMMENT

Low agricultural product prices, coupled with movies and other media romanticizing the West, are partially credited for the resurgence of families wanting to experience farm and ranch lifestyles while vacationing. The number of dude ranches, bed and breakfast farmhouses, and family ranch vacations available throughout North America has increased since the 1990s, as a response to market demand. Instead of encouraging all participants to diversify their operations and possibly find hidden value in existing production, or to expand current tourism businesses, the Montana Farm and Ranch Recreation Business Workshop series supplies its workshop participants with expert information, practical examples, and the tools with which to make informed decisions.

---

1 To access further resources, visit the Montana State University Web site at **www.montana.edu/~wwwpb/ag/ranch.html** and read about *Running that Extra Business Along with Your Ranch or Farm*. Links found on the site include *Tips on succeeding in farm recreation* and *Farm and ranch recreation videos*.

KEY TERMS

recreation business
farm tourism
workshop series
rural development

economic diversification
industry input
partnerships
feasibility assessment

 www.travelmontana.state.mt.us

DISCUSSION QUESTIONS

1. How did the workshop program's approach succeed in the buy-in of business owners facing a challenging situation?

2. Explain how the workshops developed over time. What kind of feedback contributed to the evolution of the program?

3. Choose an industry which is in a situation like Montana's, and explain how the workshop format might be applied. What modifications would you suggest?

Canada
Rocky Mountaineer Railtours

Submitted by: Janice Greenwood

ORGANIZATIONAL LEADERSHIP IN TOURISM

… The leadership role of one individual transformed this passenger rail tour company into a profitable business venture focussed on comfort, efficiency, economy, marketing, and minimal overhead.

LEARNING OUTCOMES

1. Explain the benefits of a diverse Board of Directors in a privately owned company.

2. Identify the role of an executive committee in managing corporate change.

3. Explain the role of guest feedback in developing a growth management strategy and a strong corporate culture.

OVERVIEW

Rocky Mountaineer Railtours is the largest privately owned passenger rail service in North America, with sales offices located in 18 different countries. During the operating season, the company employs 330 employees. With an on-board team of specially trained staff, this full-service tour operator offers specialized rail tours through Canada's West and the Canadian Rockies. Guests experience the most magnificent scenery in the world as they journey on two-day, all-daylight rail tours from Vancouver, British Columbia, to either Jasper, Banff, or Calgary, in the province of Alberta.

In 2000, the company welcomed 75 000 guests aboard its 148 train departures, taking place between mid-April and mid-October, with additional special winter departures in mid-December. Rocky Mountaineer Railtours also operates Two River Junction, a dinner and musical revue in the city of Kamloops, which is where the company's operations and maintenance facility is situated. As part of its many services, Rocky Mountaineer Railtours provides 40 independent package tours of the region.

Peter Armstrong, president, chief executive officer (CEO), and principal of Rocky Mountaineer Railtours, started the company in 1990. At that time, the federal government cut VIA Rail's (Canada's national passenger railway's) subsidized program, and privatized the daylight service, originally begun in 1988 as a tourist product. Peter Armstrong assembled a team of former railroad executives and leading tourism experts who imparted 120 years of combined railroad experience to the newly established company. Today, Armstrong's vision is to turn Rocky Mountaineer Railtours into the premier provider of Canadian tourism travel experiences. He is committed to developing and offering unique, quality vacation products in Canada.

IMPLEMENTATION

Structure and Leadership

With the same vision that continues to drive the organization today, Armstrong remains president and CEO of the company he founded. Complementing his leadership, he has developed a strong team of advisors. These employees guide the company's development within their area of expertise. This has fostered the growth of a strong core group of stable, knowledgeable, enthusiastic, and well-trained staff.

Although the company is privately owned, Armstrong instituted a formal Board of Directors. The directors consist of outside advisors whose purpose is to provide expert advice and mentoring for the president and the executive committee. The company executive also has the support of an experienced group of consultants and advisors, from all industry sectors. Armstrong recognized early on that individuals outside of tourism organizations have much to contribute to Rocky Mountaineer Railtours' business approach.

The nine-member executive committee is led by a chief operating officer with thirty years of experience in the hospitality industry. Responsible for forming the company's growth strategy objectives, the committee pays close attention to media and public relations efforts, and forges good relationships with clients, suppliers, financial institutions, and venture capital partners. The committee members are vice presidents from the following departments:

- guest services
- finance
- operations
- human resources
- sales
- marketing
- communications
- administration.

Through guidance and investment, each of these departments is capable of making autonomous decisions, while remaining closely connected to the company. Reflecting on the success of the Rocky Mountaineer team, Armstrong says: "There are some people who say they can do it alone but I was never able to do that. Even when you don't have partners, your employees often serve the same function because so many of the good ideas you get, come from them."

While many of Rocky Mountaineer Railtours' employees are seasonal, the return rate of on-board staff is close to 80 percent. The company credits staff loyalty to the low rate of turnover. Staff value the company's close-knit corporate culture, pride in providing quality service, and the knowledge that every employee's opinion is valued.

Communication

Rocky Mountaineer Railtours' two major audiences are employees and guests. As the company has grown over the last ten years, the president's ability to communicate individually with all these people has lessened. The importance of communicating with these audiences, however, has not.

Despite corporate growth, communication is still viewed as a two-way process. What guests tell Rocky Mountaineer Railtours is as crucial as what Rocky Mountaineer Railtours shares with guests.

There are 160 employees in guest services alone, all committed to providing quality service. All guests are asked to complete a comment card after their journey, as customer suggestions provide valuable information and help the company to continuously improve service. Ten thousand personal letters are sent out annually to ensure that guest comments and suggestions are properly recognized.

Internal communication is also a priority for the company. An internal monthly newsletter is sent to all employees and important stakeholders in the company. This newsletter includes a regular column written by the CEO, explaining some of the concepts behind his policies and visions. Annual employee opinion surveys are also undertaken to identify employee concerns and company successes.

Decision Making

Characteristic of the company's entrepreneurial spirit, fostered by the company CEO, business development ideas are encouraged from the staff and executive. Recognizing that service and product delivery is the ultimate measurement of guest satisfaction, many innovations in rail travel have been introduced into the marketplace by Rocky Mountaineer Railtours.

The introduction of GoldLeaf Service in 1995 is perhaps the most successful decision made by the company since beginning the rail service five years earlier. The service, explains Armstrong, is a direct result of listening to customer feedback: "Guests told us they wanted a dome coach. They told us they wanted freshly prepared meals. They told us they wanted an outside observation deck. When you look at our GoldLeaf dome coaches today, you see all these features."

Over the past five years, the company has commissioned the design and construction of 10 bi-level dome coaches, with 70 seats on the upper level and 36 dining room seats on the main level. The coach also carries a galley where gourmet menu selections are prepared. Built at a cost of $3.4 million per car, complete with rear observation platform, these were the first new passenger railcars built for the Canadian market in over 40 years.

Typically, staff quickly embraces visionary and business development ideas that are made into a workable plan. In 1999, a core group of experienced employees structured a charter agreement with Laidlaw Canada to provide branded motorcoach service for Rocky Mountaineer guests throughout the Canadian Rockies. Not only does this service provide a seamless transition during the guest's tour experience, but service and quality control is retained by Rocky Mountaineer Railtours. By the end of the first year, a profit was realized.

In a similar way, Two River Junction Dinner and Musical Revue was created in Kamloops, BC, based on an idea to provide a dinner and entertainment venue for Rocky Mountaineer Railtours guests. A manager was appointed with autonomous decision-making power and company support. In five years of operation, over 100 000 guests have experienced the traditional western Canadian menu, complimented by a lively and entertaining musical revue.

Empowerment

The Valued Idea Program (VIP) encourages employees to bring forth workplace improvements. The program solicits and recognizes suggested policies and procedures on a quarterly basis. An annual employee awards program, the President's Awards, is announced at the season ending celebration attended by all employees. In 1996, the President's Award was presented to an employee who initiated a program to donate unused food to local food banks, rather than dispose of the meals at trip end. This commitment is continued to this day.

Overall, guest comfort and safety continues to be a central focus of the company. More than 120 on-board attendants receive three weeks of intensive training before each season on every topic from best practices to emergencies. Similar programs are available for Kamloops and Vancouver employees. A training centre has been developed within company headquarters, ensuring that employees are trained to provide quality service in a safe environment.

RESULTS

More than 99 percent of guests have rated Rocky Mountaineer Railtours as meeting or exceeding expectations. Also of note, 99 percent of guests would recommend the Rocky Mountaineer experience to a friend or relative.

More than 70 000 guests experienced the Rocky Mountaineer and its 40 tour packages in 2000. Over 10 seasons, this is an increase of 1 000 percent. The efforts of the company contribute well in excess of 100 000 hotel-room nights per year to the western Canadian economy. Financial statements for 1999 concluded that Rocky Mountaineer Railtours' total impact is $192.6 million—directly and indirectly—on local economies. The annual impact in terms of jobs is estimated to be a total of 2 469 person-years of employment.

The entrepreneurial spirit and commitment to guest services that defines Rocky Mountaineer Railtours is a testament to Armstrong's leadership and organizational style. As the company moves into its second decade of operation, the company's core strengths in communication, decision making, and empowerment will ensure the continued growth and success of the company.

WTTC Human Resource Centre COMMENT

Good leaders understand that communication is not just a one-way process. It requires feedback from the recipients, as well from employees. Peter Armstrong built the leading railtour company in North America by combining strong personal vision with effective team-building approaches. The service culture that has resulted at Rocky Mountaineer Railtours relies on staff passing on the values and beliefs of the CEO to both their colleagues and the guests. Armstrong's clarity of purpose in his leadership approach to building sustainability—matched with the uniqueness of the product on offer—has led to the success of Rocky Mountaineer Railtours.

KEY TERMS

leadership   personal achievement
chief executive officer   empowerment
decision making   communication
tour operator   value-added
corporate culture   venture capital

 **www.rockymountaineer.com**

DISCUSSION QUESTIONS

1. Explain the importance of gathering guest and employee feedback and the impact this information has on a) employee training, b) company operations, and c) guest service.

2. What economic advantages does Rocky Mountaineer Railtours gain by offering additional services such as Two River Junction (the dinner and musical revue in the city of Kamloops) and branded motorcoach service? What other value-added services and products could the company provide?

3. How would you characterize the leadership approach of Peter Armstrong in building a strong team culture at Rocky Mountaineer Railtours?

United Kingdom
Glendola Leisure

Submitted by: Alex Salussolia

GLENDOLA
l e i s u r e · l i m i t e d

CUSTOMER LOYALTY BUILT THROUGH QUALITY SERVICE

... Improving business performance through effective and structured training and development.

LEARNING OUTCOMES

1. Explore the advantages of including managers and supervisors in the creative design of training programs.
2. Recognize how new and revised training programs enable staff to become more focussed and capable of providing a better, more efficient standard of service.
3. Describe the benefits of varying training formats according to training needs.

> *"Our overriding philosophy is simple: The leisure business depends on people—whether they are employees or customers. We will continue to recruit the best people available and groom them effectively through training and development. This will ensure that customers receive a warm welcome and a high standard of service."*
>
> *Foundation Group*

OVERVIEW

Established in 1973, Glendola Leisure is the pub, club, and restaurant-operating division of the Foundation Group (a privately owned company managing a range of leisure operations in the United Kingdom [UK] and Europe). Its portfolio includes the renowned World's End Pub in Camden, North London, the Bootsy Brogan's chain of pubs on the River Thames in Putney and London's East End, and Waxy O'Connor's (the award-winning Irish pub in the heart of London's West End). Glendola Leisure also operates a number of clubs and bars in the South of England and has added the Rainforest Café to its list of properties. Over the next 10 years, the Foundation Group has an agreement with Rainforest Café to open five more restaurants in the UK and Ireland.

In 1994, Glendola Leisure realized it needed a training strategy to retain and improve its entrepreneurial edge within a highly competitive and difficult marketplace. The company chose to implement the UK's national standard, Investors In People (IIP), as it provides an effective training and development structure and is designed to improve business performance. Glendola Leisure considered several possibilities, but IIP offered the most suitable and flexible approach. IIP's human resource management standards are recognized as a government national training standard throughout the UK.

IMPLEMENTATION

IIP paid for a recognized consultant to evaluate Glendola Leisure. The consultant conducted a gap analysis to establish which of the company's business objectives did and did not meet IIP objectives. A strategy was then designed to fill in the "gaps." Next, an action plan was developed and this led to the design and implementation of various programs.

For example, induction programs were revised for employees hired into the areas of bar, floor, kitchen, cellar, supervisory, and management. In addition, front line, supervisory, and management training programs were redesigned so that they could be offered through both group and individual training sessions. New programs were incorporated in all Glendola Leisure properties over a three-year period. To make sure standards were being met, and to identify areas needing improvement, all training programs were evaluated twice a year on an ongoing basis. Staff also had to meet statutory requirements such as health, safety, food hygiene, and licensing.

By restructuring training, Glendola Leisure clearly defined areas needing improvement, and focussed accordingly. The company integrated training and development into the day-to-day business, and designed its training format as a part of the "company culture," rather than a specific or separate program. This philosophy is emphasized throughout the company, to highlight the importance of daily improvement both in the workplace and in terms of personal development.

During training restructuring, Glendola Leisure faced one specific challenge. The new training programs required managers to put into practice set procedures. Typically entrepreneurial in nature, company managers were not certain to accept structured procedures. As a way to gain gradual acceptance, the action plan set very loose time scales. Glendola Leisure felt it was more important to introduce the plan at a cultural level, and did not want to appear too hasty. Managers needed time to accept the action plan and give their support. Including managers and supervisors in the creative design of training programs helped to develop a feeling of ownership and acceptance.

As a compromise, the training format varied according to training needs. While skill development might take place at the work site, a classroom setting may have incorporated video presentations, role-playing, and instruction with employee interaction. Instruction ranged from a few weeks to a few years, as training is considered an integral part of the business life at Glendola Leisure.

Appraisals were developed for all levels of employment, and communication meetings were introduced at all units. An evaluation framework was set up to measure the outcomes of training and development activities. Regular reviews were introduced with unit managers, the human resource manager, and the senior team to assess the effectiveness of all programs. The cost of developing the entire program was £50 000 (GBP).

RESULTS

All Glendola Leisure outlets achieved an increase in sales. As a result of the new training, staff became more focussed and could offer a better, more efficient standard of service. Glendola Leisure measures its success in the following achievements:

- 40 percent increase in all outlets' business performance;
- 40 percent reduction in turnover as monitored in the company's payroll;
- increase in operation standards (measured through the comments Glendola Leisure receives from its mystery shopper, who visits the outlets on a regular basis, comparing like for like);
- fewer customer complaints; and
- an increase in staff morale and commitment. (Glendola Leisure has an external consultant who meets with staff to review their training program and work attitudes. Responses are compared from year to year.)

Glendola Leisure was pleasantly surprised by how warmly staff accepted the new programs. Staff perceived the action plan as being of personal benefit to them. For Glendola Leisure, training became a day-to-day function of the business.

WTTC HUMAN RESOURCE CENTRE COMMENT

The Investors In People standard ensures that clear business objectives are set and communicated to staff. This helps employees to better understand the direction of the organization and their part in its success. Glendola Leisure not only recognized that it is good business to invest in training, but realized that training had to be an integral part of all operations at every level. The company took advantage of an existing national tool (IIP) to provide the basis for company-specific programs. By establishing training evaluations, Glendola Leisure is capable of identifying areas for future improvements.

KEY TERMS

national training strategy
company culture
gap analysis
business objectives
performance appraisal

entrepreneurial
service standards
mystery shopper
Investors In People

 www.foundationgroup.co.uk/altindex.htm

DISCUSSION QUESTIONS

1. List several ideas or structures to ensure that management and supervisors are delivering newly implemented programs. What are the advantages of establishing accountability?

2. Discuss two advantages of integrating training into the day-to-day business operations as opposed to creating a specific or separate program.

3. To measure company operation standards, you use a mystery shopper who visits your outlets on a regular basis, comparing like for like. List 10 items that the mystery shopper should evaluate while at your pub or restaurant.

United States
Continental Airlines

Submitted by: Michelle Meissner

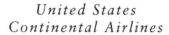

FROM "WORST TO FIRST": LESSONS FROM A HIGH-FLYING AIRLINE

> . . . Organizational restructuring with good leadership and communication is secured through employee buy-in.

LEARNING OUTCOMES

1. Analyze a restructuring approach addressing business planning and a human resource strategy.

2. Outline key priorities in the turnaround of a major travel product.

3. Identify the importance of employee support and commitment in corporate restructuring.

OVERVIEW

In 1994, Continental Airlines was experiencing severe operational challenges. The United States Department of Transportation surveys rated it tenth among US airlines in on-time performance, baggage service, and customer complaints. The company had filed bankruptcy twice in the preceding 10 years, and was on the verge of a third, and possibly final bankruptcy in the fall of 1994. There was constant change in senior management. Ten chief executive officers came and went in as many years. By the end of 1994, employee morale was at an all-time low, which was reflected in high numbers for lost time, job injury claims, and voluntary turnover.

To rectify the situation, a new management team was formed. In fall 1994, the management team quickly assessed the company's service, financial, and employee operations. Unanimously, the team agreed on what was needed to turn the airline around. The Go Forward Plan was born.

IMPLEMENTATION

The first step in introducing the Go Forward Plan was to make all employees aware of the role they played in meeting the company's new business objectives. In July 1995, and every year since then, all directors and vice presidents met at Houston headquarters for a two-day leadership conference. The purpose of this conference was to explain the objectives of the Go Forward Plan, and to secure a personal commitment from each leader to inform their teams about the plan.

The Go Forward Plan addressed financial matters, company infrastructure, service issues, and employee morale. The plan is based on the following four cornerstones:

- **Fly to Win**—Flying to destinations that make money. The company focussed on increasing revenue by attracting business travellers and reducing its distribution costs.
- **Fund the Future**—Responsible for reducing its debt structure. Continental Airlines began investing in its hubs and working towards "owning its markets."
- **Make Reliability a Reality**—The operational cornerstone. This initiative focussed on the airline's on-time performance, customer service, and inflight products.
- **Working Together**—Continental's people strategy: to create a company where employees enjoy coming to work. This objective was no small feat considering the history of relations between management and employees.

Having a sound business strategy was a good start, but without buy-in and commitment from employees, the plan did not stand a chance. To ensure employee participation in the Go Forward Plan, two cash incentive programs were introduced. These were:

- Profit sharing: employees' compensation was tied to the financial performance of the company through profit sharing.
- On-time bonus program: every time the airline is measured in the top three for on-time performance, employees receive a $65 (US) bonus payment. When the airline is in the number one slot, each employee receives a cheque for $100 (US).

The company directors and vice presidents (the team leaders) monitor the effectiveness of the Go Forward Plan. These leaders are evaluated on how well they communicate the program's goals and objectives, and how well they explain individual staff members' responsibilities. Evaluations take place each December, in the form of a 10-question survey called the Leadership Communication Survey. All employees complete the survey, and results are tied directly to the leader's bonus plan.

RESULTS

The Go Forward Plan has been a tremendous success. Under the Fly to Win cornerstone, Continental has recorded 24 straight quarters of pre-tax profit. As a result of restructuring its destinations, the carrier has been able to strike alliances with Northwest, Alitalia, Air France, and Virgin Atlantic. Continental is leading the industry in revenue per available seat mile, and has increased its business-to-leisure ratio to over 50 percent. Through leveraging technology, the carrier has reduced its distribution costs, and provided easier access to its product through the Internet. To its benefit, Continental flies the youngest fleet in the industry.

Fund the Future accomplishments are significant. The company has a healthy cash balance, while purchasing new aircraft to reduce operating expenses. In 1999, Continental consolidated its headquarters in Houston, Texas. Continental has doubled the revenue out of the carrier's three major hubs—Houston, Cleveland, and Newark—while achieving industry-leading profit margins.

Make Reliability a Reality has aided Continental in receiving the J.D. Power and Associates award for service four out of the last five years, including winning both the long and short haul award in 2000. This is the first time an airline has ever won back-to-back awards. *Air Transport World* (*ATW*) magazine named Continental "Airline of the Year" in 1996. Continental consistently ranks in the Department of Transportation's surveys as one of the top five carriers, and was the number one carrier for on-time arrivals in 2000.

> *"You can make a pizza so cheap, nobody wants to buy it."*
>
> Gordon Bethune, CEO and Chairman of the Board
> Continental Airlines

Working Together has been the cornerstone that has shaped Continental's winning culture. Named to FORTUNE *magazine's* "100 Best Companies to Work for in America" for the last three years, the airline has become a place where people enjoy coming to work every day.

In its February 2001 issue, *ATW* magazine announced Continental Airlines as recipient of the "Airline of the Year" title in its Industry Achievement Awards series. Continental received this distinction in 1996 as well, and is the only airline to win the title twice in such a short time frame. The article states: "The hallmark of any highly successful enterprise is consistency, the ability to perform at a superior level over an extended period of time. Continental Airlines has demonstrated such consistency for more than half a decade, an era that includes its selection as *ATW*'s 'Airline of the Year' for 1996. Six years is a long time for any company in any industry, but it's an eon in the airline business, a sector marked by rapid change and vulnerability to the economic cycle that can wreck even the best-laid plan."

Continental has increased employee compensation from 73 percent of industry market to 100 percent, while absorbing increasing benefit costs. Voluntary turnover at the airline has decreased from 31.2 percent in 1995 to less than 6 percent last year. Continental received over 130 000 employment applications in 2000.

WTTC Human Resouce Centre COMMENT

The process by which Continental Airlines has travelled from one of the lowest-rated airlines to one of the best is a model of good practice. The restructuring strategy was sound, but it could only succeed if the employees bought into it. The pay-for-performance program provides a monetary incentive, which is distributed fairly through profit sharing. Employees feel they are part of the process of fundamental change for this huge corporation. A sense of employee ownership in change processes is essential for any tourism human resource development strategy.

KEY TERMS

employee morale
monetary incentives
hubs
business plan
corporate restructuring

cornerstone
turnover
Department of Transportation
profit sharing
employee buy-in

 **www.coair.com**

DISCUSSION QUESTIONS

1. Pick one of the four cornerstones of the Go Forward Plan. Describe, in your own words, the challenge involved, and the results.

2. What other employee incentives might be considered to further strengthen buy-in?

3. How did Continental Airlines structure things so that it could be sure that the Go Forward Plan would be delivered and monitored effectively?

Scotland
Nevis Range

Submitted by: Marian Austin

AN OPEN MANAGEMENT SYSTEM

. . . By implementing an open management system, the company developed a caring, committed, and multi-skilled workforce.

LEARNING OUTCOMES

1. Define the philosophy of an open management system.
2. Explain the benefits of a positive approach to staff appraisals in an open management system.
3. Explain how a ski resort initiative may provide a new economic base for a region.

OVERVIEW

In 1970, the small Scottish town of Fort William experienced dramatic change. The town's pulp mill closed and its aluminum works were modernized, resulting in 3 000 people left without work. At the time, the town population was 11 000.

New development was necessary to create jobs and redefine the base industry for sustaining this Scottish Highland area. Working with the existing tourism industry, Nevis Range Development Company plc (Nevis Range) introduced a plan that would create access to ski slopes in the area.

To proceed with the development venture, a sum of £13 million (GBP) was raised through a group of local businesses, six Scottish financial institutions, government grants, and a European Development Fund.

Nevis Range opened in 1989 with a parking lot, cable car, restaurants, a gift shop, ski rental facility, ski school, and six ski lifts. Breathtaking views of Ben Nevis and the surrounding mountains are accessible year round from the gondola cable car.

In the last four years the company has doubled the size of the ski area and spent £1 million (GBP) on the upgrading of facilities to achieve new heights as a year-round tourist attraction. Helping Nevis Range meet an even wider range of leisure and sporting experiences are the newly added:

- snowboard hire
- crèche
- five new lifts
- mountain bike hire
- downhill mountain bike track (allowing experienced mountain bikers to take bikes up in the gondola and cycle down a three-mile track).

Nevis Range employs approximately 50 people during the summer season and 120 in the winter ski season. For Nevis Range, this means that employees and management are encouraged to share business-related views and ideas, regardless of their job titles. Communications within Nevis Range flow within an open management system. For example, departmental meetings typically follow management meetings (which are held twice a week), encouraging input and discussion on topics in a timely matter. In periods of financial loss, this management process is more difficult. Nevertheless, staff are included in company dialogue, even when business results are negative. The company's philosophy is to operate under the belief that good communications grow from a caring, sharing, and committed workforce.

IMPLEMENTATION

To successfully monitor an open management system, management sought the aid of the program Investors In People (IIP), Scotland. IIP is a United Kingdom government program designed to help businesses adopt modern management practices. The company's commitment to IIP reflects its own philosophy. IIP's management solutions focussed on increasing staff loyalty and commitment.

With assistance from IIP staff, Nevis Range developed a new and easily revised management plan, with clear lines of communication to staff throughout the ski field. Departmental managers received train-the-trainer training, thus reducing training costs in the long term. It was necessary to tie all training to business objectives, to record progress, and to review the effectiveness of the training. For budgetary reasons, it was also necessary to prioritize external training.

Nevis Range achieved IIP status in 1995 and was reassessed in 1999. During the re-accreditation, their review showed that some of the original structure had been too ambitious and changes were made accordingly.

Staff Training

The efforts that management made in providing external training to staff reinforced their commitment to employee development. For financial reasons, however, the cost and benefits of providing staff with outside training were re-evaluated. In response, the Scottish Vocational Qualifications program, offered throughout the company, was scaled down because the program was found to be too complex and time-consuming for many departments.

As for other staff training, all supervisors and management continue to attend Tourism Training Scotland's quality service programs. These one- and two-day seminars, targeted specifically at tourism business, teach participants how to create a more positive service strategy. In addition, new employee orientation programs are reviewed annually and include an in-house customer care module.

Staff Appraisal

The initial staff appraisal scheme, once unpopular, is now viewed with enthusiasm. Prior to reassessment, staff appraisals were conducted through informal discussions about the company, with emphasis placed on each individual's role within it. Appraisal paperwork has changed to encourage discussion, and to allow for positive feedback. This modification has reduced "judgmental" feelings previously expressed by employees.

> *"I used to dread carrying out appraisals because I dislike confrontational situations, but now that the staff and I realize that this is an opportunity for a quiet chat, I have discovered that some of the barriers come down and I get ideas from the staff as well as them getting ideas from me."*
>
> *Kevin Byrne, Engineering Manager*
> *Nevis Range*

Customer Service

A central goal of the entire company is to provide quality customer care. In the ski industry, the product is directly affected by weather conditions, and, therefore, much is out of the company's control. Having a reputation as a friendly visitor attraction is essential. It is possible to minimize guest disappointment with the right service.

For example, instead of avoiding an awkward situation—such as a ski lift breakdown—operators are encouraged to chat with customers and to provide an explanation about the delay. Customers have commented on how much they appreciate this kind of service, despite being delayed. Experienced lift operators participate in seasonal staff training to help new employees understand Nevis Range's service culture.

To monitor guest feedback, the company's publicity department conducts regular customer surveys. Summer questionnaires are distributed periodically to customers with their lift tickets. Those who complete the survey have their names entered in a prize draw designed to encourage participation. Various winter questionnaires are also distributed. The company has a questionnaire available at all times at every Scottish ski area. Customers who have registered their e-mail address with Nevis Range's Web site are also e-mailed questionnaires. E-mail surveys typically have a high rate of return.

RESULTS

Nevis Range was the first ski company to achieve the IIP, Scotland award. To date, four of its competitors also have also received accreditation. Not being the "new" ski company any longer, there is constant pressure to improve while facing the challenge of maintaining and running dated equipment. Staff and management are all involved in any decisions affecting change to programs and equipment.

The ski industry operates in an uncertain financial climate. The fact that Nevis Range has survived 11 years, with very mixed winter fortunes, is clearly due to the company's dedicated and motivated employees.

As a result of management style and training programs, permanent staff can now be described as a flexible and multi-skilled workforce. For example, the winter ski patrol manager is in charge of an environmental program in the summer. Similarly, the winter piste machine drivers maintain the ski lifts in summer.

Staff understanding of the company's aims, ambitions, and challenges is important to the success of Nevis Range. This message is communicated through managers' meetings, meeting reports, and minutes available to all staff, as well as through an in-house newsletter.

Positive factors to date include:

- a reasonably stable summer business, supporting a year-round tourist destination and providing employment for core staff;

- reasonable business returns for 1999 and 2000, allowing the company to purchase its debt and stabilize its financial future;

- construction of an additional summer bike track through European Community grants and lottery funding (since it is more motivating for staff to work where developments are taking place rather than in a zero-spend environment);

- rated one of the top 10 visitor attractions in Scotland; and

- repeated compliments from visitors about staff friendliness.

WTTC HUMAN RESOURCE CENTRE COMMENT

Despite a difficult start-up period caused by winters with little snow, Nevis Range's perseverance paid off. Seeking outside help and investing in train-the-trainer and customer service programs created clear communication lines and a positive evaluation system. Diversification and expansion of Nevis Range facilities complemented the open management system and, collectively, these initiatives have helped to make the ski area one of the top 10 visitor attractions in Scotland.

KEY TERMS

open management   staff appraisal
multi-skilled   customer service
departmental communication   Investors In People
service culture   train-the-trainer

 www.nevis-range.co.uk

DISCUSSION QUESTIONS

1. Cite other examples of tourism developments that have allowed for successful community economic transitions.

2. Discuss the pros and cons of an open management system when a business is facing difficult economic times.

3. Should customer feedback be part of a staff appraisal session? How would you incorporate feedback in a positive manner?

Celebrating Cultural Differences: Cross-Cultural Training, Multi-Cultural Skills and Awareness, and Cultural Interpretation Training

United States
Sheraton Hotels & Resorts Hawai'i

Submitted by: Kayomi Kaneda, Dr. Franz Broswimmer, and Michiru Tamanai

Sheraton
HOTELS & RESORTS
HAWAI'I

INTERCULTURAL COMMUNICATION TRAINING

… A hotel's diverse intercultural workforce learns to appreciate cultural differences by responding appropriately to one another and exceeding guest expectations.

LEARNING OUTCOMES

1. Interpret how staff training in cultural sensitivity improves the quality of the guest experience.

2. Recognize that an understanding of behaviour and expectations can improve communication and cooperation within the workplace.

3. Explain how a program is constructed and designed to facilitate understanding between hosts and guests.

OVERVIEW

In the hotel lobby of the Sheraton Hotels & Resorts Hawai'i, a *lei* greeter warmly welcomes the newly arrived guests with the Hawaiian island greeting of *aloha*. To the delight of the Japanese guests, the *lei* greeter can speak English and some Japanese. Typically, the Sheraton Hotels & Resorts Hawai'i (Sheraton Hotels) greeter will speak English to the younger Japanese guests, as they appreciate practising their English. The older Japanese travellers, asking for directions, are grateful as the greeter politely responds in Japanese, using the appropriate gestures.

The above scenario is an example of a staff member culturally sensitive to the needs of the Japanese traveller. It is the goal of the Sheraton Hotels' Japanese Culture and Language Program to create a more tolerant workplace.

Sheraton designed a cultural program in response to the increasing number of Japanese hotel guests frequenting Hawai'i during the mid-1980s. In 1990, Sheraton Hotels, located in Waikiki, started offering Japanese culture and language courses to teach employees basic language and intercultural skills to meet Japanese guests' expectations. To oversee the program, a director was hired to provide in-house Japanese language and culture courses on a regular basis.

Since 1998, Starwood Hotels & Resorts Worldwide has managed Sheraton Hotels & Resorts Hawai'i. The Japanese Culture and Language Program was expanded to include diversity training courses two years later. The program was renamed the International Program to reflect the Japanese culture, language, and diversity training classes it encompassed.

The diversity training courses cover a broad range of issues such as ethnic diversity, gender, age, and disability. The program is designed to help Sheraton Hotels' employees who have a range of multicultural backgrounds to work together effectively in a cross-cul-

Sheraton Hotels & Resorts Hawai'i

A *lei* greeting and expression of *aloha* is shared with a Japanese guest at Sheraton Hotels & Resorts in Hawai'i.

tural setting. Ultimately, Sheraton Hotels' guests will benefit from being served by a team of culturally sensitive hotel staff.

IMPLEMENTATION

Collectively, Sheraton Hotels' four Waikiki properties employ approximately 3 715 staff. Of these, the hotel estimates that the 2 200 employees in direct contact with guests are the candidates most suited to participate in the Japanese culture and language classes. These include staff from the departments of valet parking, bell desk, front office, guest services, concierge, security office, housekeeping, engineering, restaurants and bars, pool services, telephone operators, and the doormen. To date, 1 000 staff members have participated in the program. This encompasses nearly 50 percent of all front line employees!

During orientation, new employees have the opportunity to learn about Japanese guest expectations. The Japanese culture and language classes provide "tips" for successful intercultural communication. The standard 40-minute session highlights four basic points for culturally appropriate guest interaction. These include:

- *Greet the guests in English*—Some Japanese guests may want to use English as a part of their foreign travel experience.

- *Give immediate acknowledgement to the guests' requests*—Japanese guests are used to receiving services promptly and do not recognize a system of waiting in line in the hotel lobby.

- *Attend to positive facial expressions, tone of voice, and postures*—Most guests appreciate positive non-verbal communications, such as a smile and pleasant tone of voice.

- *Understand the differences in cultural meaning between American gestures and Japanese gestures*—Many North American gestures carry different symbolic content in Japan and may offend customers.

Japanese Culture Training

The Japanese culture course is the most important training element of the International Program. Japanese guests have high service expectations and require more from Sheraton Hotels because of the hotel's name value and prime location in the centre of Waikiki. To exceed Japanese expectations, employees need to understand the guests' cultural values. Misunderstanding behaviour often results in hotel staff prejudging guests wrongly.

The goals of the Japanese culture course are to:

- learn the Japanese guests' hotel service expectations;

- understand Japanese cultural needs, such as communication styles;

- be aware of and practice tolerance towards guests' cultural differences and varying behaviour patterns; and

- learn cross-cultural communication skills through shared and comparative cultural study.

Participants achieve these training goals through classroom learning and hands-on application in daily operations.

Japanese Language Training

After completing the introductory Japanese culture course, employees can further their cultural knowledge by taking the Sheraton Hotels' two-hour Japanese culture and language session. This course illustrates how to:

- apologize appropriately to Japanese guests (phrases and manners);
- understand indirect verbal and non-verbal communication styles of Japanese guests; and
- read body language so as to offer assistance.

The manuals developed for the Japanese culture and language course were based on a thorough needs assessment. Training goals and delivery are customized from information gathered from surveys, interviews, and departmental observations (derived from job shadowing).

The major difference between the Sheraton Hotels' language program and a conventional school program is that the hotel's curriculum is designed for adult learners and is hotel-specific. To date, program directors know of no comparative intercultural in-house training in either the United States or Japan.

Because many employees strive to take Japanese training sessions during or between their shifts, learning time is limited. Rather than focussing on vocabulary memorization or grammar, the trainer focusses on job-related sentences, creating a fun learning environment for participants. This technique includes using actual guest incidents and sharing both the students' and the trainer's own cross-cultural experiences. This encourages employees to immediately make use of Japanese phrases when assisting guests.

Course participants benefit from interacting with Japanese guests and sharing those experiences with other participants from different departments and properties. The program trainer encourages brainstorming and problem solving during the Japanese culture and language sessions. The class allows participants to act as catalysts, thereby suggesting new ways to improve customer service.

RESULTS

Since the introduction of the Japanese Culture and Language Program in 1990, Sheraton Hotels has successfully raised employees' intercultural awareness and improved communication skills with Japanese guests to better meet guest expectations. Feedback from hotel employees having participated in the training is positive. According to a standard survey conducted at the end of 2000, 99 percent of course participants rated the Japanese culture and language sessions informative and helpful in the workplace and intended to continue their studies.

Sheraton Hotels in Waikiki continues to be one of the most popular hotels in Hawai'i among Japanese visitors. In 2000, Japanese guests accounted for approximately 65 percent of all guests at four properties in Waikiki.

WTTC Human Resource Centre COMMENT

This program not only improved staff cultural and language skills when serving Japanese guests, but also created a communications and problem-solving network. By encouraging employees to understand Japanese culture, a more tolerant workplace has evolved. Initially designed for staff to provide better service to the Japanese traveller, this program is easily adapted to include training in any foreign culture.

KEY TERMS

bilingual	intercultural communication
culturally sensitive	diversity training
intercultural skills	service expectations
collaboration	cross-cultural
non-verbal communication	job shadowing

 **www.sheraton.com**

DISCUSSION QUESTIONS

1. List three reasons for teaching employees the language and cultural skills deemed necessary to provide a high level of service to Japanese guests.
2. As a trainer in this program, what kinds of techniques would you use to teach the required cultural skills?
3. Considering current economic conditions and changing inbound travel patterns, what other multicultural courses would you add to the existing program?

Malaysia
Hilton Batang Ai Longhouse Resort

Submitted by: Rina Ganguly

Hilton
Batang Ai Longhouse Resort

ENGLISH LANGUAGE TRAINING: AN EFFECTIVE APPROACH

… Developing an English language skills training program for an indigenous population "from the ground up."

LEARNING OUTCOMES

1. Recognize the importance of developing in-house programs that directly address the needs of the audience.
2. Explain why individual competency levels in English language training foster self-confidence and employee development.
3. Describe why it is important to develop a language training program which allows employees to proceed at their own pace.

OVERVIEW

The Hilton Batang Ai Longhouse Resort is a 100-guest-room resort built around 11 timber longhouses traditionally designed to follow the architecture of the local Iban tribe. Built on native Iban land, the resort is situated on the shores of a freshwater mountain lake, surrounded by mountains in Sarawak (a Malaysian state on the Island of Borneo). It is a four-hour drive along the Pan Borneo Highway from Sarawak's capital of Kuching.

Prior to opening in March 1995, Hilton International committed to hiring the native peoples inhabiting the area. Most resort positions required English language fluency, since employees were expected to work with supervisors, participate in skills training sessions (offered in English), and communicate effectively with resort guests. As a result, in-house training needed to address language issues and skills training in a culturally sensitive manner.

With little outside contact, the Ibans' level of spoken and written English varied from marginal to fluent. Although some English language skills were taught in area schools, the opportunity to practice was limited. For Hilton International, hiring indigenous peoples with minimal language and formal education created a challenging training opportunity.

Hilton Batang Ai Longhouse Resort's human resource department drew upon resources from their corporate head offices, as Hilton International is a global corporation with properties worldwide. Management at Hilton Batang Ai Longhouse Resort needed to know how to respond to as well as assimilate language and cultural challenges encountered when working with indigenous populations. As a result, resort staff established their own standards of English language requirements, beyond that of simply learning everyday English. Language training thus concentrated on basic hotel vocabulary (common language used by all hoteliers) and more specialized communication specific to employee duties. For example, employees working in areas where telephone skills are necessary learned more about telephone English. Similarly, food and beverage as well as housekeeping staff learned vocabularies specific to their jobs.

IMPLEMENTATION

While structuring resort management, Hilton Batang Ai Longhouse Resort quickly established a training department with an area designated specifically to English language training. Three months before opening, an Australian teacher and a local Chinese assistant were hired to teach English, on-site. The two English teachers coordinated the training program and were responsible for determining the instruction format, collecting appropriate teaching materials, and developing a resort-specific manual. If they required additional assistance, the resort's personnel supervisor was available.

During job orientation sessions, staff language competency levels were determined through a simple process of both oral and written tests. Employees were assigned departments relative to their skills and interests. Department supervisors continuously observed language competency levels, while staff learned new job skills and English.

During the initial orientation, staff were tested (in both practice and theory) to place them at appropriate class levels. Employees were then divided into three groups based on their language skills. Groups initially included a mix of staff from all departments, which enabled employees to:

- gain insight and knowledge of each other's jobs;
- promote teamwork; and
- foster positive working relationships.

All groups had the same general materials and covered similar study topics. However, the depth of study varied depending on the group's English competency levels. Teaching materials included workbooks, textbooks, videotapes, audiotapes, role-playing, and flashcards. Resort function rooms were set up in a classroom-style format for small groups of six to seven participants. Classes were held during afternoon shift changes, which averaged 45 minutes in length. Although courses were not mandatory for all staff, they were considered compulsory to those who needed language improvement. The learning of vocabulary, correct word pronunciation, and practical word definitions were key areas of concentration.

As employees met established levels of English language proficiency, language groups were restructured according to departments. Subsequently, job-specific skill training increased. Staff concentrated on vocabulary building by focussing lessons on language and terminology specific to particular areas of work. For example, dining staff concentrated on cutlery terms. Housekeeping staff concentrated on room amenities and furnishings, learning to differentiate between a "cotton ball" and a "cotton tip," or a "hand towel" and a "face towel." In turn, language training reinforced departmental skill training.

During staff training, many individuals found difficulty in remembering new and unfamiliar words. Word definitions were reinforced through practice and hands-on experience. It was important to make sure that there was constant reinforcement while trainees were learning vocabulary and pronunciation. According to one of the pioneer staff (who is now working in food and beverage operations), he never once felt bored during the on-the-job lessons. He looked forward to language classes. Many of the original students recall their first encounters with the program as an experience which was fun, worthwhile, and unforgettable.

Along with job-specific training, Hilton Batang Ai Longhouse Resort also has on-site property training programs for environmental studies, local nature education, and gardening. Due to the resort's unique surroundings, guests want to learn more about the flora and fauna of the island through guided walking tours. Because nature gardening and environmental studies is an important part of the resort, the on-site interpreter handles interpretation and English training. Currently, the naturalist has three trained staff able to take guests on nature walks and interpret local gardening activities.

Language training was not without incident during the months of English classes. Both students and teachers recorded many humorous incidents. On one occasion, the on-site teacher was invited to travel upriver to a celebration at an Iban longhouse. En route, she wished to take a photograph and asked her student to stop the boat. Her words to "wait, wait" were recognized by the boat operator, who promptly overturned the boat. In the Iban language, *wit* means overturn!

RESULTS

The Hilton Batang Ai Longhouse Resort has earned a five-star AAA rating and attracts an international clientele of adventure travellers, special interest groups, and incentive travel groups primarily from Taiwan, Japan, Germany, North America, Europe, and Australia.

Today, 90 percent of the resort's 65 employees belong to Iban, Sarawak's largest native group. To this day, Hilton Batang Ai Longhouse Resort continues to provide language proficiency lessons for staff to improve their conversational English. The hotel does not, however, hire staff members who have no prior English skills. The program is ongoing and continues to be modified to accommodate employees' needs. To date, one trainer works full-time in language training at the resort, using instructional materials adapted from the Malaysian education syllabus.

Language improvement tests are occasionally administered. These tests include both oral and written formats and evaluate employee communication skills, although guest feedback is considered the most important measure of guest service. Currently, the resort ties incentives for improvement directly to guest service excellence.

WTTC HUMAN RESOURCE CENTRE COMMENT

Language—whether written, verbal, or gestured—is the basis of communication and the key to the success of all staff training programs. When English is a necessary second language, job-specific training must include English language proficiency. In this Malaysian good practice, Hilton Batang Ai Longhouse Resort hotel trainers used a two-step approach to building the Ibans' language skills. First, basic English language training is delivered in short yet continuous classes according to individual competency (not area of work). This practice fosters teamwork and interdepartmental knowledge of hotel operations. Next, vocabulary specific to an area of work is taught, along with new job skills. The high percentage of local employees is testimony to the success of this good human resource development practice.

KEY TERMS

language training
communication skills
indigenous peoples

cultural relations
competency levels

 **www.hilton.com**

DISCUSSION QUESTIONS

1. Describe the two-step process this company used in English training.

2. Explain how this training program helped to build employee morale and foster communication between staff.

3. What criteria would you set for three levels of English language competency (level one, level two, and level three) if you were the manager of this property?

Worldwide
Four Seasons Hotels and Resorts

Submitted by: Ellen DuBellay

FOUR SEASONS
Hotels and Resorts

MONTHLY CULTURAL AWARENESS PACKAGE

… One hotel's approach to improving its staff's cross-selling skills and cultural awareness of "sister" hotel properties.

LEARNING OUTCOMES

1. Recognize that a human resource department is capable of conducting in-house functions other than training.

2. Restate how an international company can communicate the cultural differences of thousands of employees through a simple, relatively inexpensive, and easily managed information program.

3. Indicate why a company would implement a program that informs employees of the size, scope, and opportunities within the organization for which they are working.

OVERVIEW

Four Seasons Hotels and Resorts currently manages 51 properties in 23 countries under the Four Seasons and Regent brand names. Considered to be the world's leading operator of luxury hotels, the Four Seasons Hotels and Resorts (Four Seasons) family has added many new properties over the last few years. In 1999, new properties were opened in: Las Vegas, Nevada, and Scottsdale, Arizona, in the United States; Punta Mita, Mexico; Paris, France; and London at Canary Wharf, England. One year later, a Four Seasons property was opened in the Middle East, and many more properties will enter the marketplace in 2001.

In 1997, the Four Seasons corporate office (called "home office") created a Cultural Awareness Program to circulate information about sister properties and explain the cultural activity surrounding each property. By circulating information about changes to existing properties, new developments, and local culture, employees are better informed of Four Seasons' properties worldwide.

Specifically, the *Cultural Awareness Program's* objectives are to:

* make employees aware of the Four Seasons global corporation and the opportunities for international transfer;

- spread information about, and promote, the cultures wherein Four Seasons properties operate; and
- improve employees' cross-selling techniques by educating staff of sister properties.

Each Four Seasons property that participates in the program develops its own cultural awareness package. The package is property-specific and includes information about the hotel and its surrounding area. Items typically included are:

- destination profiles
- hotel fact sheets
- maps, posters, and photos
- national flags and recipes
- taped music cassettes
- country or property area videos
- local papers
- decorative items such as locally made ribbons and gift wrapping paper.

Many hotels also include a questionnaire or quiz relevant to the information sent in the package. This quiz can be in the form of question and answer, multiple choice, or in the format of a crossword. Employees are encouraged to take the quiz as there is a prize for answering all questions correctly.

"People, Product, and Profit—all in one package."

IMPLEMENTATION

Four Seasons' home office personnel oversee the Cultural Awareness Program. Participation is voluntary, although home office staff is responsible for generating interest in the program and encouraging other Four Seasons properties not currently participating in the program to do so. Home office staff monitor the circulation of the cultural packages through an annual schedule. Packages that have been circulated are kept in storage at each property in a cultural library (or, where this facility has not yet been developed, in the human resource department). Each year, home office staff update the program's annual plan and distribute it to all Four Seasons properties.

It is the human resource director at participating properties who develops the hotel's cultural package, with the involvement of the property's planning committee members— particularly, the director of marketing and the public relations department. Generally, public relations and marketing personnel work with the human resource department, and with planning committee members, by generating ideas and supplying information for the cultural package. When a hotel develops its cultural package, the packages are pre-addressed to the receiving properties and then sent in bulk via courier or regular mail to home office for distribution.

The cost of running the program is minimal. Expenses for developing the cultural awareness packages include:

- **Contents**—Most of the package materials relating to area culture and location are obtained for little or no cost from local tourism authorities or through airlines and other venues.
- **Prizes and decorative items**—Prizes are largely purchased through the hotel gift shops at cost (with no mark-up).
- **Duplication**—Most photocopying and printing is done in house, keeping costs low.
- **Staff time**—Shipping costs are minimized through use of the company courier service.

RESULTS

The contents of the cultural awareness package provide all properties with colourful, interesting, and informative materials, some of which can be kept for the staff bulletin board. Several properties have taken the initiative of expanding the program by serving special theme meals in the staff restaurant in honour of the cultural package circulated that month. For example, an Italian meal theme might be featured when Four Seasons Hotel Milan's cultural package arrives from home office.

In terms of morale, staff is eager to undertake the challenging quiz questions within the package, particularly when prizes are attractive!

Feedback gathered from human resource directors has been very positive. Home office reports that overall, properties are very receptive to participating in the Cultural Awareness Program. Scheduling, however, must be flexible due to on-site projects and emergencies. One year, for example, a back-up activity was needed. Instead of the planned monthly package, home office sent all properties an international knowledge quiz. The quiz contained questions concerning the geography, history, and culture of all Four Seasons properties previously featured in the program. Unexpectedly, this quiz was well received and may be included as a permanent part of the Cultural Awareness Program.

WTTC HUMAN RESOURCE CENTRE COMMENT

The Cultural Awareness Program builds on the Four Seasons Hotels and Resorts' corporate culture by increasing employee knowledge of other accommodation locations and the cultures surrounding them. Global product knowledge is important for employees in this multinational company. Its communication strategy—which encourages each property to collectively share its unique cultural characteristics—is partially responsible for Four Seasons and Resorts' rapid expansion. An element of fun and surprise adds to the appeal of this program.

KEY TERMS

multicultural
communication
public relations
cultural awareness

corporate culture
cross-selling
internal promotion
international transfer

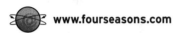 **www.fourseasons.com**

DISCUSSION QUESTIONS

1. Develop your own cultural awareness package for a Four Seasons property (real or imagined) residing in your city or town. What would it include? How would you make your package exceptional?

2. Upon receiving a cultural package, what other ways can the monthly theme be incorporated into a property? Discuss your ideas.

3. As an employee of a large travel corporation with offices worldwide, what information and incentives would convince you to transfer to another country?

◼

United States
Kā'anapali Beach Hotel

Submitted by: Lori Sablas

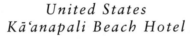

APPRECIATING CULTURAL HERITAGE

… The Kā'anapali Beach Hotel shares an appreciation for Hawaiian culture with both staff and guests through a program called Project Po'okela (Hawaiian for excellence).

LEARNING OUTCOMES

1. Evaluate how guest and host both benefit from understanding and appreciating cultural values in the delivery of a service product.

2. List the significance of employee input in developing a company mission statement.

3. Discuss the role of non-traditional educational approaches, methods, and resources in developing an in-house cultural program.

OVERVIEW

The 430-room Kā'anapali Beach Hotel is located on a stretch of white, sandy beach along the sunny western shores of Maui, Hawai'i, in the heart of the world-famous Kā'anapali Beach Resort. Situated on a 10-acre tropical courtyard, characteristic of a gracious Hawaiian estate, the Kā'anapali Beach Hotel embodies the Hawaiian meaning of hospitality, and shares the *aloha* spirit with its guests while delivering quality service.

In 1986, the hotel's general manager recognized the importance of preserving the area's heritage. A local expert was hired to teach the hotel's 300 employees the essence of Hawaiian culture. To do this, he developed a program called Project Po'okela (Hawaiian for "excellence"). At the same time, the hotel's mission statement was rewritten to include and celebrate Hawaiian cultural values.

Over time, the classes taught in Project Po'okela were formalized and renamed the "Ke Kula O Ka Po'okela," or the "School of Excellence." The investment in training affected areas within the hotel in ways management had never anticipated. By placing an overall emphasis on delivering Hawaiian hospitality, or *ho'okipa*, employees and management changed the way they interacted with each other and with guests. From a business standpoint, the marketability of the hotel increased, and so did the bottom line.

IMPLEMENTATION

Project Po'okela started as a half-day workshop. All management and staff attended this initial workshop, which focussed on defining and explaining basic Hawaiian values. Shortly thereafter, the hotel's mission statement was redrafted to incorporate key values naturally linked with Hawaiian hospitality. Employees were asked to participate in the rewriting of the mission statement, so that they would feel committed to a set of values which they had helped to develop. The new mission statement stresses values such as *ho'okipa* (hospitality), *aloha* (love), and *kōkua* (helpfulness). Kā'anapali Beach Hotel's mission statement positions the hotel as "a place where [staff] are recognized and rewarded for [their] achievements."

When the program first started, key staff members were sent to workshops on different islands throughout the state of Hawai'i to learn about Hawaiian culture. Employees also participated in internships at the Bishop Museum on Oahu and at the Bailey House Museum on Maui. These internships were co-sponsored by the Waiaha Foundation, which is a not-for-profit organization dedicated to the perpetuation of Hawaiian culture. During this time, the hotel began building an in-house collection of books and materials on Hawaiian culture.

Initially, the hotel general manager oversaw Project Po'okela. In 1989 a separate Po'okela department was formed to administer cultural training at the hotel, and a director was hired to provide staff with regular support. After three years, less outside assistance was required and classes were designed and taught internally by the hotel staff. Class subjects cover Hawaiian geography, religion, mythology, economics, technology, and the native Hawaiian diet. Many non-traditional educational approaches and methods have been used over the years, from hiking through Maui's rain forest to visiting historical sites and participating in a hands-on archeological dig.

Every employee is required to attend classes on company time since the classes are considered to be an integral part of each employee's training and development. Since 1986, hotel employees have participated in almost 50 different classes on Hawaiian history, culture, and values.

The Poʻokela project strives to include and empower employees at all levels throughout the Kāʻanapali Beach Hotel. Every aspect of class training, including the production of workbooks, is done in-house. The sales and marketing department produces all promotional and advertising material, utilizing the talents of employees and their families, and, in many cases, incorporating actual quotes from guests.

In addition to developing and teaching the Poʻokela classes, staff have also designed programs to share the Hawaiian spirit with hotel guests. For example, the hotel invites guests to share in free Hawaiian activities such as *lauhala* weaving, in which guests learn one of the oldest and most important crafts of old Hawaiʻi. Using the leaves of the *hala* trees (*pandanus* or screw pine) found in the hotel's gardens, guests create their own handmade bookmark.

Other activities include *ti*-leaf skirt making, *lei* making, *hula* dance classes, *lau* printing, garden tours, *haku*-flower *lei*-making, pineapple cutting, and Hawaiian art legacy tours. Employees also serenade guests in the hotel's lobby and courtyard throughout the week. A sunset torch-lighting ceremony and a complimentary *hula* show are performed nightly.

RESULTS

After investing time and energy to educate hotel staff about the importance of their host culture, hotel management reported positive results in employee relations, marketability of the property, and company bottom line. Since the Project Poʻokela program started in 1986:

- The resort's annual labour turnover has been reduced by 27.4 percent to an annual rate of 9 percent, the lowest on the island of Maui.
- Incidents of sick leave abuse have been reduced by 45 percent.
- Worker's Compensation payout has been reduced by 43 percent ($66 500 [US] in 1985 to $37 000 in 1999).
- Hotel Association Charity Walk contributions increased 62 percent ($8 000 [US] to $13 000 in 1999).
- Maui United Way contributions increased 423 percent ($7 800 [US] to $33 000 in 1999). Hotel employees give three times more per person than the employees of any other hotel on the island.

Management believes this blending of important cultural values with good business practice is responsible for the Kāʻanapali Beach Hotel being featured twice in *Condé Nast Traveler* magazine's "Top 50 Tropical Resorts" in the world, and locally as "The Most Hawaiian Hotel in the State" by the Waiaha Foundation. Most recently, the Travel Industry Association of America, as part of its annual National ODESSEY Awards program, presented the hotel with the prestigious Cultural Heritage Award in the Travel Promotion division.

For the fourth year in a row, the Kāʻanapali Beach Hotel Employee Choir has taken first place honours in the statewide Hospitality Industry Song Contest. The contest coincided with the release of the hotel employees' second music CD, *E Hoʻomau I Ka Poʻokela*.

Music is at the heart of what makes Kāʻanapali Beach Hotel so unique. The production of the music CD was in response to guest requests for Hawaiian music to take home. Hotel employees from all departments gather to sing Hawaiian songs for hotel guests, an ongoing effort to preserve and perpetuate Hawaiian culture that has evolved into a source of pride for the employees.

The song competition is part of the Native Hawaiian Tourism and Hospitality Association annual conference. The Kāʻanapali Beach Hotel choir includes union employees, middle management, and senior executives from the housekeeping, accounting, Poʻokela, food and beverage, culinary, sales, rooms, grounds, human resources, guest services, and executive departments. The new music CD is available for purchase in the hotel's gift shops and in music stores throughout Hawaiʻi.

WTTC Human Resource Centre COMMENT

The Kāʻanapali Beach Hotel clearly demonstrates that authentic benefits as well as financial gain are possible through cultural training programs. Programs such as this benefit cultural preservation and community service. Former US President George Bush designated the hotel a "Point of Light for the Nation," in recognition of its employees' volunteerism and community service and for exemplifying his belief that "from now on in America, any definition of a successful life must include serving others." This spirit comes from the heart and is part of the hotel's daily work life. Weaving together Hawaiian heritage and local lifestyle, the Kāʻanapali Beach Hotel cares for its guests in many thoughtful and personal ways that ensure repeat business.

KEY TERMS

cultural training	service excellence
values	preservation
heritage	mission statement
empowerment	authentic

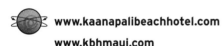 **www.kaanapalibeachhotel.com**

www.kbhmaui.com

DISCUSSION QUESTIONS

1. As an employee at the Kāʻanapali Beach Hotel, list the advantages you personally gain when demonstrating traditional crafts and activities to hotel guests.

2. The Kāʻanapali Beach Hotel provides an authentic cultural experience. Assess the indirect benefits this travel product has on Hawaiʻi as a tourist destination.

3. As a staff member of the Poʻokela department, what outside resources would you use to teach staff about Hawaiian geography, religion, mythology, economics, technology, and the native Hawaiian diet?

Canada
'Ksan Historical Village & Museum

Submitted by: Beverley Clifton Percival

LIVING CULTURE INTERPRETED

… An association which represents and seeks to preserve a living culture forges alliances with surrounding communities.

LEARNING OUTCOMES

1. Analyze the significance of preserving and truthfully portraying the lifestyle of a living culture.
2. Interpret the significance of a cultural centre to First Nations young people and elders.
3. Explain how staff are encouraged to retain current skills and facilitate, whenever possible, learning opportunities.

OVERVIEW

The 'Ksan Historical Village & Museum opened to the beat of Gitxsan drums on August 12, 1970. Located in Hazelton, British Columbia (BC), 'Ksan Historical Village & Museum ('Ksan) is built within the boundaries of the Gitxsan territory, and stands where the village of Gitanmaax has existed for centuries. 'Ksan was created to preserve and portray the true lifestyles of the people who have always lived in the region.

As a cultural centre, 'Ksan is committed to presenting the richness of Gitxsan culture, and to promoting economic opportunities for local First Nations peoples of the Upper Skeena River region. To support these goals, 'Ksan operates a museum and a gift shop and offers guided tours of several buildings which house examples of Gitxsan history and culture.

'Ksan Historical Village & Museum is owned and managed by the 'Ksan Association. The association is registered as a non-profit society under the Societies Act of BC and is therefore under legal sanction to operate as a non-profit organization. The 'Ksan Association has a Board of Directors made up of both Gitxsan and non-Gitxsan volunteers from the communities surrounding 'Ksan. This helps the association to ensure it meets the needs of the communities it represents and serves.

'Ksan management trains staff to provide quality interpretive programs for guests, while at the same time advocating and supporting the community's pride in their culture. A key focus is maintaining the integrity of the cultural interpretation program. 'Ksan is continuously challenged with maintaining its role as a steward of traditional, performing, and visual arts.

IMPLEMENTATION

In the 1950s, a group of people formed a committee to address a common concern— the physical protection and sharing of items that are part of Gitxsan material culture.

Two Gitxsan men, Simgigyet Hanamuux (Jeffery Johnson) and Amlaxyeltxw (Albert Douse) were very instrumental in this process, along with Margaret Sargent, who was the mayor of Hazelton at that time. It was agreed that the Gitxsan culture would not be presented in the standard museum style, but rather in a way that would present the history as a part of a living culture. This complemented the beliefs of the Gitxsan elders, who maintained that the culture had been "sleeping" and was now "awakening and gathering strength." Through the work of Gitxsan members, and with assistance from a former mayor of Hazelton, a place to house and present such items was built.

The first building, the Skeena Treasure House, was erected on the waterfront of Old Hazelton in 1959. A curator was hired from the Fireweed clan in the village of Gitsegukla. She was trained to care for the collection, and did so for several years. The committee soon realized that the building was too small. They sought funding and by the late 1960s were successful in securing provincial and regional monies for replicating a traditional Gitxsan village.

The interpretive village was completed and opened to the public in 1970. The centre represents the cultural traditions of the surrounding Gitxsan villages of Gitanmaax ("People of the Torchlight Fishing"), Gitsegukla ("Place near the Mountain"), Gitwangak ("People of the Rabbit"), Gitanyow ("Place where the River Narrows") Ansbahyaxw ("Hiding Place") and Sigit'ox ("Place Behind the Mountain"). It is from these communities that 'Ksan recruits staff to share their history and culture with all visitors.

Employee Recruitment

'Ksan is staffed by paid employees. Six staff members were initially hired during the seasonal months of June through August. Over the years, the size and structure of the association has grown. Nineteen staff are now employed during 'Ksan's peak season of May through September. High school and post-secondary students are hired as support staff for the summer months.

'Ksan management feels fortunate in that it has been able to recruit members of the Gitxsan nation, who actively participate in the traditional Gitxsan governance system. 'Ksan calls this the feast system, and this system is something that 'Ksan represents in its displays and audio tour.

The Gitxsan have a matrilineal society (lineage through the mother), which is made up of four clans: Wolf, Frog, Eagle, and Fireweed. Each clan is made up of several houses; a chief, with wing chiefs acting as advisors, heads each house. House membership supports and directs the actions of the chief and wing chiefs. Feasting is a central component of Northwest Coast First Nations social, political, and economic worlds. All business of the Gitxsan is conducted at these public events and activity is witnessed and validated by the attending guests. All business is conducted according to strict protocol and members are cognizant of how they should conduct themselves.

Many on-site staff at 'Ksan are active in the traditional governance system. These staff members bring their pride and understanding of this system to their job and are able to effectively and accurately interpret Gitxsan traditions to their guests.

Staff Development and Training

During the remainder of the year, there are three permanent, year-round positions which include the executive director, curator, and bookkeeper. These team members hold post-secondary education in administration, accounting, and arts. It is this team that trains all seasonal staff. Senior staff positions function six months of the year, and include a tour coordinator, two senior cultural interpreters, and a grounds person.

The 'Ksan Association's Board of Directors also has a role in staff development and training. Board members want to ensure that all staff members are skilled and, whenever possible, will work with staff to facilitate learning. Many learning opportunities are provided in seminars offered through organizations in which 'Ksan has membership. These include certification bodies such as Northern BC Tourism, Aboriginal Tourism BC, Upper Skeena Tourism Association, Canadian Museums Association, and the BC Museums Association. Workshops and seminars allow staff to enhance their knowledge and learn new skills—benefiting both the organization and the individual.

On-site staff training and development includes:

- *First Host* training for developing customer service skills;
- the use of video and print resources in service training;
- access to on-site resources; and
- hands-on training in sales and cultural interpretation.

> *"We have been very fortunate to maintain a good pool of people interested in working here and being ambassadors of the nation. Given the fact that we have 40 000-plus visitors each season we are always concerned with the quality of product, and with service delivery."*
>
> 'Ksan Historical Village & Museum

Cultural Considerations

The job of 'Ksan's cultural interpreters is to showcase parts of Gitxsan material culture for guests visiting the village. This is achieved by conducting guided tours of the grounds in groups of two to 30 people. Skills required include:

- excellent oral skills
- in-depth knowledge of Gitxsan culture and history
- knowledge of the Gitxsan language (an asset)
- ability to facilitate large groups
- ability to work under time constraints
- presentation skills
- customer service

- working with diverse groups
- ability to answer questions
- retail skills.

'Ksan's cultural interpreters have had many unforgettable experiences. In their own words, here are a few:

"I have had people lock us in from the outside.... so I had to keep talking to the group for about 15 minutes till the next group came along."

"People expect to find us walking around in leather shifts with cedar capes and smiling for pictures."

"This guy had totally researched copper and had 10 questions about how we got copper and what we used it for."

"Sometimes I am not sure if I can answer the same question for the tenth time that day, but I smile and give a clear and meaningful answer because I know that I am an ambassador for our nation."

'Ksan houses a Performing Arts Group which acts as a cultural ambassador for the Gitxsan people. The group has performed throughout the province, across Canada, and around the world demonstrating the richness of Gitxsan culture through traditional song and dance. The 'Ksan Performing Arts Group has worked with 'Ksan for over 28 years and continues to be a fundamental component of this institution. 'Ksan Performing Arts group was initiated by 'Ksan, and thus shares a common history.

Cultural skills are learned through provincial and federal youth work internship opportunities, similar to service training. Staff learns about artifacts, cultural significance, and interpretation by working on-site with the curator of the museum's collection. This experience is both stimulating and rewarding to students of the Gitxsan nation. Perhaps more importantly, staff partake in cultural mentoring and, as cultural interpreters, pass on this traditional knowledge to guests.

As a result of continuous training, 'Ksan operates with a team of qualified and satisfied staff each year. At the end of peak season, there is a closure session for all seasonal staff. At the same time, senior staff conducts informal staff appraisals. Management encourages staff to provide feedback for future planning and educational development. Results are presented to the board of directors for review. Comments made by staff include:

"This is a very demanding, yet stimulating and rewarding job."

"I have really increased my knowledge about my cultural heritage and identity as a Gitxsan in a wonderful way."

"Studying First Nations studies at college is good, but coming and working in a place like 'Ksan puts knowledge into vibrant action—that is a worthwhile summer job!"

"Each year as I come back I am amazed at the new things I learn about the Gitxsan and the many travellers that come to visit us for a variety of intriguing reasons."

"Sharing my culture with the world instills pride and strength in my identity as a Gitxsan and allows our cycle of life, learning, and knowledge as a nation to evolve, grow, and flourish."

RESULTS

When presented with authenticity and spirit, cultural interpretation becomes an important avenue for educating a visiting public and reinforcing the soul of a culture. A growing interest in cultural tourism provides for opportunities in many communities. Through education, training, and empowerment, staff is able to handle the humorous and unique issues that relate to culture, product, and service delivery. Training and development at 'Ksan are approached with these issues in mind:

- presenting the Gitxsan culture in a positive way;
- presenting culture with authenticity and integrity;
- providing employees with the support they need in an often hectic and frenetic environment; and
- providing interpreters with information that is relevant and reflects the past, present, and future of the Gitxsan culture.

'Ksan is dedicated to providing staff with a meaningful work experience. Management constantly aim to improve operations, provide value to the visitor, and respect those whom they represent in the community.

On-site, 'Ksan has developed a resource of materials in the form of books and videos. Staff is encouraged to acquire new information on a regular basis, either by personal involvement in Gitxsan society, interviewing others, or through their own research.

Staff also engages in regular group discussions about terminology and an understanding of the Gitxsan world view. Behind the scenes, 'Ksan is in the process of integrating Gitxsan terminology and actual language in informal ways. Terminology is often integrated into the tour when answering questions or elaborating on concepts. For example, the term *halayt* (healer) is explained and used while touring the Frog House display. *Hawal* refers to the contributions of goods and money in the feast hall and *Limx Oiy* is a song for important occasions such as a death feast. The latter terms are introduced while touring the Wolf House. New words and terms are constantly introduced and circulated to strengthen indigenous vocabulary.

There is relatively low turnover at 'Ksan. All senior interpretive staff and the grounds person have been with the organization for many years. Summer students return year after year and 'Ksan continues to receive a steady number of applications annually.

WTTC HUMAN RESOURCE CENTRE COMMENT

Interest in visiting authentic aboriginal cultural centres is high in Canada. 'Ksan stands as one of the earliest community-directed centres. Service training and the cultural education of young Gitxsan employees provides enriched cultural understanding, together with valuable employment skills. 'Ksan helps to sustain traditional art and dance while, at the same time, building understanding of the Gitxsan governance system. Visitors benefit from interaction with a living culture that continuously reinvents itself while keeping traditional practices alive.

KEY TERMS

culture
aboriginal tourism
cultural interpreters
steward

First Nations
feast system
indigenous
authenticity

 **www.ksan.org**

DISCUSSION QUESTIONS

1. Cultural interpreters portray the lifestyle of a living culture. Discuss the importance of preserving cultural heritage from the perspective of descendants of the living culture, the surrounding community, and tourists.

2. Think up three ways that 'Ksan could create additional value for their product and new economic opportunities for the community by working with local businesses.

3. What personal development opportunities and employment skills are young people building by working at 'Ksan?

United States
National Park Service

Submitted by: Dave Ruppert

CULTURAL TRAINING IN NATIVE LAW FOR NATIONAL PARKS INTERPRETATIVE GUIDES

… A course developed for the National Park Service and designed to improve park/tribal relations and to raise the quality of park educational programs regarding Native American histories and cultures.

LEARNING OUTCOMES

1. Identify the National Park Service's process for ensuring the accurate and appropriate portrayal of Native American history, culture, and law.
2. Describe interactive processes for developing and updating instructional program content.
3. Describe national benefits from National Park Service interpretative programming.

OVERVIEW

Visitor education is a vital element in the National Park System in the United States. Education programs (referred to within the National Park Service as visitor interpretative programs) are designed to ensure that visitors, now and in the future, will experience and learn from the unique history and character of each park. With over 386 million recreational visitors to the nation's 384 park units throughout the country (1998 figures), the combined interpretative programs of the National Park Service can be seen as one of the world's largest classrooms for educating tourists.

The history of Native American peoples is a large component of many park interpretative programs, as these peoples once lived in and used the area now set aside as a park. Domestic and international visitors alike have a strong interest in Native American history. Although parks are often set aside to preserve the natural wonders of a given place, cultural history is also important. Almost every park in the system was once used and/or occupied by Native American peoples.

Park interpretative programs strive to provide visitors with accurate information about Native Americans. Native peoples also want to improve the education programs in parks by having stereotypes of Native peoples and cultures replaced with a more accurate picture of Native history and contemporary Native life.

With assistance from the federal government, the National Park Service instituted a course in the history of Native American law and tribal relationships, titled: *American Indians and Cultural and Natural Resources Management: The Law and Practice Relating to Federal Land Management.* The course was developed as an inter-agency initiative for federal land managers and cultural and natural resource management specialists. Many federal agencies and bureaus from the Departments of Agriculture, Energy, Interior, and Defense were partners in helping put on the course and in sending participants.

IMPLEMENTATION

The purpose of the training course is twofold. First, the course provides detailed information to federal agency staff, so as to accurately inform them about the contents and history of Native American law. Secondly, course content covers the consequential federal responsibilities towards Native American resources on Native lands and on non-Native federal lands. The course also educates National Park Service interpretative guides so they can conduct more accurate tours for park guests.

The three-day course was originally coordinated through the Denver Service Centre of the National Park Service. The course materials, curriculum, and class presentations were developed and presented by Dr. Raymond Cross (from the University of Montana Law

School) with the assistance of a team of law students. In addition, Dr. Stephen Pevar, an attorney with the American Civil Liberties Union specializing in Native American law, also lectured on aspects of Native American law. Key individuals from each of the partnering agencies were involved in planning the course, including tribal liaisons. Tribal governments were invited to co-host the course, and tribal members were invited to attend as participants.

Class sessions consist of both lectures and "workgroups" in the morning and afternoon. The lectures cover the principles of Native American law, to provide participants with some familiarity with the language and purpose of specific treaties, laws, presidential executive orders, and court cases. Each lecture is followed by a breakout session, when the class is broken into workgroups (with about 15 participants in each group) in which a real management issue or problem is discussed.

Discussion focusses on applying what was learned in the morning session. These sessions are facilitated by law students from the University of Montana and by a federal employee familiar with the issue at hand. The purpose of the afternoon session is to apply the law in ways that find satisfactory resolutions to the given problem before the conflicting parties reach court. All workgroups are given the same issues to resolve, and, during the last hour of the day, individual groups present the solutions they find to resolve the problem. If there is time, Dr. Cross will provide the actual outcome.

Group dinners and other activities are held in the evening. During the first year, in 1998, the course was co-hosted by Yellowstone National Park, and the park provided various tours. In 1999, the course was co-hosted by the Wind River Shoshone and Arapaho tribes, who generously hosted dinners and traditional dances for course participants. In 2000, the Yakama Indian Nation co-hosted and provided dinners and dances.

On the last day, the entire group participates in a round table covering some of the issues that arose during the course. At this time, course evaluations and suggestions on course improvements for the following year are collected. Typically during this session, many representatives from tribes and agencies offer to serve as host for the following year.

The course targets personnel in all federal land managing agencies and is voluntary for all. Participants in the course have included employees from the United States Forest Service of the Department of Agriculture, the Interior Department Bureaus of Reclamation, Land Management, and Indian Affairs, and the Fish and Wildlife Service, as well as branches of the Department of Defense. To date, response has been positive and there are more people wanting to participate than slots available in the course. In addition, representatives of tribes throughout the western and eastern United States also attend the course. Tribal members have been very receptive to partaking in and hosting the course and it is important to note that tribal members are involved not only as participants, but also as teaching resources—for example, facilitators, coordinators, and knowledgeable agency employees.

Course content provides an overview of the history and development of Native American law in the United States, and an analysis of important legal cases that shaped federal Native American policies from the 18th century to the present. Agency partners contact tribes that they consult with on a regular basis to notify them of an upcoming course. This will change as time goes on and a more formal system for encouraging tribal participation will no doubt replace the present system.

The costs for the first year were covered by a grant from the National Park Service. These grants are normally provided for only one year to get training programs off the ground, or to test new ideas in training. The grant covered participant tuition, contracting services for the University of Montana, and Yellowstone National Park expenses in hosting the course. Some tribal representatives were also provided with their travel and living expenses. Subsequent courses have been supported through tuition charges to agency participants.

RESULTS

The first course was limited to 80 participants. By limiting course participants during the first year, course providers could experiment with different methods of adult education. Lectures to the entire group provided background information on the history of relations between tribes and the federal government. At other times, participants were broken into small discussion groups in which Native and federal agents reversed roles while discussing cases involving conflicts.

A lot of "second guessing" goes on, especially among agency employees who know how the system works and doesn't work. The problems presented in sessions are recent controversies, but disguised with new names. Agency employees know they are real, but few know how the conclusions came about. That is, they may know the outcome since they are familiar with the issue, but they often don't know the process by which the outcome was reached. The process of getting to the end result is often the most important aspect of the workgroup discussions.

Depending on where the course is held and the tribal co-host, agency personnel and tribal representatives share reports regarding nearby and contemporary or ongoing conflicts between tribes and agencies. This allows relevant discussion to ensue. In addition, case studies used for discussion are tailored to issues that are relevant to the co-hosting tribe or the area where the course is held. The small class size makes a combination of these approaches possible, and enables agency and tribal representatives to get to know one another on a more personal level, thus fostering cross-cultural communication.

The primary purpose of the course is to make government land-management personnel aware of Native American history and way of life. The program, however, is responsible for improving agency relations with tribal peoples and affects the quality and quantity of interpretation and education programs offered to the public. In its fourth year, course coordinators plan to design methods of determining the program's effectiveness by assessing its success in making such changes.

Students are given an evaluation sheet to fill out at the end of the course. The principal course instructors and the agency coordinators use these participant evaluations to adjust instruction methods and the content of course materials. One important suggestion already implemented is joint hosting of the course by Native Tribal Offices and partnering federal agencies, whereby a few agencies work together and provide staff, space, time, and material support to make the course happen.

A long-term goal of the course is to affect changes in the interpretative and public education programs of the National Park Service (and other agencies) to benefit park tourists, as well as visitors to other federal or public lands. Since these programs are periodically evaluated, redesigned, and changed, it is hoped that participants will improve the accuracy of information provided to over 286 million visitors to the National Park System each year.

WTTC Human Resource Centre COMMENT

Recent years have seen an increased desire from visitors to US national parks to learn more about Native American history and culture. This increase has been paralleled by an increase in activism by Native American peoples to ensure that information about their past and contemporary cultural lives is honestly and accurately provided to the visitor. Changes to the National Park Service's public education programs in parks need to be reviewed and upgraded to remove old cultural stereotypes and improve the accuracy of information provided to park visitors. This course is attempting to do just that.

KEY TERMS

cultural history
visitor interpretative programs
tribal relationships
cross-cultural communication

aboriginal tourism
educational tours
breakout session

 **www.nps.gov**

DISCUSSION QUESTIONS

1. Discuss the approach used to ensure accuracy and authenticity in the teaching program.
2. Explain the use of case studies as a tool for teaching Native American law.
3. What are some of the public benefits of the National Park Service's programs on Native American history and culture?

Indonesia
Four Seasons Resort Bali at Jimbaran Bay

Submitted by: Minie Brodtman

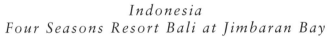

MAKING TRAINING TRANSLATE

. . . When opening a new resort in Bali, Four Seasons human resource staff met the challenges of training, communication, and cultural differences by developing a Self-Access Language Training Centre.

LEARNING OUTCOMES

1. Explain the advantages of establishing a language-based Self-Access Centre on-site.
2. Recognize why it was important for Four Seasons Hotels and Resorts to provide uniform service worldwide.
3. Explain why staff who are in the process of increasing their English language skills can benefit from cross-training in sister properties located in other countries.

OVERVIEW

In the early 1990s, the island of Bali was slowly evolving into a world-class, five-star travel destination. Travellers came to the Four Seasons Resort Bali at Jimbaran Bay for the cultural experience it provided, and for the island's luxurious white-sand beaches and lush tropical rain forests. As travellers became more demanding, the resort realized it needed to service guests on the same level as its "sister properties" in North America.

When the Four Seasons Resort Bali opened in 1992, many staff applicants spoke no English, had never travelled off the island, and were unfamiliar with Western customs and world cuisine. Four Seasons' human resource trainers flown in from North America soon realized that the standard training procedures, which had transplanted so well in the past, would not import well into this particular cultural setting. Most of Four Seasons' training materials had been developed for use with young Americans with some college training.

Although many staff members were hired from the local hotel school, their English language skills were not at international standards. Four Seasons Resort Bali had an official English-speaking policy and, before the resort opened, employees needed to demonstrate a minimum level of English language proficiency. Trainers quickly realized the immediate need to improve communication skills in order to provide good training to the Balinese and Indonesian staff members.

Human resource staff immediately put staff through an intensive English training program, administered through a makeshift training centre. Over time, the resort established a permanent self-study language facility for staff to increase their English levels on a voluntary basis, to the calibre expected by luxury-bound travellers.

IMPLEMENTATION

The Four Seasons Resort Bali created a permanent language lab in 1993. The lab was established to help individual employees strengthen their English language skills. This library-like study centre, located adjacent to the resort's human resource offices, is officially called the Self-Access Centre.

The centre's goal is to create an environment for employees to build their language skills on their own. Due to busy schedules and varying language skills, it was wiser to offer a voluntary environment as opposed to traditional, structured language classes.

The Self-Access Centre, which cost $50 000 (US) to create, is set up like a classroom. It features learning tools such as headsets with audio learning cassettes, tape players, a TV/VCR with video language programs, computers with computer learning games, and a large selection of English books and magazines. All levels of language instruction are available, from elementary to advanced. Learning modules were developed by the Indonesia Australia Language Foundation (IALF) and native speakers working within the centre.

Self-learning methods are available for four languages, namely, English, Japanese, French, and German, as are teacher attachments. (Teacher attachments are individuals contracted from the language schools and are not permanent staff of the resort). Centre materials are continuously updated by the teacher attachment from IALF and funded in part by the 2 percent Fund for Training & Development. Government mandates this fund to improve the language skills of local people so they can better compete with other nationalities. The fund averages $3 300 (US) monthly.

Since the Self-Access Centre was first opened, two more computers have been installed, with access to the Internet. Computer courses are now available to all qualifying staff at a local educational institute, and are also funded by the 2 percent Fund for Training & Development. The courses provide participants with the basic computer knowledge necessary to develop supervisory and management skills.

The resort's policy for new hires requires that each potential employee pass an English language test. The test score, along with the interview, determines whether that person will be hired. If the applicant is hired, he/she is automatically placed in one of five language levels coded by colours: green, blue, red, yellow, and orange. Each level is broken down into 10 modules or sections. Employees are tested upon completion of each level.

The resort offers staff a financial incentive to progress to the next level. An employee achieving a successful test score is awarded a monetary bonus and receives a certificate at an awards ceremony attended by all staff. The bonus increases, incrementally, based on the language level (*rupees* 100 000 to *rupees* 250 000, or $40 to $100 [US]). Employees are also acknowledged for the amount of time spent in the Self-Access Centre. Each month, one staff member is recognized for their time, with a certificate presented at the Employee of the Month ceremony.

RESULTS

The success of a self-study centre rests largely on the personal motivation of the "students." At the Four Seasons Resort Bali, the program worked well because employees were motivated to excel. Employees who juggled erratic work schedules appreciated the flexibility of the program. The centre was structured in such a way that all employees, regardless of their current English language skills, could push themselves to improve.

At the Four Seasons Resort Bali at Jimbaran Bay, there is a common understanding that staff are being trained and prepared for more challenging positions. Staff are motivated because they know resort management appreciates their hard work. This message is positively communicated monthly at the awards ceremony attended by the resort's planning committee.

Of the resort's employees, 24 percent have moved up at least one language level. To date, the resort has paid out $8 000 (US) in employee bonuses. Although staff has transferred to Australia, the Maldives, Singapore, Malaysia, and the United States, turnover remains at 1 percent—the lowest on the island!

Many staff members in food and beverage, spa, and housekeeping take advantage of an annual assistance program promoting cross-training. Through this program, local employees gain valuable experience working for the Fours Seasons chain in Singapore, Malaysia, and the Maldives, for six months at a time. Obviously, improved English skills make an employee more eligible for this valuable training experience.

The resort continues to be highly regarded by travellers worldwide and is proud to be the recipient of many travel awards. Most recently, Four Seasons Resort Bali welcomed in the year 2001 ranked as the "Number One Resort in the World" in the seventh annual "Gold List" of *Condé Nast Traveler* magazine.

WTTC HUMAN RESOURCE CENTRE COMMENT

Four Seasons Resort Bali's example illustrates how standardized training programs do not import seamlessly into foreign cultures. Organizations training overseas will encounter a range of training challenges in communication and cultural differences. Sensitivity to each other's cultures is necessary for a successful enterprise. With a little ingenuity and flexibility, Four Seasons' human resource trainers and human resource department staff were able to turn a potentially crippling situation into a positive and successful venture.

KEY TERMS

English language training   sister properties
communication   cross-training
standard training procedures   incentive
language skills   self-study

 **www.fourseasons.com**

DISCUSSION QUESTIONS

1. List six advantages of cross-training in a foreign country.

2. As the human resource manager, what criteria would you establish to determine whether an employee met a minimum level of English language proficiency?

3. What other incentives would encourage staff to continuously practice English language training voluntarily?

United States
Outrigger Hotels and Resorts

Submitted by: Pila Kikuchi and Ka'aipo Ho

INCORPORATING TRADITIONAL VALUES AND CULTURE

… Outrigger Hotels and Resorts preserves the cultural values of its host community by incorporating these values into staff training and the organization's corporate culture.

LEARNING OUTCOMES

1. Describe how a value system may be defined and incorporated into the culture of a hotel.
2. Interpret distinct cultural values which may be applied to guest service.
3. Identify how a value-based model may be adapted to different settings.

OVERVIEW

Outrigger Hotels and Resorts of Honolulu has made Hawaiian hospitality the heart of its organizational culture. Through a company-wide initiative it calls *Ke 'Ano Wa'a* (translated as "The Outrigger Way") employees are instructed in Hawaiian heritage and the *aloha* (Hawaiian for love) island spirit. This training initiative is a staff training program, integrating cultural learning into daily staff interaction with guests, co-workers, business associates, and families.

The program was developed in 1994 with the guidance of the late Dr. George Kanahele, President of the Waiaha Foundation. The Foundation is dedicated to bringing "Hawaiianess" back to Hawai'i. With the assistance of an outside company, hotel managers organized, analyzed, and incorporated operational improvements into existing training programs to better train staff. Since Outrigger Hotels and Resorts has acquired properties in the Pacific region, the program has also been expanded and adapted to the cultures of the many places where the company now does business.

IMPLEMENTATION

Ke 'Ano Wa'a began by developing a *Hui Mana'o* (team of thought), or executive committee. The executive committee rewrote the Outrigger Hotels and Resorts of Honolulu's (Outrigger) mission statement as follows:

Outrigger Hotels & Resorts

Sharing Hawaiian culture through song is standard entertainment at Outrigger Hotels & Resorts Honolulu.

> "We will grow together as the leisure hospitality company of choice, providing our employees [with] an opportunity to be their best, our guests with distinctive hospitality and value, and our owners with promised results, working as a family in harmony with the culture and environment of the places where we do business."

Next, hotel employees wrote and edited a values statement, which would become the benchmark for all workplace actions. The values statement is a list of eight Hawaiian values, stated both in name and concept. They include:

K	KĪNĀ'OLE (flawlessness)
E	Equality (KAULIKE)
A	A'O (to learn and to share)
N	NĀMEA HO 'OKIPA (hosts)
O	'OHANA (family)
W	WAHI (place)
A	Accountability (KULEANA)
A	ALOHA (love)

These values are embraced by every employee and are a vital part of Outrigger's corporate culture. As suggested by an employee on the values-drafting committee, making the values into a mnemonic device (a formula easily remembered) has made it easier for everyone to learn. The values have been translated into Chammoro in Guam, Marshallese in Majuro, and Fijian in Fiji for employees of Outrigger properties throughout the Pacific.

Reinforcing Outrigger values is an important part of the Ke 'Ano Wa'a process. Workshops and seminars educate employees as to the ongoing importance of *Ho'okipa* (hospitality) in a business setting. These workshops highlight Hawai'i's unique culture and include information on local history and area geography. The five workshops are delivered through the following series:

- *Sense of Place* covers the concept of a reciprocal relationship between *Wahi* (the place), *Mea Ho'okipa* (the host), and *Malihini* (the guest). It also includes a history of Waikiki before the area became a popular visitor destination.

- *Mea Ho'okipa* discusses the qualities and behaviours of the ideal host.

- *Aloha the Integrating Force* pulls all of the above together into a single vision for action.

- *Aloha the Guest* explains how a special relationship should exist between host and guest. The host is the caretaker of the guest and each has responsibilities.

- *Kīnā'ole* (flawlessness) discusses the traditional Hawaiian concept of perfection and how this concept can be applied to the provision of hospitality services that meet guest expectations.

RESULTS

Outrigger Hotels and Resorts of Honolulu has invested over $1 million (US) in developing and implementing the Ke 'Ano Wa'a process, which has now been operating for more than six years.

At a pilot hotel, early results from the property indicated that:

- Turnover and absenteeism rates were halved.

- Guest "intent to return" increased by 14 percent.

- The number of guests who would recommend Outrigger to others increased by 19 percent.

In more recent findings, 89 percent of Outrigger guests said they would stay at the same Outrigger hotel and 92 percent said they would visit another Outrigger in the future. Ninety-four percent of Outrigger guests surveyed would recommend Outrigger hotels to friends or family. Also, the majority of guests judged the quality of a stay at an Outrigger hotel to be equal or superior to a stay at other major hotels.

Outrigger Hotels and Resorts has been widely recognized for its dedication to the cultures and traditions of the places where it does business. In Hawai'i, Outrigger has been awarded numerous "Keep It Hawai'i" awards. These awards, sponsored by the Hawai'i Visitors & Conventions Bureau, honour businesses and individuals dedicated to preserving the unique culture and *aloha* spirit of Hawai'i. In addition, Outrigger has won numerous other awards for merit, community visual and performing arts, and heritage preservation.

The Outrigger Guam Resort has also been recognized numerous times by the Guamanian community for its dedication to the perpetuation of the local Chamorro culture. In May 2000, the Outrigger Guam Resort was presented with the Guam Visitor's Bureau's Award of Excellence for the "Hafa Adai Spirit."

WTTC Human Resource Centre COMMENT

The Ke 'Ano Wa'a process shows that authentic, traditional hospitality values can form the basis of a successful and vibrant corporate culture. Building a sense of pride in local culture and heritage extends the program beyond the immediate goals of guest service and procedural improvement. The program encourages cultural appreciation while also enhancing the appeal of the destination to travellers.

While the costs of a project of this magnitude may be limited to all but the largest enterprises, the results suggest that all businesses could profit from reinforcing traditional cultural values. Local heritage and cultural organizations hold a wealth of information and may have existing programs that support similar initiatives.

KEY TERMS

cultural values

mission statement

benchmark

corporate culture

mnemonic device

host

heritage preservation

 **www.outrigger.com**

DISCUSSION QUESTIONS

1. Why did Outrigger Hotels and Resorts of Honolulu create the Ke 'Ano Wa'a initiative?
2. List other ways by which one might incorporate cultural aspects of a host community into an accommodation product.
3. Describe how learning more about the host culture might enhance a staff's daily relationships with guests and co-workers.

chapter seven

Training for Service Quality: Mentoring, Coaching, Peer Training, Multi-Skilling, and Customer Service Training

Canada
Tourism British Columbia

Submitted by: Jenni Hopkyns

SUPERHOST FACE-TO-FACE

. . . Building on the 15-year success of SuperHost, the revised SuperHost Face-to-Face program was developed to reflect new realities in British Columbia's tourism and hospitality industry.

LEARNING OUTCOMES

1. Identify marketplace factors which led to the expansion of the original SuperHost program into a family of workshops.
2. List the key points of customized workshops that are designed to meet the needs of individual businesses.

3. Recognize the importance of early market research in customizing customer service workshops.

OVERVIEW

SuperHost was first introduced in 1985 to prepare British Columbia's (BC's) tourism workforce to host the world at Expo 86. Since then, over 400 000 British Columbians have participated in SuperHost training and have helped to establish BC's world-class reputation for service.

SuperHost is recognized internationally. American Express selected SuperHost as its customer service training program, which was promoted in 10 different Asian countries. Tourism agencies in England, Wales, Scotland, New Zealand, and Australia, as well as the state of Alaska and the Canadian provinces and territories of Ontario, New Brunswick, Nova Scotia, Prince Edward Island, the Northwest Territories, and Newfoundland also have the license rights for delivering the SuperHost program. After 15 successful years, the front line training program was revised to meet the changing needs in BC's tourism and hospitality industry.

An increasing number of international travellers visit BC. This requires tourism and hospitality employees to be aware of cultural differences and expectations. The growing market for visitors with disabilities or special needs also demands a high level of sensitivity. The SuperHost Face-to-Face family of workshops was designed to help employers better train staff to meet the needs of these and other travellers. The workshops include:

Fundamentals (One-Day Workshop)

This workshop identifies and explains basic skills which are necessary to provide excellent customer service in the workplace. During the one-day session, trainers focus on the practical application of different tools and techniques to achieve quality customer service.

Japanese Service Expectations (One-Day Workshop)

For years, Japan has been BC's largest overseas market. This workshop provides participants with a better understanding of the needs, preferences, and expectations of this valuable market segment.

Customers with Disabilities (Half-Day Workshop)

Participants learn how to deliver superior service while respecting the needs and requirements unique to customers with disabilities. The workshop is designed to increase participants' awareness about this growing market segment.

> *"The SuperHost Customers with Disabilities training program is designed to give front line staff the opportunity to look at the broad range of disabilities and special needs. And when these special needs are met you get repeat customers."*
>
> *Joe Couglin*
> *BC Office for Disability Issues*

Service across Cultures (Half-Day Workshop)

This workshop offers participants a better understanding of the diverse cultures that make up BC's international pool of tourists (Japan, Hong Kong, Taiwan, South Korea, and Germany).

Service in Health Care (Full-Day Workshop)

As Canadians' expectation for service excellence grows, Canada's health care system is being pushed to change in many ways. Through this workshop, participants gain a greater understanding of the communication process and learn how to provide caring service to patients and their families.

IMPLEMENTATION

Tourism British Columbia conducted extensive market research and industry consultations in the design and development of the SuperHost Face-to-Face product line. Responding to current industry needs, the stand-alone workshops can be combined in any order with great success.

The workshops are delivered through a "hands-on" approach. Interactive learning is supported through role-playing and group work. The trainer's role is to work as a "guide on the side" while providing tips and techniques for good service. By encouraging group participation, the trainer delivers an energizing and enjoyable workshop relevant to all attending.

Tourism British Columbia delivers the SuperHost Face-to-Face workshops through a network of community representatives. Sixty-three organizations are able to arrange for the delivery of SuperHost Face-to-Face workshops in BC. Local ownership of the training has proved to be a great strength for the program. The target market is small tourism businesses (under 50 employees). Representative organizations have strong ties to the local business community, ensuring that the program reaches this market effectively.

To ensure the SuperHost Face-to-Face product line is delivered consistently, an operations guide was developed for representative organizations. This guide details ongoing certification requirements for trainers, as well as periodical monitoring to ensure that quality workshops are delivered throughout the province.

SuperHost Face-to-Face is also delivered by teachers of grade 11 and 12 tourism programs, and in career preparation programs. Over 100 schools within BC have certified teachers who deliver workshops. Several post-secondary institutions also incorporate Superhost Face-to-Face into a wide variety of tourism and hospitality programs. Certificates in all the Superhost Face-to-Face workshops are excellent for student résumés, as the tourism industry recognizes the value of this internationally-known training program.

Early market research clearly indicated that employers wanted greater flexibility in "off-the-shelf" training products. In response to this need, Tourism British Columbia introduced the option of a "customized" workshop. Custom workshops specialize the "generic" or standard curriculum package. To support flexibility within the curriculum there are three optional sections within the SuperHost Fundamentals workshop. All trainers are trained to customize SuperHost Fundamentals using the SuperHost Needs Assessment Process.

Recognized SuperHost Business Program

The Recognized SuperHost Business Program was launched in January 1997 to encourage businesses to commit more resources to customer service excellence training. The program recognizes businesses that provide continuous training in one or more of the SuperHost Face-to-Face workshops to at least 60 percent of their employees.

Upon meeting the program requirements, a business may then display the SuperHost decal and a certificate on property. The business is also licensed to use the Recognized SuperHost Business logo in any of its advertising and promotion. Businesses recognize the value of SuperHost training and often require SuperHost certification as a prerequisite for job applicants.

RESULTS

During its first year of operation, 22 500 people participated in a SuperHost Face-to-Face training program in BC. Participant and employer feedback on the SuperHost training has been collected through quantitative and qualitative research. Results show that:

- 96 percent would recommend the workshop to their co-workers.
- 96 percent learned a new customer service technique(s) that they used on return to their place of work.
- 65 percent of supervisors indicated that they noticed an improvement in morale and service levels after the workshop(s).

"SuperHost gets everybody on the same page and sets the standard. Fundamentals is an excellent workshop—it was fun, effective, and informative. Thanks!"

Tom Freitag, General Manager
Manteo Resort

"It was probably the best seminar I ever attended. It should be compulsory for everybody in the service industry."

Don MacArthur, STC Operator
BC Transit

"I took the SuperHost Service across Cultures workshop and I really enjoyed that it brought my awareness to the diversity of cultures that are coming to BC for tourism. I would definitely recommend it!"

Shawn Kisling
Raintree Restaurant at the Landing

Frontline Management Solutions (One-Day Workshop)

Another result of the successful workshop series was the creation of a new one-day workshop for supervisors and managers called Frontline Management Solutions. Training Services of Tourism British Columbia developed this one-day workshop for supervisors and managers in response to repeated requests by the tourism and service industry for such a course. The purpose of this workshop is to support the supervisors of front line staff. For a business to deliver quality customer service, managers also require training in providing quality customer service. Frontline Management Solutions is all about how to get the best return on the most important investment—the people who serve the customer directly.

Continuing in the SuperHost tradition of providing practical, fun, and insightful information, Frontline Management Solutions is designed to work closely with the SuperHost Face-to-Face product family. This workshop offers a hands-on approach to learning, and helps participants discover how to:

- build a team, and make it a winning one;
- challenge, motivate, and reward winning performances;
- make training decisions that work;
- use your leadership style to your advantage;
- manage change; and
- hire the right person and then keep him or her.

Implementation of Frontline Management Solutions

For one year, Training Services worked closely with an industry-based working committee of 14 people. This committee, which represented all sectors and both large and small operations, provided valuable feedback and direction for the course content. Three pilot workshops were held in three different locations in BC to test course relevancy. All currently certified SuperHost trainers were asked to apply to deliver the new product. Of the applicants, eight experienced facilitators were selected. Tourism British Columbia trainers are BC-based professionals with extensive hands-on experience in various areas of the service industry. They are recognized as leaders in management training and help to create the dynamic workshop environment.

Tourism British Columbia promotes, administers, and delivers Frontline Management Solutions directly. The 63 local organizations—representing SuperHost throughout the province—partner with Tourism British Columbia to bring the workshop to all communities. These organizations receive a 15 percent commission for promoting the workshop locally.

Frontline Management Solutions can also be customized for an organization to enhance the organization's morale and teamwork.

Results of Frontline Management Solutions

In December 1999, Tourism British Columbia conducted an expanded evaluation of Frontline Management Solutions. This in-depth evaluation measured learning, on-the-job applications, business results, and return on investment.

The key findings indicated the following:

- 97 percent felt that they received value for the time and registration fee incurred.
- 92 percent would recommend the workshop to other managers.
- 88 percent saw an improvement in morale and teamwork among staff.
- 79 percent found they had a more effective hiring process.
- 69 percent saw enhanced profitability.
- 71 percent saw a growth in repeat business.
- 28 percent reported the workshop contributed to a decrease in employee turnover.
- 69 percent reported the workshop contributed to an increase in employee productivity.

Since launching Frontline Management Solutions over two years ago, over 1 200 participants have benefited from the workshop.

Testimonials for Frontline Management Solutions

"It has answered a lot of the needs our managers had—great program. The other SuperHost programs are terrific, but how do the managers tie everything together? Frontline Management Solutions is helping us to do that."

Mark Andrew, General Manager
Westin Bayshore

"One of the best things about Frontline Management Solutions is actually the trainers. The Tourism BC trainers are some of the best in the world. I have seen trainers nationally and internationally, and these people are at the top of their game."

Mike McDaniel, Director of Human Resources
Pacific National Exhibition

"Frontline Management Solutions is a great program—it really involves everyone in the course. There's a lot of involvement and participation in the group, a lot of activities, a lot of brainstorming and sharing people's ideas in the group. So you're really participating in the learning and learning from each other, not just the instructor."

Kristi Strickland, Human Resources
Capilano Suspension Bridge

WTTC Human Resource Centre COMMENT

Originally developed to meet a specific need, SuperHost is proof that a quality service program can remain relevant in a changing industry. By reinvesting in market research and continually seeking input from clients, the program continues to upgrade and diversify its services. SuperHost has trained hundreds of thousands of people around the world, and has been a key element in the growth of British Columbia's strong tourism industry.

KEY TERMS

front line training

service excellence

special needs market

train-the-trainer

cultural differences

early market research

career preparation

certification

 **www.HelloBC.com**

DISCUSSION QUESTIONS

1. List the key reasons why the SuperHost program was redefined and expanded.

2. Explain how the SuperHost program goes about customizing a workshop series for an individual business. What are the benefits of a customized delivery to the business owner?

3. Changing economies and an ageing population base are two factors which affect inbound travel to Canada. Brainstorm three new workshop topics that could help the Canadian tourism industry meet future customer service needs.

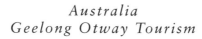

Australia
Geelong Otway Tourism

Submitted by: Roger Grant

**GEELONG
OTWAY
TOURISM** INC.

CHANGING REGIONAL VIEWS

. . . Measuring key performance indicators to reflect quality, not volume.

LEARNING OUTCOMES

1. Explain the role of a customer service strategy within a destination marketing plan.
2. Describe the role of partnerships in developing a destination marketing plan.
3. Explain the role of customer service training in the transition to niche markets.

OVERVIEW

Geelong Otway Tourism is a regional tourism body established in May 1993 to provide leadership to the marketing and industry development of the Geelong Otway region of Australia. With a population of 250 000, Geelong is a bustling metropolis located on the shores of Corio Bay in the state of Victoria.

Traditionally a summer holiday destination, Geelong attracts almost three million overnight visitors per year, with an additional five million day trippers per annum. Over the years, Geelong has established itself as a popular tourist destination in the region.

Regional visitation patterns reflect dramatic peaks in the number of summer visitors and significant falls in the number of winter visitors. The seasonal variations hurt the region's commercial district and affect the area's environmental sustainability. To combat the seasonal fluctuations and to encourage visitors, businesses typically offer volume incentives and price reductions during slower months.

Geelong Otway Tourism became involved with designing a new approach to address the challenge of seasonal instability. With seven staff members and 16 board delegates, the Geelong Otway Tourism Board proposed a new plan. Instead of encouraging mass tourism, the tourism board suggested that the industry focus on quality, innovation, and customer responsiveness.

The tourism board proposed relying on industry leadership and partnerships to bring about a radical shift in planning and communication.

IMPLEMENTATION

Geelong Otway Tourism staff developed a strategic business/marketing plan. A niche market strategy identified not only the needs of the tourism industry, but also the needs of the wholesale and retail travel industry. Consultants were hired to conduct focus groups and market research.

A plan was developed in three months. The consultants recommended the plan be phased in over a three-year period. The plan was subject to a formal annual review process, to be conducted by the Geelong Otway Tourism Board.

Funding for the proposed marketing and development programs came from five sources:

- Geelong Otway Tourism's industry membership fees
- state and federal government grants
- private sector sponsorship
- local government financial support
- industry contribution via direct advertising.

A partnership was established with local government and tourism bodies to put into effect the regional marketing and development plans. The business plan examined the regional overview, as well as:

- proposed future marketing, infrastructure, management, leadership, and industry partnerships;
- defined the economic benefits of tourism to the community; and
- provided analysis and role statements.

The marketing plan identified:

- target markets
- market influences
- sustainable competitive advantages
- regional marketing strategies
- product zone marketing and development
- performance targets.

The business/marketing plan recommended that Geelong's tourism industry stop marketing to the masses, and instead focus on attracting specific niche markets. Niche markets defined in the marketing plan were: backpackers, cultural tourism enthusiasts, and those interested in nature-based ecotourism. The marketing plan outlined strategies specific to the needs of these markets, including: planning goals, market analysis, industry trends, infrastructure development needed, industry training, marketing, and integrated strategy development. Niche market strategies focussed on providing for the total experience.

Along with these changes, industry was encouraged to consider the style of customer service provided. Good customer service was redefined to mean meeting not only the physical needs of customers, but also emotional and environment needs specific to that particular niche market. It was important that all operators recognize that they were not simply providing a bed, meal, or means to get from A to B. They were providing an experience that favoured style and ambience over service and facilities.

An extensive training needs analysis study identified the need for customer training programs throughout the region. Of the total budget, 30 percent was dedicated to industry consultation and training. Under the direction of its board, Geelong Otway Tourism staff implemented the development/marketing plans. To encourage industry participation, training is heavily subsidized by Geelong Otway Tourism. Businesses pay only a small amount to contribute to the cost of the venue. Trainers are experts in the field and local industry operators.

RESULTS

Geelong Otway Tourism no longer measures the region's success by simply counting the number of guest arrivals. The board views the measurement of growth through bookings, employment, the commitment to return, and positive word of mouth advertising as most important.

Since 1993, bookings have increased by almost 50 percent for area hotels, motels, and guest houses, and almost 30 percent for caravan parks. Employment growth has also defied national and regional trends, with major growth in employment in the off-season winter months.

Industry and municipal partners are reassured by the results. Tourism is now one of the major economic platforms of the city and surrounding region. Most businesses immediately accepted the Geelong Otway Tourism Board's new marketing and development plans. Those that have not embraced these changes are welcome to attend local forum presentations to initiate change. To keep informed, members receive newsletters and detailed progress reports following board meetings every six weeks.

WTTC HUMAN RESOURCE CENTRE COMMENT

This good practice provides a framework for any region intent on developing an environmentally sustainable and economically viable tourism industry. With a small staff and guidance from a board of directors made up of industry representatives, Geelong Otway Tourism facilitated a radical shift in its planning and communications approach.

KEY TERMS

mass tourism	market research
industry partnerships	niche markets
tourism board	high and low season
regional planning	regional tourism body
focus groups	volume incentives
infrastructure	subsidized

 **www.greatoceanrd.org.au**

DISCUSSION QUESTIONS

1. What market forces caused Geelong Otway Tourism to move to a niche market approach with a focus on customer service?
2. Explain the benefits of partnerships in putting the strategic marketing plan together.
3. Explain the role of improved customer service in meeting the goal of a total quality experience. How would you encourage the participation of small area businesses to train front line staff?

The Bahamas
The Bahamas Ministry of Tourism

Submitted by: Bradley Bain

THE BAHAMAHOST PROGRAM

… A nationally developed and subsidized customer service training program has generated a professional workforce in the Bahamas.

LEARNING OUTCOMES

1. Identify key customer service topics relevant to all sectors of a country's tourism industry.
2. Describe benefits of a customer service-based alumni association.
3. Explain how national front line training programs can establish a benchmark for knowledge and professionalism, helping to support a destination's competitive advantage.

> *"Over the past 20 years, Bahamahost has come to mean much more than a training program; it has become a watchword for quality and a service mindset that symbolizes excellence in customer service in the nation, at all levels and at all times."*
>
> *Prime Minister Hubert A. Ingraham*
> *The Bahamas*

OVERVIEW

Bahamahost is a training program developed to upgrade the customer service skills of front line employees in the service sector. The program was designed to meet industry demands for highly skilled, better informed, and technically prepared workers in the Bahamas. The program's aim is twofold. Firstly, Bahamahost creates self-awareness and fosters positive attitudes among those individuals working in tourism. Secondly, the program increases an individual's self-confidence by teaching participants general knowledge on points of interest and events in the Bahamas.

This self-improvement program is offered—through a series of lectures—to business, professional persons, and grade 11 and 12 students. Bahamahost enables participants to:

- increase their knowledge about the Bahamas;
- develop interpersonal relationship and communication skills;
- improve customer service skills;
- gain a working knowledge of the tourism industry; and
- foster teamwork and networking.

First developed under the leadership of the former Minister of Tourism, the Honourable Clement T. Maynard, a study determined that a comprehensive training program would be most effective. Initially adopted from Jamaica, the program content was restructured by the Bahamas Ministry of Tourism staff, at a cost of $40 000 (US). In 1978, Bahamahost was completed. It incorporated the importance of personal fulfilment, national pride, and the high professional business standards of the Bahamas hospitality industry to help improve the quality of visitor services in the Bahamas.

IMPLEMENTATION

Bahamahost is offered twice a year in two separate sessions, from January to June and from September to November. Classes average 25 participants and are held on-site. By offering both day and evening courses during the week, the program accommodates professionals, students, and working parents. With no marketing budget, word-of-mouth and telephone contacts are the only means of advertising the program.

The 19 core courses cover information about the history, culture, and geography of the Bahamas. Course topics include:

- **Introduction to Bahamahost**—an introductory course where participants become acquainted with each other and are provided with a program overview.
- **History of the Bahamas**—an illustrated review of Bahamian history that builds confidence in dealing with visitor questions.
- **Geography of the Bahamas**—a review of the major tourist destinations within the 700-island archipelago covering such topics as natural history, formation of the islands, rainfall and temperature data, climate, population, agriculture, and industry.
- **Civics and Government**—a two-part course focussing on the evolution and present form of government in the Bahamas, including political parties, the election process, the constitution, and national symbols.
- **Culture and Folklore**—This course develops an appreciation of Bahamian culture. The nature and role of folklore are explained in this brief review of Bahamian culture, heritage, community, and lifestyle.
- **History of Tourism**—a two-part course offering a brief historical review of the Bahamian tourism industry, with a focus on organizations involved in the development of the industry, including the Ministry of Tourism.
- **Tourism and the Bahamian Economy**—Emphasis is placed on the role and importance of tourism in the Bahamian economy, examined using basic economic

concepts. Tourism product development, the competitive position of tourism in the Caribbean, and the direct economic relationship between tourism and jobs in the Bahamas are highlighted.

- **Promoting the Bahamas**—a review of marketing concepts including the marketing mix, the need to maintain market share, and cost factors involved in promotions.

- **Attitudes and Professionalism**—a short course in human psychology examining attitudes in the workplace and the need for professionalism in the service industry.

- **Effective Communication**—This course discusses how to develop effective communication skills for career and personal success while recognizing listening skills as an integral part of the communication process.

- **Handling Complaints**—The course develops an understanding of the value and importance of a complaint while building skills to handle complaints effectively.

- **Frontier Formalities**—a course to familiarize participants with customs and immigration rules and regulations governing the border. United States Customs and Immigration officials discuss departures from the Bahamas to the United States, and vice versa, and include information about dutiable items and violation codes.

- **Basic First Aid**—Instruction in first aid covers basic procedures for different emergency situations.

- **Flora of the Bahamas**—an overview of the hundreds of colourful flowers, trees, and plants of the Bahamas. Instructors explain the particular significance, or special interest, of flora as well as discuss the practice of bush medicine, which has been used for decades.

- **Fauna of the Bahamas**—In an introduction to the indigenous animals of the Bahamas, participants learn about natural habitats and the role that animals play in the balance of nature. Also covered is an overview of national parks and the conservation practices of the Bahamas.

- **Visitor Relations**—Participants are introduced to the visitor relations unit of the Ministry of Tourism, which is in charge of handling visitor complaints.

- **People-to-People**—People-to-People is sponsored by the Ministry of Tourism and is a community involvement venture for visitors to the islands of the Bahamas.

- **General Information**—a guest service information course providing participants with facts about local tourist activities and general information specific to visitor needs.

- **Professionally Guided Tour**—This course is designed as an interactive tour covering points of interest and historic sites in residential and commercial areas.

Classes build upon each other, so participants must complete all 19 core courses offered within each session. Sessions last seven weeks and average 49 instruction hours. Public service drivers' sessions span 10 weeks, averaging 70 instruction hours. Lectures are supplemented by audiovisual material, handouts, reference literature, role-playing, group discussions, and printed teaching aids. Each session includes a quiz, covering topics introduced in the previous session.

To pass the program, participants must achieve 70 percent on all exams, including a final exam. During courses, participants must also be good team players, have positive attitudes, be punctual, partake in activities and discussions, and have a good attendance record. In a ceremony at the end of the program, all successful graduates receive a certificate and pin certifying the individual is a Bahamahost graduate.

Employers pay a small fee per person to help cover program costs. The Bahamas Ministry of Tourism subsidizes the program by paying a portion of instructor salaries and by providing training materials and supplies for the program. The trainers and associate facilitators the Ministry hires assist in course delivery. Program trainers are industry educators and permanent staff members of the Ministry of Tourism. Associate facilitators must be graduates of the Bahamahost program and have excellent communication skills. The Ministry invites instructors from educational and vocational institutions—as well as successful business leaders—to deliver lectures on the core course topics.

Where applicable, additional auxiliary courses of a more technical nature (relating to specific careers or fields) are offered. A total of 33 auxiliary courses are available, addressing attitudes, professionalism, and service, for staff such as: public service drivers; hotel employees; glass-bottom boat and marine operators; retail sales associates; and management.

RESULTS

To date, over 19 000 persons are qualified Bahamahosts, representing all segments of the tourism industry. Graduates include public service drivers, glass-bottom boat and jet-ski operators, hotel and restaurant workers, straw business persons, braiders, police, defence force personnel, immigration and customs officers, government employees, airline personnel, professional sales persons, and many others.

Bahamahost graduates are invited to join the National Bahamahost Association (NBA). The NBA has a membership totalling over 100 and is a private sector initiative made up of former Bahamahost graduates. This association provides a means to recognize and distinguish individuals who have excelled in their contribution to the service industry. The association promotes high standards of excellence and encourages members to be role models for future graduates. Activities organized by the NBA include community projects and a self-development series.

WTTC HUMAN RESOURCE CENTRE COMMENT

Human resource training and development can play an important part in nation building. In the Bahamas, the Ministry of Tourism chose to incorporate a training program which went considerably beyond service to include elements of culture, history, geography, folklore, civic duty, and safety. This comprehensive approach was complemented by the National Bahamahost Association, which maintains the industry professionalism established in the program among the graduates. The program also links together all those professionals who come into contact with tourists, and provides a common level of customer service quality.

KEY TERMS

train-the-trainer

self-improvement

service excellence

industry awareness programs

professional association

alumni

www.bahamas.com

DISCUSSION QUESTIONS

1. Describe the benefits to the individual, to the industry, and to the country of a graduates' alumni association for a customer service training program.

2. What do you consider to be the most important customer service skills in the Bahamahost program? Why?

3. As an employer, what might you do to encourage staff participation in the Bahamahost program?

Australia
Gledswood Homestead

Submitted by: Marcus Testoni

Gledswood Homestead

TEAM LEADERSHIP BUILDS MULTI-SKILLED WORKFORCE

… Using job rotation, staff is trained in many areas under the supervision of a qualified team leader building a committed team of multi-skilled workers.

LEARNING OUTCOMES

1. Explain how train-the-trainer systems can reduce an operation's overall training cost over time.

2. Describe the benefits of a multi-skilled workforce in the operation of a tourist attraction.

3. Describe how cross-training supports team building and customer service quality.

OVERVIEW

Built in 1810, Gledswood Homestead is a colonial farm in New South Wales, Australia. Just one hour's drive from the centre of Sydney, this attraction is an experience in genuine Australian bush life. In addition to being a popular tourist attraction, the site hosts a range of special functions, from wedding receptions to business conferences.

The Homestead's staff of 100 employees entertains more than 120 000 international visitors each year. Employees demonstrate first hand farm activities such as mustering, milking, boomerang-throwing, and shearing. They also conduct trail rides, sell country crafts and gifts, guide visitors through the residence, and serve Aussie tucker and wines at the Country Eating House.

It is essential that employees at Gledswood Homestead are able to work well in a variety of areas. Without multi-skilled employees, more staff would be required and training costs would escalate. This visitor attraction also has limited internal promotion opportunities, and the nature of the operation requires staff to perform many different functions throughout the year. With the assistance of government programs, Gledswood Homestead was able to implement a training strategy to develop a multi-skilled workforce in a team-based work environment.

IMPLEMENTATION

The owners of Gledswood Homestead are the first to admit that they had their share of challenges and disasters while implementing new training strategies. With government programs offering mandatory spending in the late 1980s (which was equal to 10 percent of employee payroll) Gledswood Homestead embraced the idea of furthering staff training by applying for industry assistance. During this period, Tourism Training Australia (TTA) led the way in developing industry standards and training materials as Australia's advisory board for national industry training.

TTA was established in 1982 to develop a flexible and effective training system for the tourism and hospitality industry. The organization brings together a large number of training partners, including government, unions, private and public training providers, industry associations, students/trainees, and universities. For Gledswood Homestead and many other Australian tourism businesses, TTA has been a major resource in developing tourism training structures over the last 10 years under the original training demonstration program.

Train-the-Trainer Courses

During work hours, all eight team leaders at Gledswood Homestead completed train-the-trainer courses off-premises through the Restaurant and Caterers Association. This training is now a standard course easily found throughout Australia. Gledswood Homestead paid for team leaders to take the seven-day course, which could be completed in a week-long session or by attending seven days over seven weeks. Over the years, a number of employees have become industry-accredited trainers, which allows for team leaders to now be trained on-site under a mentoring system.

Over time, train-the-trainer courses have reduced training costs for Gledswood Homestead. An example is in the job rotation training program. Job rotation was first introduced to allow team leaders to train each employee as they passed through specific job

Gledswood Homestead

Dining in Gledswood Homestead's Country Eating House.

areas. This training was the first step in developing a multi-skilled workforce. Because the company experiences little turnover, the need for job rotation has decreased over the years.

Hiring

Because of the innovative nature of the workplace, careful attention is paid to staff selection. Vacancies are advertised in local newspapers and all applicants who meet the specified requirements are interviewed. Interviewing is first conducted by the general manager and then by a panel of three staff members, including someone from the section with the vacancy.

According to the owners, "We ask lots of questions that seem strange but we are looking for people we want to work with. We want the right person. Involving co-workers, not just team leaders and managers, is real interesting as they often see things that others don't." Gledswood Homestead takes its time selecting new associates.

Staff Training

All general staff receive tour guide training so that all employees are able to conduct tours of the property. By sharing historical knowledge of Gledswood Homestead, all staff are equipped to answer visitor questions.

One team leader is the on-site training officer responsible for running induction sessions for new staff. The training officer organizes orientation sessions, compiles training materials, and coordinates with other team leaders. Every new associate visits each work area of the property under the direction of a team leader.

Staff can also take speciality courses on- and off-site, depending on need and availability. On average, staff take advantage of the opportunity and complete the courses on personal time. For example, staff members who took wine appreciation training sessions helped increase wine sales in à la carte dining. Staff was more knowledgeable and better able to promote the product in the Country Eating House. Another specialty program attended by some staff was Japanese language and culture training courses. These courses helped increased the staff's ability to meet the expectations of this international market.

Management will pay a portion of course fees provided that employees agree to let their progress be monitored while participating in employer-funded courses. If a course is not successfully completed, management asks for staff to reimburse the course tuition.

Monitoring

Monitoring and feedback are two important elements of measuring Gledswood Homestead's quality of service. Three service areas which are monitored include the number of visitors, customer satisfaction, and productivity.

Service quality is assessed through restaurant and shop productivity via systematic customer surveys and spends-per-customer. For example, the number of covers and wage costs are used to evaluate restaurant productivity. The number of tourists and the dollar value of sales measure shop productivity.

Customer satisfaction is gauged through staff feedback, discussions with customers, return visit counts, and biannual surveys. As a result of monitoring and feedback, changes are regularly made to existing operations to improve service quality and customer service. Gledswood Homestead's staff, who are empowered to check satisfaction and correct problems on-site, further enhance customer satisfaction.

Team Building

The team atmosphere is cultivated through staff discussions during team meetings, which are held every two weeks. The first step is to make sure that new employees are eager to join the company as team players. If after the first two months it is obvious that the individual is not a team player, they are let go. According to management, "You know you have a team when the staff have social functions with partners, and turn up on days off to make sure that fellow workers are alright."

RESULTS

Since 1990, Gledswood Homestead has won two Australian Tourism Awards for Excellence and 11 State Tourism Awards for Excellence. In 1999 the Tourism Council of Australia nominated Gledswood Homestead as "The Best of the Decade in Tourism Excellence for Heritage and Cultural Tourism."

The multi-skilled workforce developed at Gledswood Homestead makes flexible working hours possible to meet individual staff needs and help reduce employee turnover. This also improves staff morale and creates a more positive work environment. As a direct result, employee turnover remains at 11 percent.

A significant number of employees have become industry-accredited trainers, many of whom are nationally licensed workplace assessors. Gledswood Homestead can now provide on-the-job training recognized anywhere in Australia. This gives staff further recognition, raising performance standards, and entrenching a culture of learning. Survey results indicate that staff friendliness is considered Gledswood Homestead's greatest asset.

Like other employers who invest in staff training and have a qualified team, Gledswood Homestead has had a few key staff poached. More often it is younger staff members who are more enticed by offers to work in the city. For Gledswood Homestead, once someone has come to the decision to leave, they are supported.

WTTC HUMAN RESOURCE CENTRE COMMENT

This good practice demonstrates the effectiveness of employee empowerment, where employees are provided with the skills and given the responsibility to influence their own work environment. Small operations could benefit from implementing these practices, which do not have the heavy overhead costs often associated with extensive training programs.

KEY TERMS

multi-skilled	monitoring
team building	train-the-trainer
job rotation	hiring
workplace assessors	leadership
industry-accredited	induction session
performance standards	

 **www.gledswood.com.au**

DISCUSSION QUESTIONS

1. Discuss the advantages of having a multi-skilled workforce.

2. As a team leader, what are the advantages of empowering employees in your department?

3. Explain how cross-training has supported employee retention at Gledswood Homestead.

Canada
Hotel Association of Canada

Submitted by: Tony Pollard

HOTEL ASSOCIATION OF CANADA
ASSOCIATION DES HÔTELS DU CANADA

PREPARING FOR THE SPECIAL NEEDS HOTEL MARKET

... A program aimed at training hotel staff to better accommodate the growing market of seniors and travellers with disabilities.

LEARNING OUTCOMES

1. Describe the benefits of training staff to deal with visitors with special needs and to provide barrier-free access.
2. List and evaluate Access Canada's four barrier-free access levels.
3. Describe strategies for training hotel staff to adjust to the emerging market of travellers with disabilities.

OVERVIEW

The market of affluent seniors, combined with the growing number of persons with disabilities venturing into international travel, is expanding rapidly. Between 1990 and 2020, the seniors market is expected to grow from 25 to 37 percent of the total market in the US alone. The disabled market is estimated at 27 percent of the total North American market.

To accommodate these expanding markets, the Hotel Association of Canada (HAC) is promoting Access Canada, a program intended to: define building and service standards for four levels of barrier-free access to hotel facilities by travellers with special needs and provide awareness, training, and communication materials to help staff deal effectively with these visitors.

The Access Canada program has been officially endorsed by the International Hotel Association. In addition, the United Nations (UN) has presented the program as a model to all UN countries, stating that the program "meets or exceeds all international standards on serving the needs of seniors and persons with disabilities."

IMPLEMENTATION

The Access Guide

The hotel operator's guide to barrier-free access provides hoteliers with building specifications and service requirements graded to meet four types of special needs: agility, sight, hearing, and mobility.

Four levels of access have been defined:

- **Level 1**—aimed primarily at travelling seniors who have special needs due to slight reduction in vision or hearing capacity and/or some problems with agility, but do not require wheelchair-accessible accommodation.
- **Level II**—aimed at travellers with moderate disabilities.
- **Level III**—aimed at travellers with more severe agility, hearing mobility, and vision disabilities, and independent wheelchair users.
- **Level IV**—aimed at travellers with severe disabilities.

Hoteliers can be certified for any of these four levels. A hotel must review the specifications for facilities, equipment, and services, and then make adjustments as necessary. Authorized inspectors evaluate the facilities and provide certification at the appropriate level rating. This rating is included in hotel rating guides and, increasingly, is being marketed by associations of both seniors and travellers with disabilities.

Access Training

To meet the service requirements of travellers with special needs, Access Canada has developed a bilingual interactive training program on CD-ROM, a training video, and a self-training manual available in both English and French.

Objectives of the training are to:

- increase interpersonal skills in relating to travellers with special needs
- raise staff awareness of the range of service requirements by hotel patrons with special needs;
- enhance staff knowledge of the hotel property, services, and facilities; and
- raise staff comfort levels in relating to patrons with special needs.

The program content includes sections on:

- *Disabled guests and their special needs,* which helps staff to recognize disabilities, communicate comfortably and effectively, and understand how to meet the special needs of every guest.
- *What makes a hotel accessible,* which examines the equipment and features of a hotel from the perspective of guests with special needs.
- *How to provide the best possible service,* where staff learn how to address individual needs of guests based on their special needs.

Each section includes a review quiz that allows users to assess their own level of learning and review material not fully absorbed.

RESULTS

Ensuring barrier-free access broadens the appeal of an establishment to include the grow-ing market of persons with special needs. Access training helps hotel staff become more confident and more efficient in serving customers with special needs. Instead of worrying about saying or doing the wrong thing, staff are able to address and meet the needs of guests and provide the best service possible. As a by-product, many hoteliers have found that special needs training enhances service delivery to all customers, not just clients with special needs.

Choice Hotels Canada, the largest hotel company in Canada with over 260 properties, has made Access Canada mandatory in all its hotels. The HAC expects the day will come when this is the expected norm in all of the Canadian accommodation industry.

WTTC HUMAN RESOURCE CENTRE COMMENT

Training packages are available in CD-ROM or video format. Both include a training manual to complete the exercises, as well as the operator's manual for accommodating travellers with special needs. Access Canada provides certificates and lapel pins for those who successfully complete the training program. The package retails at $160, which provides training for five employees. Each additional participant costs $89.

KEY TERMS

disabled travellers

special needs travellers

accommodation ratings

certification

barrier-free access

international standards

interpersonal skills

 **www.hotels.ca**

DISCUSSION QUESTIONS

1. Explain the significance of Access Canada's programming as it relates to the shift in market demographics over the next decade.
2. What are some of the marketing opportunities presented to hotels that have partici-pated in this program and received certification?
3. Which departments of a hotel should participate in this program? Why?

United Kingdom
Tower Bridge Experience

Submitted by: Mary Tebje

QUALITY CUSTOMER SERVICE POLICY

… Wanting its quality customer service to be consistent, measurable, and capable of being evaluated, London's Tower Bridge Experience implemented a quality service policy from the "bottom up."

> *At Tower Bridge Experience, we all work together. Even though I was lucky enough to receive an award, there are numerous examples of other staff on Tower Bridge offering similarly good customer service. It goes to prove there's no customer service without teamwork."*
>
> William Kidman, Cashier
> Tower Bridge

LEARNING OUTCOMES

1. Define customer quality service.
2. Explain the process of developing a team approach when establishing company policy and standards.
3. Recognize the benefits of a mystery shopper program in defining and monitoring in-house standards.

OVERVIEW

Tower Bridge and the Monument are two of the most famous landmarks in London, England. Both are owned, funded, and managed by the Corporation of London.

Built in 1677, the Monument has been a visitor attraction in London for over 300 years. The Monument was designed by Sir Christopher Wren to commemorate the Great Fire of London. Today, over 130 000 customers climb 311 steps to the top of this historic landmark to take in spectacular views of London.

Tower Bridge was built in 1894 and is still a vital and historic river-crossing over the Thames River. It is also home to an award-winning high-tech permanent exhibition called the Tower Bridge Experience. Attracting over 400 000 admissions annually, the Tower Bridge Experience tells the story of the original need for the bridge, and explains its design choices and the unique way that the bridge is raised when watercraft must pass below. Visitors learn more about the Tower Bridge through the use of interactive and multilingual touch-screen computers. They can also gather details about surrounding area sites.

Depending on seasonal attendance demands, both attractions are staffed by a team of approximately 45 staff—both permanent and temporary. This "tourism team" is based in the Tower Bridge, yet is responsible for visitors to both the Tower Bridge Experience and the Monument.

In 1999, a cashier at Tower Bridge Experience, William Kidman, received the inaugural London World Class Welcome Award, which is presented by the London Tourist Board. Recognized for his customer care initiatives and his beyond-the-call-of-duty visitor service efforts, Kidman credits his excellence in customer service to his participation in numerous training opportunities offered by the Corporation of London, and to the team approach adopted by all staff at Tower Bridge.

Like many tourist attractions, the Tower Bridge Experience and the Monument have customer care programs to educate and train staff in providing excellent service. Prior to developing their customer service training program, management completed a visitor audit. The audit, conducted by an external research agency, measured visitor responses to questions rating the attraction's "value for money" and "enjoyment and entertainment." Ratings were reported at 76 percent and 84 percent respectively.

With all results in, management could not determine if the scores accurately reflected the levels of service and customer care at Tower Bridge Experience. Without a customer service program, management felt they were unable to challenge these scores or set targets for improvement. It was decided that a Quality Customer Service (QCS) policy was needed, and should be designed with staff and management input in order to ensure that employees would embrace the new company principles.

IMPLEMENTATION

In designing a customer service training policy, management took a bottom-up approach involving all employees. Although senior management determined policies, employees were influential in outlining how policies would be met. During workshops, staff and management shared comments and suggestions, and worked together on designing a set of operational standards. These standards, also known as the customer care policy, would impact the staff's daily tasks and duties.

Working Towards a QCS Policy

In August 1999, the tourism management teams (and the retail manager) participated in a "back to basics" one-day workshop. This workshop was designed to review how the company's current operations and communications impacted on the visitor's experience. Teams working at both attractions concluded that in order for the Tower Bridge Experience and the Monument to set targets to improve visitor ratings, a QCS policy was needed as a benchmark for measuring service and service improvements. This "buy-in" was the first step in establishing the Tower Bridge Experience's QCS policy.

Three months later, all tourism managers (including corporate, retail, trade sales, and consumer marketing) attended an in-house "quality workshop." This workshop was designed and run by the in-house tourism manager. Throughout the workshop, participants learned:

- the meaning of the term "quality";
- why quality is so important; and
- the importance of both managers and employees to the final outcome of a quality program.

Following the quality workshop, management formulated a working QCS policy that would eventually be incorporated into the business plan. A team approach was taken to gain employee input throughout the process. Each manager would work with a small team of employees to review predetermined topics. From this, team input and suggestions would be compiled into a single document, which would then be distributed to all team members. This teamwork approach was designed to keep employees abreast of service expectations, which would soon become company policy.

Introducing the QCS Policy

In January 2000, a customer care training day was held for all members of the Tower Bridge Experience tourism department (and all security team members not on duty). It was during this day-long workshop that the QCS policy was presented to the entire tourism department. Finalized after months of work, the customer care policy was introduced as a required set of standards.

The workshop was mandatory for all tourism staff. Participants were paid their regular wages while in attendance. Session topics focussed on typical service blunders and the consequences of poor customer service. In the on-site education centre, a customer care training video was presented and group discussions ensued linking the scenarios to the working environment of staff and management present. The video and related training materials were hired from an outside company specializing in customer service training.

Role-playing was also an effective training mechanism in presenting customer service issues. Participants "put themselves in the customer's shoes" as they focussed on service areas requiring improvement. This session gave front line staff an opportunity to express their concerns and share suggestions. Handouts were distributed to reinforce key points.

To assess current service standards, all tourism department members were divided into five different teams. Led by department managers, each team examined existing standards, suggested new standards, discussed monitoring and measuring techniques, and designed operational evaluation procedures. Although some teams worked on like areas, each management team had respective duties. These included:

- **Exhibition Manager**—assessed ticket sales and transactions, visitor feedback, languages, standing instructions (internal procedures employees must follow, largely relating to health and safety, fire, bomb scares, security etc.), and operational standards.
- **Duty Managers**—Three teams focussed on assessing property signage, audio guides, Tower Bridge lift information, shift changes, area cleanliness, uniforms, rosters (the timetables by which all tourist guides know where they should be in the exhibition, at any time), maintenance, functions (corporate hospitality), and staff briefings.

- **Corporate Hospitality Executive and Duty Manager**—reviewed corporate events.
- **Retail Manager**—assessed vending, stock, training, research, and cashiers.
- **Marketing and Business Development Executives**—examined consumer events, the Monument, reception, telephones, information provision (the content and manner in which information was distributed), and current marketing strategies.
- **Department Head**—conducted group follow-up (a guiding and supporting role).

Assessment forms rated the day's workshop as extremely positive and, upon completion, participants were committed to being involved in further developing the QCS policy.

Monitoring and Measuring Techniques

Daily quality checks were established as a standard. Staff members routinely check all parts of attractions before opening. Each business day a team member, normally a tourist guide, checks the part of the exhibition they are working in. Checks include cleanliness, fabric of the building, and show content. Any faults are immediately reported. Later in the morning, the duty manager collects completed checklists and records all problems requiring repair or maintenance.

Monthly management team meetings review work in progress, and allow for groups to share developments, challenges, and suggestions in their area. Prior to proceeding with any corrective measures, a report listing the monthly meeting discussions is circulated for comment.

Evaluation Procedures

With new operational standards in place, monitoring and evaluation procedures were a necessary follow up measure.

A mystery shopper program was established to operate at least twice a year at both the Monument and the Tower Bridge Experience sites. Results from the exercise are used to establish a set of benchmarks against which management can monitor and evaluate visitor expectations and customer service. A mystery shopper program is also in effect for group bookings and corporate hospitality groups. Although an outside specialist conducts the mystery shopper program, the tourism manager designed the evaluation standards for the program. The primary aim of the mystery shopper is to evaluate the service provided from the customer's point of view before the visit, during the visit, and, where appropriate, after the visit.

In conjunction with the above, the on-site visitor audit acts as a continuous monitor at the exhibition site. This survey differs in that it provides data on the visit itself as well as the exhibition show content. It, too, is managed by an external agency that, at pre-arranged times and with a specially designed questionnaire, interviews a set number of customers. Results provide critical information on product delivery, customer service expectations, and the marketing and sales efforts.

RESULTS

Employees at the Tower Bridge Experience are eager to be included in initiatives and programs that rate quality visitor service. At present, London's local tourist board is developing a grading scheme focussed on service excellence for all area visitor attractions. A government program called Government Charter Mark (to be launched in 2001) also recognizes quality. Tower Bridge team members hope to be nominated for various awards within this program.

Measurable results stemming from the introduction of the Quality Customer Service policy are to date as follows:

MYSTERY SHOPPING SCORES (PERCENTAGE)	ACTUAL		FORECAST
Tower Bridge Experience	July 2000	Feb 2001	July 2001
Corporate Hospitality	72	80	85
Retail	90	90	90
Telephone Enquiries	48	70	80
Signage	80	85	90
Operational Standards	76	80	85
Uniforms and Staff Presentation	94	95	95
Cleanliness	94	95	95
Disability Awareness	60	75	95
The Monument			
Telephone Enquiries	77	85	90
Operational Standards	86	90	90
Uniforms and Staff Presentation	0	80	85
Cleanliness	70	75	75

The list for the Monument is not as extensive because it is a much smaller site, with fewer facilities.

Corrective action has already been taken for the areas where scores were poor. For example, casual staff at the Monument were not issued a uniform, hence the initial score of 0. These staff members have since been provided with uniforms and a name badge, so it was expected that the score would rise dramatically at the time of the next audit.

Retraining was needed to remedy the scores for "telephone enquiries" and "disability awareness." The telephone course covered the topic of "making the most of incoming calls" and was aimed at reception, administration, accounts, and group booking staff. This course was run in-house with the aid of external training tools. It looked at the role that each individual has in making that all-important first impression, as well as going on to generate sales.

To facilitate the disability awareness training, a tourist guide at Tower Bridge, John Bull, was sent on an external course—"train-the-trainer"—to learn how to conduct in-house training for front line staff. He has since successfully trained over 95 percent of staff at both sites. The two-hour course covered the essentials of the new Disability Discrimination Act and looked at practical examples of disability awareness within the tourism environment.

WTTC Human Resource Centre COMMENT

Tower Bridge Experience provides a candid and useful good practice example for any tourism business wanting to benchmark its levels of service and customer care. Having implemented evaluation and monitoring procedures into its daily operations, Tower Bridge Experience easily gathers the benchmarking criteria it needs to effectively evaluate itself. The addition of two additional training sessions, introduced to cover telephone techniques and disability awareness, shows that management was quick to accept the ratings and use them as a basis by which to improve guest services. Scores can be challenged and targets set for improvement. The continued use of mystery shoppers will provide valuable and impartial evaluations to compare with daily in-house evaluations. By continually reviewing the QCS policy, team members can all help reaffirm and redefine established targets, while also embracing new company principles.

KEY TERMS

customer service	standards
policy	audit
operational standards	communication
monitoring	quality
mystery shopper	evaluation procedures
benchmark	buy-in

 **www.towerbridge.org.uk**

DISCUSSION QUESTIONS

1. There are both advantages and challenges when you include staff members in the development of company standards and policies. List five advantages and five disadvantages. Explain your choices.

2. List five benefits of having a firm set of quality standards in place. What are the benefits at a later stage?

3. Describe how the mystery shopper program was used to influence company benchmarking and evaluation procedures.

Canada
Elmhirst's Resort

Submitted by: Anne Marshall

CROSS-TRAINING BUILDS CROSS-SELLING

... A small resort builds customer loyalty despite size limitations and labour pool shortages by developing a team of multi-skilled staff. As staff becomes multi-skilled and experiences all the services the resort has to offer, employees cross-sell resort products. This increases personal gratuities, staff knowledge, and guest satisfaction.

LEARNING OUTCOMES

1. Analyze the benefits for a small resort property in developing a multi-skilled staff.
2. Describe the concept of cross-selling.
3. Explain the advantages to staff and the resort when staff samples the services and products offered by the resort.

OVERVIEW

Family enterprise is a way of life for many Ontario resort operators. Elmhirst's Resort is a family-run operation located on the shores of Rice Lake, Ontario. Currently, four generations of the Elmhirst family reside on-site to manage the lakeside cottage resort, which began operation in 1906. Having started as a one-cottage summer fishing rental facility, this family operation grew to operate as a campground with cottages, and eventually evolved into its current state as a year-round, full-service resort. Thirty cottages now line the shores of Rice Lake.

Over the years, services were updated so the resort could cater to vacationers, conference delegates, weddings, weekenders, and fishermen from North America and Europe. The main building houses the recreational facility, conference centre, banquet facilities, and office and dining area. The unique building has great views and is equipped with the services expected by international meeting planners. Amenities and activities available to guests include mountain-biking trails, sport courts, playgrounds, all-terrain vehicle (ATV) safaris, boat and motor rentals, windsurfers, kayaks, and guided fishing trips. There is also a range of winter activities, with special packages to encourage mid-week leisure business. These packages are geared towards "couch potatoes," romantics, and those who want to sample winter activities.

Initially catering to the United States market, key markets have grown to include guests from Canada, Europe, the United Kingdom, and the Caribbean. Each year repeat business and referrals increase. Guest loyalty is built in several ways. On departure, guests who inquire about returning are guaranteed the same cottages, for the same week, the following year. Direct mail campaigns include an annual spring newsletter and a Christmas card mail-out, customized with guest photos.

In the mid-1990s, the resort began focussing on the adventure market. To attract this market, activities on and around the property were needed. At this time, Free Spirit product lines were expanded on-site. Because of the ample acreage surrounding the resort, all activities became a part of the actual resort, and were easily incorporated into the guest experience. Among the product lines is Free Spirit Air Adventures, specializing in sightseeing flights and air charters to places wild and popular. Free Spirit Riding Stable offers trail rides and riding lessons. Free Spirit Health Club, located in the main building, includes an exercise room, masseuse, tanning bed, whirlpool and sauna, and both an indoor and outdoor swimming pool. The health club attracts both in-house guests and local members.

Nearby resort operators often recommend Free Spirit activities. As these activities are offered under the Free Spirit logo, they are not necessarily associated with Elmhirst's Resort and thus are not considered direct competition.

As a result of adding the Free Spirit product line, the resort's qualified team expanded to 60 staff members, all of whom offer the guests a variety of recreational activities. During winter months landscaping and gardening positions are not required, and staff numbers are reduced to 54.

For Elmhirst's Resort, finding employees to support a year-round property in a small community is a continuous challenge. Traditionally, family members worked long hours to create a friendly, casual atmosphere. As the business grew, recruitment became more of an exercise in finding genuinely friendly candidates than a search for individuals with specific skills. With the addition of a seasonal staff to run the operation, Elmhirst's Resort acquired a new workforce who had little guest recognition, suffered from strained team dynamics, and required retraining.

IMPLEMENTATION

Staff Retraining and Development

To develop a skilled seasonal workforce, resort management hired multi-talented individuals rather than those with a focussed specialty. Training in basic skills is ongoing throughout the year. Technical training in job-specific activities is provided on-site through hospitality programs like the provincial customer service workshop series, SuperHost.

Manuals outlining required standards of service and conduct are used during staff training sessions. Customized manuals are designed in-house, with help from hospitality consultants. The manuals are reviewed and updated as necessary, incorporating new ideas and different training techniques.

All training is conducted during working hours or as a special session in the evening. Employees are paid for the hours they spend attending training sessions. The resort's human resource team provides most of the training, while some components are delivered by outside trainers.

Supervisors and managers also attend outside training courses as required to improve their own training skills. Managers are an important link in the ongoing training cycle. At annual retreats, managers are asked to research and present management skill workshops in addition to discussing the budget.

Standards and expectations are reinforced during all in-house sessions. These standards are well observed by both management and staff. Testing the effectiveness of training is done in a variety of different ways. A mentor system has proved successful, whereby managers focus on specific employees, offering insight and guidance. Owners take a hands-on approach in continually testing products and services throughout the resort. In support of this, all staff is encouraged to use the resort's facilities, and to make suggestions for improvements. For example, in the spring staff is invited to enjoy horseback riding—helping the Free Spirit trail guides in preparing for upcoming guest rides. The resort's dining room is also open to staff, and critiques are welcomed.

Staff work as a multi-skilled team, moving between departments when needed. Working as a multi-skilled team means that dining-room servers work in housekeeping on busy turnover days, and kitchen staff work on the waterfront in summer months, and on snow removal duty in the winter. Recreation staff move between dining-room service, banquet service, and housekeeping. Trail guides also serve at banquets and learn bartending.

Sustaining a multi-skilled workforce requires a certain amount of organization and structuring. At the hiring stage, candidates are advised of all available positions. Employees are encouraged to apply for those positions they are most interested in, and which meet their own work-hour needs. On hiring, employees are assigned to a "home department," and all of their work hours are designated to the appropriate department. Management runs each of the home departments as a small company. This means they are responsible for their own mini-budgets, which are directly tied to labour hours. Work-sharing is important as it helps management meet budgets, especially in slow months.

Cross-Selling

Boredom and apathy have disappeared as employees feel comfortable moving between departments. As a result, employees are better able to cross-sell the resort's various services and recreational activities on-site. For example, a fishing guide talks up the resort's dining options, restaurant servers sell floatplane flights, pilots sell shoulder season cottage stays, and a bartender promotes the ATV safari experience. The result? Sales increase and the guest experience is enhanced.

Employees are first introduced to the concept of cross-selling during orientation sessions. Staff is encouraged to experience all services, facilities, and activities offered at the resort to learn more about the resort and its products. Managers encourage employees to "be a guest of the resort" during slow times.

Cross-selling is easy for staff who share a passion for activities which the resort offers. It is natural for these employees to get excited about sharing a best fishing spot, helping organize a tennis partner for a guest, or assisting a guest with their activity itinerary. Employees with interests similar to those offered through the resort are valued highly in the interview stage.

Concepts and suggestions around cross-selling can be introduced, but employees are far more likely to participate if there is a reward. Suggesting a successful activity is always appreciated by guests, and is well supported by management. Interacting with guests in a variety of different ways—perhaps by assisting them on the tennis court during the day, and later serving them dinner at night—builds familiarity and, generally, better gratuities for the employee. Management recognizes this and supports employees in the benefits they might receive. While management is pleased with the revenue outcome of cross-selling, employees are also increasing their earning power.

Employee Development

The concept of empowerment is discussed with staff. As staff members become more aware of the many products offered throughout the resort, their ability to cross-sell and multi-skill increases. As their confidence grows, so do their earnings through gratuities.

The resort's guest-centred culture is reinforced through the actions of management. Each manager is responsible for a recreation event during the summer months. This allows management to interact with guests and provides for a variety of programs offered throughout the season. Some activities are artistic, some involve games (one manager has staged a bingo event for over 10 years), and others are athletic (such as a guided mountain-bike ride or a sailing lesson). When employees see their managers interacting with guests, it reinforces the organization's culture.

In support of employee development, Elmhirst's Resort developed a simple rewards and recognition program known as the Winners Circle. Each year employees are asked to nominate a fellow team member whom they feel best personifies the resort's mission statement. Employees may nominate from any department throughout the resort. One employee from each department is selected by secret ballot system. The ballot includes the reason for that employee's nomination. The winning employee joins the Winners Circle and receives recognition throughout the year with a special name tag, dinner rewards, and team outings to sporting events and the theatre. Winning employees also receive a Christmas bonus.

> *"We believe we are here to provide a year-round experience that fulfils the needs and exceeds the expectations of our guests. While we target diverse markets, vacationers remain our priority. We take pride in delivering an international standard of dining, accommodation, and facilities. We are a family-owned-and-operated cottage resort with a commitment to developing an exceptional team. We strive to maintain a reasonable level of profit while continuing to provide excellence in guest satisfaction."*
>
> *Mission Statement*
> *Elmhirst's Resort*

RESULTS

Although Elmhirst's Resort is susceptible to many of the same issues as a small business operation located outside a large metropolis, it is capable of incorporating change and new programs quickly and with relative ease. Recruitment is and will remain a challenge, but

Elmhirst's Resort management is confident that its new retraining and development programs will encourage existing employees to work as a team. Many high-school students choose a vocation based on their exposure to new job areas at the resort. Post-secondary students often change their major at university or college, based on their work experience.

Guest satisfaction has increased. Guests frequently acknowledge an employee by name on comment cards upon departure. Guests have the option of leaving completed comment cards in guest rooms upon check-out, delivering them to the front desk, or mailing them back to the resort. Guest comments provide motivation for front-of-the-house employees. These feedback cards, good and bad, are kept in a general spot in the main office, and are accessible to all staff for review.

Cross-selling has supported measurable returns for Elmhirst's Resort. Snowmobile safaris increased by 12 percent after employees were invited to experience the adventure. Throughout the summer of 2000, ATV safari sales grew in number each week once dining-room staff began acting as safari guides. Horseback trail-ride sales have doubled over the last two years following a program wherein staff is invited to work with the horses and become more familiar with the stables. Turnover was 41 percent in 1998, 38 percent in 1999, and 32 percent in 2000. Elmhirst's Resort's goal is to maintain a 25 percent turnover. Considering the attrition of graduating students and the number of construction positions it will need in its five-year building program, management feels this is a realistic goal given the labour pool.

WTTC Human Resource Centre COMMENT

Characteristically, small tourism operators in outlying areas cite limited resources and a shortage of qualified workers as local disadvantages. Elmhirst's Resort suffers from similar issues but has shown how focussing on the local market and working with resources at hand can translate into other opportunities. Investing in training built a more qualified team of in-house trainers capable of supporting a multi-skilled workforce. The use of evaluation techniques helped the resort monitor staff training and redevelopment. Cross-selling, which was encouraged by management as a means to discourage apathy, surprisingly matured into an all-round positive feature. Employees took pride in suggesting other activities they enjoyed or had personally experienced, thereby better servicing guest needs and increasing their earning power.

KEY TERMS

empowerment	recruitment
cross-selling	turnover
customer loyalty	seasonal employment
cross-training	retraining
multi-skilling	direct mail campaign

 **www.elmhirst.com**

DISCUSSION QUESTIONS

1. Why is a mentor system a successful training tool for small businesses such as Elmhirst's Resort? (Remember, Elmhirst's Resort's reputation was built on a friendly, casual atmosphere.)

2. What other programs or methods can a resort use to develop guest loyalty?

3. When standards and expectations are reinforced during in-house training sessions, both management and staff better observe standards. What methods can be used to monitor the effectiveness of training?

Hungary
Mirror Mirror Customer Care Program

Submitted by: Alan Godsave

GB RESOURCES

LEADING IN LEARNING

REFLECTIONS OF A TRAINING NEED IN CENTRAL AND EASTERN EUROPE

… People are the most important asset in any tourism enterprise, so quality interpersonal skills training is vital for the continued growth of the industry, especially in restructured economies.

LEARNING OUTCOMES

1. Gauge why many travel and tourism businesses in restructuring economies are reluctant to invest in front line staff training for basic service delivery.

2. Recognize the service standards and front line interpersonal skills demanded by Western travellers.

3. Describe how a front line training program may be translated and customized to meet the specific needs of a country or region.

OVERVIEW

With the end of the Cold War, many Westerners eagerly visited Central and Eastern European countries that had previously forbidden leisure and business travel within their borders. With the increase of visitor numbers in the early 1990s, many of these European countries realized there was an economic benefit to developing a tourism industry. Western visitors, however, were generally not satisfied with the service they received. Customer service standards being practised reflected what customers had considered acceptable in the days of social tourism (when everything was centrally regulated and there was no competition). Unhappy Western visitors damaged the prospects of repeat business and referrals. New sets of service standards were clearly needed!

During this period, Alan Godsave (at that time the World Travel & Tourism Council's [WTTC's] Director for Central and Eastern Europe and owner of a training consulting firm, GB Resources) was preparing tourism strategy plans for the European Union's PHARE[1] Program. He came to realize there was a need for interpersonal skills training for this region's tourism industries. While front line staff did have the technical competence to perform their jobs, they lacked interpersonal skills and the understanding of why customer satisfaction is important. Fortunately, at the same time, the WTTC member American Express had come to a similar conclusion. American Express was developing a two-day program called Mirror Mirror, focussing on just that area of human resource development.

Following a period of negotiation, the American Express Foundation[2] agreed to provide monies to pay for translating the Mirror Mirror program into the Hungarian language. Additional money was provided for training the trainers, and, ultimately, for the delivery of the courses. GB Resources became involved in the program by actively administering and evaluating program development throughout participating countries.

IMPLEMENTATION

Following a review of the original program developed by American Express, the tourism modules of Mirror Mirror were adapted to meet the needs of specific areas. Mirror Mirror needed to suit the Hungarian people and the current economic climate of a restructuring economy. In customizing the program, meditation techniques were replaced with less struc-

An interactive customer service training workshop.

tured activities such as role-playing. Role-playing helped participants retain the new information being presented to them in a non-intimidating manner. The Hungarian training program also placed emphasis on explaining the importance of each individual's role in the travel and tourism industry, while emphasizing the interdependence of all tourism sectors as a whole.

After the two-day program was tested in several pilot courses, feedback from both front line and management participants confirmed that the above-mentioned changes were necessary. In 1994, Mirror Mirror was launched in Hungary, in cooperation with the Hungarian Hotel Association. Over two days, the course taught the basics of customer satisfaction to groups of 15 to 20 participants from various front line positions in hotels and travel agency offices.

The modules within the program incorporated the following topics:

What is Tourism?

- recognizing the importance of tourism;
- understanding what tourists need and expect;
- introducing the concept of customer choice, the importance of giving value for money, and competition on a local, regional, and international level;
- defining the role of a service provider.

Customers and Service Providers

- knowing how to be a service provider and an ambassador for the country;
- recognizing the importance of presenting a professional, willing, and friendly image of service;
- understanding customer relationships;
- identifying advantages to the service provider in achieving a win-win situation;
- realizing the benefits and risks of being part of a service chain.

Observation and Feedback

- What is effective observation?
- constructive feedback.

Creating First Impressions

- realizing the importance of the initial contact in forming first impressions in customers' minds;
- showing how positive experiences, through the use of verbal and non-verbal skills, can create satisfied customers;
- defining and demonstrating the impact of positive and negative impressions on the customer and the service provider;
- practising how to observe and give useful feedback to others.

Communicating with the Customer

- practising the core skills involved in establishing the customer's needs;
- highlighting the core skills of questioning, listening, summarizing, and building rapport.

Providing the Service

- stressing the importance of giving clear information and guidance to the customer, of seeing the problem through, and of being realistic and delivering what you promise;
- recognizing the importance of body language, the use of positive words, handling emotion effectively, and of leading and pacing the customer.

Customer Service—A Challenge to Our Personality

While language skills have a bearing on the ability to deliver professional service, it is the service provider's attitude, both to customers and to him or herself, which is important. It is possible to deliver exemplary customer care without necessarily being able to speak a word of the visitor's language. What we say is nowhere near as important as how we say it! This topic area explains how to overcome personal barriers to being professional and successful, and how to develop a professional attitude and facilitate personal growth.

Evaluating Progress

The evaluation component forms the end of the formal learning segment and provides the participants with an opportunity to:

- review, assess, and react to what they have experienced;
- plan how to brief their supervisors;
- evaluate their progress in implementing actions later that will lead to improved customer service;
- partake in a personal planning session wherein participants consider and record what specific actions or changes they will make in the action plan; and
- complete a brief evaluation, to provide feedback to trainers/designers on the value of the content, the style of delivery, and their initial feelings about the course.

The program was an immediate success and word spread quickly. The material was specifically designed for two- and three-star hotels; however, four- and five-star hotels also made inquiries into the program. Sadly, it was not possible to reach all of the two-star hotels as management at these establishments "couldn't see the point of training front line staff because they only leave!"

Since those early days, Mirror Mirror has evolved and expanded into four distinct versions. It is now better able to meet particular training needs by providing a variety of training sessions, outlined below.

Two-Day Travel & Tourism

This two-day course concentrates on the importance of the participant's role in the travel and tourism industry. It also emphasizes the interdependence of the various sectors within the tourism industry. By incorporating the concept of teamwork, participants build on strong group dynamics over the two-day period. The course is ideally suited for businesses wanting to improve group dynamics and best accomplished when the entire staff is enrolled in a group session.

One-Day Travel & Tourism

Designed for regions where the travel and tourism industry is well established, this course provides a consolidated overview of the modules covered in the Two-Day Travel & Tourism course. Teamwork is emphasized less, making this version more appropriate for a mixed audience. This one-day course is also effective for establishments where management is unwilling, or unable, to release staff for more than a day.

One-Day Retail

The retail course is delivered in a shopping mall instead of in a hotel environment. Since shopping is a major component of most visitors' holidays, this course targets an important sector of the travel and tourism industry often overlooked. Course content continues to focus on interpersonal skills, but also works to improve the overall image of a professional skilled workforce.

One-Day English Language

This course was developed at the request of organizations that are focussed on inbound tourism. It provides a module on "cultural differences" as well as "words and phrases to avoid."

In addition to the One-Day English Language course, a number of clients have specifically requested versions to suit their clientele. Many modules have been developed for airlines. Mirror Mirror has even been employed by a major international accounting firm to teach their information technology personnel to be "nicer" to their internal customers!

Following the success of the Hungarian version, the American Express Foundation provided funds to launch Mirror Mirror in Romania, the Czech Republic, Poland, and Croatia—all in local languages. A Russian language version is also available.

Trainers

Many trainers hired to teach the tailored modules for Mirror Mirror courses did not have previous lecturing experience. It was felt that trainers with industry experience in travel and tourism, and good presentation skills, were best suited for the job. Just hearing someone deliver the material was not what course participants needed. Trainers who could empathize and work "with" the participants were sought after. This trainer selection policy has proven effective, as presenters have consistently received exceptionally high scores on course evaluations.

Monitoring

To ensure that the course content and delivery are properly monitored and updated, all course evaluation forms are sent to GB Resources' head office, within a week of program delivery. By analyzing trends, course content can be fine tuned, particularly in matters of cultural difference. The trainer's performance is also carefully monitored, with managers from GB Resources making regular visits to course venues and consulting with clients before and after delivery.

As for the countries that were the earliest recipients of Mirror Mirror, continued funding from American Express has enabled follow-up investigations. Report findings indicate that many tourism sectors are relying less on subsidies and moving to full commercial entities. This is particularly the case where management view staff more as an asset than a liability.

A common pattern throughout Central and Eastern Europe has been that of major multinational companies investing in staff development. Local companies have only recently accepted this wisdom. It is hoped that companies will be convinced that investing in training is worthwhile when they see the financial benefits in their bottom line.

RESULTS

By the end of 1998, over 2 500 front line staff in seven countries had participated in the Mirror Mirror program. Numerous major hotel chains have adopted the course as part of their annual training programs, and many former participants have requested places on future courses "because they enjoyed it so much."

Above all, it is the comments of the participants that provide the most important yardstick of Mirror Mirror's success:

"It is so important to think in a positive, guest-centred way."

"Now I can see the situation from the guest's point of view."

"The attitude of the trainers was super and they helped me to gain more confidence."

"The course was important because it dealt with developing communication skills, which is what our job depends on."

As part of GB Resources' policy of continuous development, a telephone version of Mirror Mirror called Hallo, Hallo has been piloted. This builds on the interpersonal skills content, and recognizes the importance of the telephone as a work tool for travel and tourism organizations. First impressions, active listening, and conflict resolution are just some of the subject areas covered.

Future Developments

Peter Foley, a United States Peace Corps volunteer working in Ukraine, requested that Alan Godsave, now Regional Director of the Central European Countries Travel Association (CECTA), pay a visit to Yalta. With experience in overseeing course delivery in Central and Eastern European countries, GB Resources will be advising on the set-up of a Mirror Mirror Program for the Crimea Tourist Region. For cost and administrative reasons, some changes to course format are advised, so appointees of the Crimean Tourist Development Council (CTDC) can successfully deliver the program. These changes will address the lack of "hands-on" trade industry experience of appointees. Appointees will receive train-the-trainer sessions and some course elements will be redesigned so a single trainer can run the course.

Unlike in the original Mirror Mirror, greater reliance will be needed on slides and workbooks to reinforce the course message to participants. When it became apparent that the Crimea needed destination marketing training, this element was incorporated into the proposal through a series of lectures for tourism managers. It is proposed that these lectures will be delivered during the consultant's visits to oversee the administration of Mirror Mirror.

At the time of writing, final approval of the program is awaited from American Express in Moscow. It is hoped that this will be forthcoming soon, since the benefits to both parties, the Crimean Tourism Industry and the sponsors, would be considerable in this important re-emerging destination.

WTTC HUMAN RESOURCE CENTRE COMMENT

For the countries of Central and Eastern Europe to succeed in restructuring their vital tourism industries, service level standards needed to be addressed. With fewer travelling restrictions, tourists now have access to the former Central and Eastern bloc countries. As such, tourism is now playing a significant role in the restructuring of these economies. With the increased competition for the tourist dollar, countries need to at least meet, if not exceed, the service expectations of visitors. Mirror Mirror illustrates the need to culturally adapt training programs to reflect regional needs, while promoting international standards of quality in guest services.

KEY TERMS

interpersonal skills training
customer service training
restructuring economies

cultural differences
monitoring
train-the-trainer

 http://home3.americanexpress.com/corp/philanthropy/economic.asp

DISCUSSION QUESTIONS

1. After reviewing the training components of the Mirror Mirror program, list 20 service standards that you think are required by Western travellers.

2. Why do you think the presentation styles for the Mirror Mirror content were modified for effective delivery in the different countries?

3. Explain the benefits to American Express of funding this project.

---

1 The European Union fund was established to aid economic reconstruction in the transitional economies of Central and Eastern Europe.

2 Special mention should be made of Connie Higginson, Vice President of the Amex Foundation in New York, Eddy Buehlmann, then American Express Vice President for Central and Eastern Europe, and his successor Colin Reeve, whose combined support successfully launched the project.

chapter eight

Setting Workplace Standards: Skill Certification, Occupational Standards, Workplace Safety, Risk Management, and Liability Issues

Canada
Coast Hotels & Resorts

Submitted by: Craig Norris-Jones

TRAINING STAFF USING INDUSTRY STANDARDS

... Management at Coast Hotels & Resorts chose national standards as a benchmark in building a service excellence program focussed on establishing chain-wide consistency.

LEARNING OUTCOMES

1. List the three steps in developing occupational standards.
2. Explain two training standards the hotel supervisor must incorporate for certification to be successful.
3. Restate the advantages to both the employer and the employee when staff are nationally certified professionals.

"Now in our third year, we are greeted with the same friendly faces as we arrive at your hotel. It is a terrific 'family' feeling. You are obviously doing a lot right to maintain such a loyal staff in a traditionally 'transient' industry."

Marilyn Barefoot
Squarepeg Inc.

OVERVIEW

Coast Hotels & Resorts is western Canada's largest chain of hotels and resorts, with 22 locations throughout British Columbia (BC) and Alberta. The chain employs approximately 1 900 front line employees. Its company mission is to establish and maintain regional networks of high quality hotels, leading their communities by:

- providing guests superior service by offering the most benefits at the highest value;
- offering a stimulating and rewarding working environment for all employees; and
- achieving a level of profitability that allows the company to continually improve and grow.

With properties located in many smaller communities throughout BC, as well as in urban centres, Coast Hotels & Resorts predominantly services the business traveller. In the smaller communities where Coast Hotels & Resorts are located, there is often no benchmark for service excellence among the competition. Consequently, Coast Hotels & Resorts based its new in-house training programs on nationally approved occupational standards and certification, developed by the Canadian Tourism Human Resource Council (CTHRC).

The CTHRC's national occupational standards are documents describing the skills, knowledge, and attitudes necessary for successful performance in a specific tourism occupation. According to CTHRC research, standards help:

- identify the skills and knowledge needed for a successful career;
- guide the development of education and training;
- assist in the selection, training, and evaluation of staff; and
- improve the quality of a product or service, which in turn generates greater consumer satisfaction.

Through a three-step process, the CTHRC develops standards for people working in Canada's tourism occupations. The first step is to gather input from groups of people currently employed in the occupation (80 percent practitioners, 15 percent supervisors, and 5 percent educators). Industry groups across Canada then validate the drafted standards to ensure that they reflect the realities of the industry. The third step is the actual writing and final validation of the standards, which is coordinated by the CTHRC and its members.

Committed to increasing the professionalism of its workforce, Coast Hotels & Resorts decided that the best way to consistently meet business travellers' high service expectations was by training all staff in programs developed for industry—by industry.

IMPLEMENTATION

As early as 1991, Coast Hotels & Resorts supported the concept of national standards and certification for hotel front line employees. At that time, Coast Hotels & Resorts donated money towards establishing national standards for the Canadian hospitality industry. The hotel also contributed many hours of staff time so employees and supervisors could provide input into the national process of developing standards.

All front line staff in the following professions at Coast Hotels & Resorts would be certified:

- food and beverage server
- front desk agent
- housekeeping/room attendant
- reservations sales agent
- bartender.

Occupational certification was also provided for supervisors and department heads in the area of their competence. Supervisors and department heads attended train-the-trainer seminars in Vancouver during the fall of 1996, to acquire the skills to coach their staff in the self-study process leading to professional certification. During the train-the-trainer seminars, department heads received a workbook with guides for coaching staff in-house.

Initially, occupational certification was implemented over an eight-month period at all Coast Hotels & Resorts located in BC. Subsequently, all Alberta Coast properties began certification in 1998. The BC initiative was first announced at a press conference at the hotel's annual hotel conference. Shortly thereafter, representatives from the provincial Tourism Education Council (TEC) visited all Coast properties in BC. During this time, department heads met to cover the administration procedures of certification. General staff attended a promotional session to learn about certification and the in-house training sessions soon to be initiated at all Coast Hotels & Resorts properties.

With self-directed materials from the CTHRC, Coast Hotels & Resorts launched occupational certification in October 1995. Between October 1995 and May 1996, all supervisors received a two-day train-the-trainer session. Following train-the-trainer sessions, supervisors were placed in a "coaching" role to work with department staff through the certification process. Registrations from all departments began gradually after each train-the-trainer session and have since grown steadily. New employees hired since 1996 have been required to enrol and successfully complete the national exam prior to becoming regular employees. Once an employee is professionally certified, Coast Hotels & Resorts reimburses the employee the cost of certification.

Achieving national certification is accomplished in three steps:

1. **National Exam**—Candidates write a multiple choice exam designed to test their knowledge of requirements found in the national occupational standards for their profession.

2. **Performance Review**—The performance review ensures that employees are able to demonstrate on-the-job the skills, knowledge, and attitudes described in the national occupational standards. The candidate benefits when his or her supervisor assists in the review and the demonstration of these skills.

3. **Industry Evaluation**—Once a candidate has passed the exam and successfully completed the performance review, a trained, certified evaluator assesses the skills and knowledge of the candidate on-the-job.

    *   A candidate must fulfil the work experience criteria set out by the TEC in their province or territory.

    *   There is a fee associated with registering for professional certification.

    *   Successful candidates receive a national certificate and gold lapel pin.

    Costs for incorporating national certification for Coast Hotels & Resorts include in-house trainers' travel expenses to Vancouver for train-the-trainer sessions. (Mileage is calculated at $0.25 per kilometre or flight costs.) Accommodation costs are based on Coast Hotels & Resorts' in-house rate per night for two nights per trainer at $50. Each trainer also receives a $25 per diem. Certification registration is $150 per employee.

RESULTS

Coast Hotels & Resorts' first certified employee registered in October 1995 and completed the process in approximately five months. As of January 2001, 450 hotel employees are registered in six occupations, and a total of 267 have completed the certification process. Since implementing the program, there is an improved atmosphere of caring and well-being among staff. Other benefits include:

*   recognition as the most financially improved company within Coast Hotels & Resort's parent company (Okabe)

*   better market performance

*   higher staff morale.

    Coast Hotels & Resorts recognizes that both management and its labour counterparts (union representatives) should be credited with keeping the interest in certification alive and the program successful by acknowledging the needs and challenges confronting hotel employees. This partnership between union and management—different from traditional hotel business hierarchies—is maintained.

WTTC HUMAN RESOURCE CENTRE COMMENT

Occupational certification is an industry-developed and driven process that helps employers assess employee skill and knowledge levels, while providing employees with motivation and recognition. Starting a certification program can make a hotel a better place to work, but time, partnerships, and management commitment are necessary to sustain long-term success. Coast Hotels & Resorts' quality of service is enhanced through training and professional certification. With benefits such as improved customer service, reduced employee turnover, greater morale and motivation, greater profits, and a knowledgeable, professional staff which is nationally recognized, we see that Coast Hotels & Resorts made a wise investment.

KEY TERMS

occupational standards

benchmark

train-the-trainer

peer training

assessment

Tourism Education Council (TEC)

coaching

self-study

industry evaluation

performance review

national certification

 www.coasthotels.com/WHC/default.asp

DISCUSSION QUESTIONS

1. Some of the benefits to employees who achieve national certification are:

   • greater work satisfaction

   • improved chances for advancement

   • mobility throughout the tourism industry

   • increased proficiency in a chosen occupation

   • greater job security.

   Choose a sector (other than accommodation or food and beverage) and explain what each of the above five advantages means to you personally.

2. What are the benefits to the tourism industry of having tourism professionals with credentials recognized throughout the Canadian tourism industry?

3. As a food and beverage supervisor, what tasks do you think the role of coaching entails?

Mexico
The Mexican Ministry of Tourism

Submitted by: Loris Estefan Chaul

NATIONAL CRUSADE FOR QUALITY AND EXCELLENCE IN TOURISM SERVICES

… All levels of Mexico's government have worked together to create a training culture for the tourism industry by developing training programs for the government, the educational institutions, business, labour, and the community.

LEARNING OUTCOMES

1. Recognize the value in customizing programs to meet the specific needs of an audience.
2. Identify the various training programs within Mexico's tourism training system.
3. Explain why a campaign that features the benefits of providing quality tourism service is of national importance to the government, the educational institutions, business, labour, and the community.

OVERVIEW

The Mexican Ministry of Tourism (SECTUR) has developed a program aimed at improving the quality of its visitor services. The training program educates leaders in tourist enterprises, the academic sector, and the community at large on the importance of providing quality tourism services.

The training program is called the National Crusade for Quality and Excellence in Tourism Services (National Crusade). It is unique in that it looks at the needs of Mexico's five key tourism sectors (government, community, business, labour, and educational environments) and customizes content and delivery to address the specific needs within each sector.

The program is a joint effort between federal, state, and municipal governments. First introduced in September 1998 by the former Secretary of Tourism Oscar Espinosa Villarreal, the program follows the policies of the National Development Plan 1995–2000. The program further seeks to consolidate the National Strategy that was put into action by former President Ernesto Zedillo.

Key objectives of the National Crusade program are to:

- create awareness in the industrial sector of the need to adopt specific safety measures;
- promote the hygienic handling of food, especially by tourist establishments;
- educate concessionaires and transportation authorities on the need to improve customer service through training;
- encourage tourism business leaders to adopt "best practices" used by leading countries in tourism; and
- set standards and procedural policies aligned with the market forces which transcend the standard six-year government term.

Much like a train-the-trainer program, the National Crusade program is the catalyst for a chain reaction. It sets off a chain of awareness to increase the general understanding of the economic benefits of tourism to local economies, and to Mexico as a whole.

Although each of the programs which make up the National Crusade vary in content and objectives, all are directly linked to five principles of total quality:

1. Quality means fulfilling and surpassing the tourist expectation.
2. The tourist measures quality. Quality is measured by satisfaction, not by self-gratification or self-appraisal.
3. Total quality means fulfilling tourist expectations 100 percent of the time.

The Mexican Ministry of Tourism (SECTUR)

A National Crusade work session in progress.

4. Quality is achieved through creating specific projects for improvement, and by designing prevention programs when necessary.

5. A commitment by all involved in the tourism industry is necessary to achieve excellence and quality.

IMPLEMENTATION

The five distinct sectors that the National Crusade targets are government institutions, educational/academic institutions, the private business sector, the labour sector, and the community. To date, 11 customized programs have been delivered to these various audiences. Examples of some of the programs, by sector, are described below.

Sector: Government Institutions

Audience: Immigration and Customs officials

Program: Video Conference for Contact Personnel

Video Conference for Contact Personnel

To better prepare immigration and customs officials, a training course was designed for those in direct contact with international visitors. The course (which was not mandatory) was delivered in a video conference format and was aired—simultaneously throughout the country—during morning work hours. The four-hour video conference was based on the five principles of total quality.

A certified professional in total quality hosted the conference, which aired in over 50 locations. Manuals were delivered in advance to all locations where the conference would air. The course structure followed the outline set forth in the manuals. Delivery was interactive in that the trainers and participants engaged in small group discussions and question/answer periods.

Between 1998 and 2000, over 1 400 immigration officers, customs officials, and workers from municipal and state tourism departments participated in the course. Conferences were promoted through Immigration and Customs Offices, which were notified of the event through formal invitations. These offices advertised the conference to employees and to State Tourism officials and their personnel. The training department of the Treasury Ministry, which has special classrooms located throughout the country, monitored the conference transmission.

Sector:	Educational/Academic Institutions
Audience:	University and intermediate schoolteachers and students
Programs:	Teacher Training—University Level
	Teacher Training—Intermediate Level
	Youth Seminars on Total Quality

Teacher Training

Training courses stressing the importance of total quality in tourism education are delivered to schoolteachers in both intermediate schools and universities throughout Mexico. Courses are delivered to groups of 25 to 30 schoolteachers over a period of five days. Each course averages 40 hours of instruction.

The seminars are designed by professionals in tourism and taught by certified teachers. Upon completing courses, participants receive an official diploma and return to their respective institutions to train colleagues, thereby generating a multiplier effect. Although teachers may increase their earning potential by acquiring the diploma, the purpose of the course is to give teachers the training skills necessary to educate students and colleagues throughout the country on the importance of providing quality service in tourism.

To date, 586 teachers have graduated from the Teacher Training programs. Sixteen courses were held at the intermediate level and 16 at the university level.

The courses are held at schools and universities throughout the country. Participants receive a manual prepared specifically for the course, and content is delivered through presentations, lectures, discussions, role-playing, and group activity in traditional classroom format. Course content for the intermediate and university levels includes:

Intermediate Level (five modules)
- philosophy of total quality within the education sector
- total quality, education, and the tourism sector
- introduction to quality in the tourism services
- leadership
- quality norms/standards.

University Level (five sessions)

- conceptualization of quality
- norms and certification
- tourism tendencies of quality in the 21st century
- quality in tourism teaching
- school business links.

Youth Seminars on Total Quality

Day-long youth seminars are also available to university students. These seminars are held in public auditoriums, convention centres, and in university auditoriums near major tourism destination areas. The content of the youth seminars was designed with input from university students in tourism. The seminars discuss:

- basic concepts of the philosophy of total quality;
- the actual experience of a service provider working with total quality standards in the tourism sector (i.e., hotels); and
- total quality in tourism education.

To date, 25 youth seminars have been held and over 10 000 university students have attended. No formal advertising program exists to promote the courses. Organizers communicate with State Tourism Authorities to report new programs being offered. University and intermediate schools that are located near cities where programs are offered are invited to attend. No formal system of feedback has been designed to monitor courses, but records of registration are kept and there is discussion about follow-up seminars.

Sector: Private Business
Audience: Corporate directors/business owners
Programs: Total Quality Model of Management
              Instructor Training
              Alternative Tourism
              Hygienic Food Handling

A number of programs have been designed for the private sector, including ones for business owners and leaders in tourism companies and corporations.

Total Quality Model of Management

The Total Quality Model of Management targets tourism entrepreneurs. This short session, usually presented during breakfast meetings, introduces business owners and company managers to a management model incorporating all five points of total quality.

The trainer gives a short slide presentation (using PowerPoint) and delivers support activities to further interpret the model. The goal is to clearly define the model. The course is also intended to encourage attending managers to consider restructuring their management styles to incorporate the five points of total quality as presented in the model.

Presentations are organized by State Tourism Authorities, which coordinate groups of 15 to 110 attendees per session. Instructors and consultants leading the sessions are certified professionals.

Program success is reflected in the number of participants who welcome an assessment of their company. Instructors will visit individual businesses to analyze their needs and to help in developing a training program based on the management model.

Instructor Training

A training instructor course targets supervisors, department directors, and training managers who work in private tourism corporations. This 25-hour course aims to improve the quality of employee training, thereby producing more knowledgeable employees. The course offers updates in the latest training techniques and prepares participants to apply these techniques in their day-to-day training activities. The course is delivered over 10 modules. Currently 81 graduates have received an Instructor's Diploma. The program was offered in coordination with the credit card company VISA until 1998.

Alternative Tourism

A 40-hour training course is available to tour operators and service providers. The course introduces methodology and techniques, encouraging operators to offer their guests greater variety. The course is delivered in four specific modules: tourist animation; ecotourism; adventure tourism; and rural and ethnic tourism. To date, eight alternative tourism courses have been held and over 700 people have attended.

Hygienic Food Handling

The Tourism and Health Program (H Award Program) aims to improve hygiene practices and the quality of service throughout Mexico's food and beverage industry. The program targets hotels and restaurants that cater to tourists and to Mexico's general public. Businesses that qualify for the program work with a professional consultant, or receive training directly from a SECTUR professional. Trainers and management work together to address all aspects of food handling within the business. The objective is to upgrade hygienic procedures in food service. Key personnel within the business are also included in the training.

Establishments that successfully complete the entire program may qualify for the H Award certificate. This certificate verifies that the standards of sanitary conditions and food handling meet the rigorous criteria set forth by the program. Interest in this program is increasing. Sixty-six training courses have been completed, resulting in 1 300 trained instructors ready to manage personnel within their own companies.

Sector:	Labour Sector
Audience:	Airport service providers in direct contact with tourists
Programs:	Contact Personnel Training
	Instructor Training

Contact Personnel Training

A three-hour interactive session is offered to airport workers who have direct contact with visitors to Mexico. Such workers include taxi drivers, certified tourist guides, and baggage handlers. The sessions are free and non-mandatory, and help workers deliver better service by incorporating the five basic points of the total quality philosophy.

State Tourism Authorities target appropriate participants by inviting members of associations and unions for airport taxi drivers, baggage handlers, and tour guides to attend. Sessions are offered on a permanent basis and are delivered in classrooms at major airport locations. Presenters use manuals, videos, and group activities to create a positive learning environment.

At the end of the course, attendees receive an official diploma and are asked to complete a feedback form. Comments are analyzed to improve content and delivery in future courses. To date, 181 courses have been delivered to over 5 000 individuals. Of this total, over 1 000 workers were trained at the Mexico City International Airport.

Instructor Training

Within the labour sector, a 30-hour course targets training agents and those involved in human resource management. Sessions focus on educational technologies and the adult learning process. Participants receive training in how to prepare their own in-house materials for future courses focussing on tourism-related topics.

Sector: Community
Audience: Fifth and sixth grade elementary school students
Program: Tourism Culture for Children

Tourism Culture for Children

The Tourism Culture for Children program targets fifth and sixth grade students who live in major tourist destinations. The objective of the program is to share the concept of total quality in tourism services. The program is directed at young children as they are the future workforce for Mexico. Thus far, the program has been delivered in 18 different states throughout Mexico, and is in great demand.

Program content is shared with the young students through an interactive video and booklet and a comic book entitled: *What about the tourist?* The information is presented in classrooms or larger group settings if adequate supervision is available. Classes are two hours or less.

The program runs with the help of State Tourism and Education Authorities. Program materials are issued to state authorities, who distribute the materials to selected schools. Materials then become the property of the schools.

RESULTS

The National Crusade for Quality and Excellence in Tourism Services program has been the main project for Mexico's Department of Development of Tourism Culture for the last three years. The program was fully launched by September 1998.

Content for all eight training programs was developed over a five-year period, under the umbrella of the National Crusade. Throughout this time, specific training needs were identified and documented by researching each sector.

More and more states within Mexico have been requesting that National Crusade courses be delivered in their areas. Many of these areas are not considered major tourism destinations. Some Mexican States (Colima, Nayarit, and Sinaloa) have even launched a smaller version of the program called State Crusades. Limits on both human and financial resources have forced program organizers to prioritize actions in order to provide programs to areas most in need.

The Tourism Minister and other SECTUR officials promote the National Crusade program when attending official reunions, trade meetings, and conferences. Several Latin American countries have expressed interest in developing similar programs. The Ministry holds close relations with numerous countries, and SECTUR offers information and consultation to those interested in the program. With constant requests for more courses, it is hoped that this project will continue despite anticipated changes to the government.

WTTC HUMAN RESOURCE CENTRE COMMENT

Tourism is moving to centre stage in many large-scale national economies. Mexico is using an integrated approach to service quality, creating a "multiplier effect" in the sharing of information. With limited resources available, the combination of a national program profile and a train-the-trainer approach optimizes the development of a national training culture for Mexican tourism.

KEY TERMS

national training culture
train-the-trainer
multiplier effect
service training
awareness

video conference
total quality
customized
workshops
assessment

 **www.mexico-travel.com**

DISCUSSION QUESTIONS

1. Of the many programs offered through the National Crusade, would any be applicable to your tourism community? Explain.

2. Choose one of the sectors discussed in this good practice and brainstorm additional training programs that might improve the quality of tourism services to that sector.

3. What is the importance of each of the five sectors (government, educational institutions, business, labour, and community) to the tourism industry? Explain how they can all work together to improve the quality of tourism services provided to visitors.

Australia
Accor Asia Pacific

Submitted by: Kelly Bennett

PROGRES Success

... Success is achieved by providing on-the-job, computer-based training that leads to an industry-recognized accreditation for front line staff.

LEARNING OUTCOMES

1. Assess the benefits for a company in training staff in the workplace with computer training programs that are nationally accredited.

2. Explain the personal and career benefits to staff when they are trained, one-on-one, by individuals working in the industry.

3. Recognize how the computer-based training platform gives Accor Asia Pacific a competitive edge.

> *The biggest reward for Accor Asia Pacific has been the personal successes of trainees who have completed the PROGRES program.*

OVERVIEW

Accor Asia Pacific (Accor) is the largest and fastest-growing hotel group in the Asia-Pacific region. Its range of properties enables the company to offer accommodation styles and locations to suit every traveller. These accommodation properties include the Sofitel, Novotel, Mercure, Ibis, All Seasons, and Formule 1 brand hotels.

Currently, Accor operates 134 hotels (which amounts to 24 599 rooms) in 15 countries. In western Australia alone, the company has 20 hotels and manages approximately 1 800 employees.

To assist in training employees, the company committed to a working partnership with a registered training provider. In 1997, Accor and Adroit Operations worked together to develop the PROGRES traineeship program. The program is a self-paced on-the-job training system. Graduates achieve a nationally accredited Hospitality Operations Certificate II. The level II training specializes in:

- front office
- food and beverage
- housekeeping
- kitchen attending.

While PROGRES was being developed, Australia's federal government was revising vocational education and training policies. This was in response to poor traineeship results from traditional educational environments. Research showed that many graduates of traditional schools were overlooked in their search for jobs due to their lack of work experience. In short, their technical knowledge and skills were considered to be too general.

Throughout PROGRES training, professionals currently working in the industry, as opposed to classroom lecturers, teach participants on-the-job. Successful trainees learn specific skills and knowledge to do the job, as well as problem-solving skills and industry knowledge to consistently exceed guest expectations.

IMPLEMENTATION

PROGRES was launched in various hotels on the east coast of Australia in early 1997, and then introduced to western Australia later in the same year. The training program is based on Australia's national competency framework. This allows each hotel to accurately measure staff skill levels against national standards, which is necessary in order to offer a national accreditation.

The Smartwork computer system (developed by Adroit Operations) is the tool which delivers the PROGRES training program. Overall, the program is delivered on an individual basis, although some elements, such as the self-paced modules, are delivered in a classroom session. Trainees learn skills on-the-job, in one-to-one situations. For Accor, the individual training program complements its existing training for new staff, which is also delivered one-to-one. The training takes place in such a way that individual skill levels can easily be assessed against both established service levels and the needs of the customer.

Smartwork is operated on an intranet, with the main server located in Adroit Operations' office. Adroit Operations developed the basic program, and with their assistance, Accor tailored the package to suit its company's needs. In most cases, Smartwork was installed on an existing computer in each Accor hotel. However, because trainees must be able to access the system 24 hours a day, every hotel allocated one personal computer for the program and purchased a server to run the system and communicate with Adroit.

Up until January 1998, when the program was running live at each Accor hotel, Adroit Operations oversaw the training for the first wave of system administrators, trainers, and prospective trainees in the Smartwork program. The program was implemented in the company's three hotels in Perth, Australia over a six-month period. Each individual implementation took approximately two months. The start-up process for each system included training on the system, hardware and software installation, and customizing the system to meet each hotel's individual needs.

The only manuals required were initial training manuals on how to use the system, and a detailed guide for the system (one per property). These were all produced by Adroit Operations. The initial system training was also conducted by Adroit Operations, with assistance from Accor's human resource team.

The human resource managers in each Accor hotel are known as enterprise coordinators. There is also a dedicated PROGRES coordinator in the Sydney Office to handle any issues relating to the program and to act as a liaison between Accor and Adroit Operations. Adroit Operations handles any information technology problems. Hardware problems are either outsourced or answered by one of Accor's two information technology managers in western Australia.

The program was initially available to all staff regardless of skill and experience. Now, the program is used primarily for new staff. The program is not mandatory. New employees have three months after they commence to choose to join the program.

Accor has found the program to be useful in assessing employee performance and, because the computer program reflects each hotel's current standards and procedures, Accor uses the program as the "minimum requirement of service" to rate employee performance.

Smartwork is owned by Adroit Operations. Because the program is easily customized, other hospitality companies are using it for similar programs. The program is capable of incorporating photographs, layouts, maps, videos, copies of hotel forms, and any other company or hotel-specific information that may assist in completing the traineeship.

The Smartwork program offers numerous benefits to both the employee and the employer. Program benefits for employees include the following:

- Successful trainees receive a nationally accredited qualification that will assist in building a career within the hospitality industry, as well as help further the trainees' education while at work.

- All training is on-the-job so there is no need to attend external courses.

- Trainees receive credit for skills that meet national competency expectations.

- The program ensures that all on-the-job skills training delivered in hotels is consistent and related to hotel and industry standards, with specific outcomes defined for each skill or competency.

- There is no charge to employees for participating in the program.

- PROGRES trainees are paid at full pay, as opposed to trainee wage rates.

- Managers, supervisors, and trainees are committed to achieving successful outcomes.

- The program accommodates trainees with limited English skills because of its flexibility and Adroit Operations' provision of interpreter services.

Program benefits for the employer include the following:

- There is high morale within each hotel department.

- Skilled employees are able to use problem-solving techniques and understand the reasoning behind policies and procedures, thus ensuring employees have a full understanding of their role and how it relates to the overall success of the hotel.

- The program results in lower staff turnover.

- A discount on payroll tax payments is made for each new trainee who meets the state training authority's eligibility criteria.

PROGRES trainees learn on-the-job and at their own pace, without the structure of semester time frames. Trainees have 12 months to complete the program. High achievers, or those with considerable hospitality experience, have finished the program in less than six months. Hotels do not incur down time, as trainees learn during work time.

During implementation, each hotel is responsible for ensuring that:

- all departmental trainers complete the train-the-trainer program so they are qualified to teach PROGRES trainees;

- at least one senior person achieves Access assessor accreditation, as the assessor is the person responsible for maintaining the integrity of the program and acts in an auditing function; and

- all assessors, trainers, and trainees can competently operate the Smartwork system.

The PROGRES traineeship is available in all Accor properties with more than 100 rooms. In the future, Accor hopes to offer a similar system to the smaller, regional hotels.

RESULTS

Accor credits the program for many improvements in its operations and training. As a direct result of the program:

- Staff better understand the competency levels required to perform specific duties.

- Employee skill level assessments are more accurate and timely.

- Staff complies with exacting hotel service standards and business principles.

- Management realizes the benefits of participating in staff development and training.

- Training content can be easily customized.

New employees who meet the eligibility criteria are able to participate in the PROGRES traineeship. Employees are given 12 months to complete the program. This strategy has resulted in reduced employee turnover as it offers employees an incentive to complete their first (and often difficult) year with a new employer. Trainees report that the benefits far outweigh the option of leaving the company to seek employment elsewhere.

PROGRES encourages staff retention. Trainees are more committed to the organization because they feel they are part of a company that is committed to their personal career development. Trainees also know they are more likely to be considered for internal promotions as they successfully complete the program and develop better qualifications.

Accor fosters a learning culture and demonstrates tangible career rewards for staff remaining committed to the company. The following table lists the trainees to date that have successfully completed the program in each hotel:

	HOUSEKEEPING	FRONT OFFICE	FOOD AND BEVERAGE	KITCHEN
Mercure Hotel Perth	10	5	4	1
Novotel Langley Perth	4	6	3	n/a
Hotel Ibis Perth	14	5	6	1

Accor won the award for "Industry Training—Private Sector" at the Western Australia Tourism Awards. This award recognized its excellence in training through the PROGRES traineeship program.

WTTC Human Resource Centre COMMENT

The computer-based training platform gives Accor a competitive edge. By being able to customize training content, the organization is more flexible and capable of accommodating necessary operational changes even on a day-to-day basis. Accor is perceived as a good employer because it supports employee training and provides career planning and development within the organization.

Company advantages include flexibility, personal mentoring, no training down time for the hotel, and access to important theoretical and practical learning for employees. Alignment with the Australian national qualifications framework ensures portability of credentials, but the hotel's commitment to staff promotion and advancement has ensured reduced employee turnover. Additional benefits include a training tax benefit and an evolved learning culture within the company.

KEY TERMS

traineeship	national standards
on-the-job training	skill competencies
accreditation	staff assessment
computer training software	down time
career development	vocational education

 **www.accor.com.au**

DISCUSSION QUESTIONS

1. Explain how computer-based training can support consistency in an international hotel chain.
2. How does Accor Asia Pacific improve its international competitive edge through this type of training program?
3. How does Accor Asia Pacific use the PROGRES training program to attract and keep a top-quality workforce?

Scotland
Isle of Eriska Hotel

Submitted by: Beppo Buchanan-Smith

IMPROVING QUALITY THROUGH CROSS-TRAINING

… Using national occupational standards and cross-training to build a successful employee culture.

LEARNING OUTCOMES

1. Recognize the key elements of a train-the-trainer system.
2. Outline the benefits of an outside appraisal and assessment process.
3. Describe the design and start-up of an employee appraisal system.

> *"We aim to offer five-star service and facilities within the parameters of a 17-bedroom Scottish country house hotel."*
>
> *Beppo Buchanan-Smith, General Manager*
> *Isle of Eriska Hotel*

OVERVIEW

One of Britain's best and most historic family-owned-and-operated country house hotels is the Isle of Eriska Hotel, located in Argyll, Scotland, on the Isle of Eriska. This country house, originally built in 1884, is located in the centre of the 300-acre island, accessible by a private bridge and a one-and-a-half-kilometre drive. Originally built and used as a private home, the house was purchased by the Buchanan-Smith family in 1973 and was converted to a hotel the following year.

The hotel, featuring 17 ensuite bedrooms and numerous public rooms, has been refurbished four times since opening. Other buildings on the island are used for staff accommodation, maintenance sheds, or leisure attractions. The island itself has been divided into two regions. One region is dedicated to golf, tennis, and other sports, while the remaining acreage is protected as a natural setting, and features wildlife among unspoiled flora and fauna.

Throughout the first 20 years of operation, the Isle of Eriska Hotel was open for seven months each year. During this time, the hotel employed between 15 and 25 employees. In the winter months, only three staff members were retained to work in property maintenance and hotel reservations.

In 1993, the owner decided to operate the hotel on a year-round basis, allowing for a better return on property investment and more year-round work for employees. The hotel thus increased its employment to a total of 35 staff (20 permanent positions and 15 seasonal positions).

At the same time, the hotel hoped to improve its guest service by providing standardized training to all staff. Management decided that staff training could no longer be conducted in an ad hoc manner and worked to develop a formal system of training. Eventually, the Isle of Eriska Hotel would increase both its guest return business and guest length of stay. These increases were due to better staff training, good communication, and valuable support provided for both seasonal and permanent staff.

IMPLEMENTATION

To assist in restructuring the hotel's training system, specialists were occasionally employed to tutor senior management and to aid in developing Eriska's own "in-house" trainers and assessors. Internal changes began with the creation of a Management Board. The Management Board was made up of senior staff members (those responsible for the business in the absence of the owners). Board members used the Scottish Investors In People (IIP) standards to identify weaknesses within the business and to develop systems to strengthen these areas. IIP is a government program that focusses on human resource development for local businesses.

After determining a weakness in internal communications, IIP introduced a simple yet effective system of communication between staff, management, and departments, with no disruption to daily business activity. The Management Board supported the new system and began by conducting weekly meetings with department heads. Information generated at each meeting was compiled and distributed monthly to all departments and top management. Shortly thereafter, communication within the hotel had improved.

In terms of staff progress, it was decided that frequent employee appraisals would be a good way to ensure that employee skills were being improved upon in their respective areas. Thus, all staff members, including management, began receiving appraisals each month, normally coinciding with employee pay periods. Offering monthly employee feedback further supported the new communications system, and often helped to identify problems early. During each employee assessment, training requirements were reviewed and staff attitude, activity on the job, and teamwork abilities were discussed. Department heads led the discussions, with the hotel owner present at each appraisal. Staff appreciated their individual appraisal sessions, and managers better understood the importance of setting aside time for consistent and focussed feedback.

In terms of internal training, changes were initially complicated. The hotel chose to follow the Vocational Qualification structure, which helps a business retrain key management and then trains them to train others within the business. A considerable amount of work was necessary to certify enough in-house trainers and assessors. Once enough trainers were on hand, it became possible to delegate duties.

A system was designed whereby each department conducted four weekly meetings, in which training requirements were identified and discussed. A fifth meeting was devoted to determining appropriate rewards for achievement. The Isle of Eriska Hotel presently has five different trainers on property, one in each department. All department heads participate in outside trainer courses as required.

Today, employees are hired as general staff and receive training in all departments. This system of cross-training provides each employee with an understanding of the entire hotel, and builds personal confidence about their own role within the business. For management, it offers flexibility in moving staff to areas of need throughout the operating season. This system also creates a strong multi-task foundation, enabling the hotel to operate in a self-sufficient manner.

As hotel staff began to understand how training made a difference in the overall business, and to their personal development, they saw that systematic training in all departments was key to the success of the hotel. Staff quickly rallied behind the initiative and gave their full support.

By using a formal system of cross-training, management is more confident that new employees understand their individual roles. This creates an atmosphere where employees feel important and part of a team. Cross-training also helped trainers to match individual strengths to tasks at hand, and to identify areas of weaknesses. By empowering staff and by giving them a voice, the number of employee suggestions increased. Hotel management was confident that employees shared the business's goals.

The Isle of Eriska Hotel was fortunate to have the support and acknowledgement of IIP, which helped to identify challenges and to design systems for change. The hotel's progress was further assessed by IIP through the use of an external benchmark (an example outside of the business). The hotel also made use of a local enterprise company (a government agency responsible for encouraging local business). This company paid for the necessary support during the hotel's reorganization of its training programs. This helped the hotel meet its training requirements quickly and efficiently.

The Isle of Eriska Hotel is now open for approximately 11 months of the year. It employs both seasonal and permanent staff and incorporates a variety of individual training plans to meet staff members' needs. The hotel is a registered Vocational Qualification Centre (where employees learn as they work, and receive accreditation for their efforts). The hotel adopted this system as a form of incentive training, enabling staff to achieve vocational qualification for their achievements. Rewards ensure that trainees respect their superiors and show that management are devoted to an individual's improvement.

> *A system of self-policing allows for individual self-evaluation, helps trainers to identify and encourage employee focus in working towards vocational awards, and includes financial incentive.*

RESULTS

After increasing the hotel's operational season, the owners' hands-on approach has diversified and a more formal attitude has been adopted. However, by continuing to follow the established business and training guidelines, the business has grown successfully without affecting the atmosphere of the property.

Over the last 10 years (1990 to 2000), the hotel has doubled its occupancy, and last year it welcomed more guests than ever before.

Since 1997, the hotel's annual occupancy has increased approximately seven percent. Throughout this period, the "return-guest ratio" to new business has remained constant at 60 percent. The "average stay-time" of guests also increased to three days. These figures show that customers value the product the hotel offers. Both staff and management believe that by working together the hotel offers the guest a consistently high quality experience.

For a service business, it is essential that employees learn and grow during their employment. With a staff-to-guest ratio of one-to-one, each staff member understands that the business survives because of the customers. From management's standpoint, the staff is an intricate part of the guest's experience. It is management's job to match the three key parts of the puzzle—the place, the personnel, the customer—and make sure they are in harmony.

WTTC HUMAN RESOURCE CENTRE COMMENT

The Isle of Eriska Hotel is achieving its quality objectives through the development of a comprehensive standards-based cross-training structure. This has helped to establish a high level of self-sufficiency within the business. Using the external benchmarking of IIP, the hotel provides incentive training and individual attention to staff needs. Through a focussed and coordinated training plan, the Isle of Eriska Hotel has achieved a high level of staff productivity, consistency in quality guest service, and increased business.

KEY TERMS

cross-training	train-the-trainer
vocational qualifications	assessment
incentives	Investors In People
communication	multi-task
accreditation	occupational standards
benchmark	

 **www.eriska-hotel.co.uk**

DISCUSSION QUESTIONS

1. What are the three areas which the Isle of Eriska Hotel chose to concentrate on in restructuring their human resources plan? How do they interconnect?

2. What kind of set-up for staff appraisals did the Isle of Eriska use? How might this be positive/negative?

3. What other kinds of incentive programs might this family-owned-and-operated business consider?

Ireland
CERT—The State Tourism Training Agency

Submitted by: Ethna Murphy

STATEWIDE TOURISM TRAINING THAT WORKS

… Ireland's state training agency develops comprehensive tourism training programs to increase industry's competitive position.

LEARNING OUTCOMES

1. List the four qualities of CERT's training programs.
2. Recognize the importance of combined efforts between state training agencies and industry training programs.
3. Recognize the importance of continued training for tourism professionals.

> *"To foster the attainment of world-class service in tourism and hospitality through building capability. We will achieve this by developing and providing high quality training and consulting support services based on a commitment to adopting and promoting principles of best practice."*
>
> *Mission Statement*
> *CERT*

OVERVIEW

Ireland's State Tourism Training Agency (CERT) has been working to create partnerships between state training agencies and tourism industry training programs since 1963. CERT was originally established to help in developing a highly skilled tourism workforce. This objective is met partly through ensuring that high operational standards exist throughout the industry. For Ireland's travel and tourism industry to be internationally competitive, employers must have access to a labour pool of qualified staff who are able to anticipate and meet the needs of the 21st-century traveller.

As Ireland's state tourism training agency, CERT offers training designed to build a workforce with strong technical skills and the ability to succeed in management. Training is typically: needs driven, in order to meet the group's training needs and job requirements; flexible, to accommodate full- and part-time staff; developed in partnership with industry; and accountable through national certification.

To succeed in training, CERT's range of services includes:

- identifying employment, training needs, and future development needed for national training structures and programs;
- recruitment, training, and formal education in schools;
- assistance in career planning;
- on-the-job and specialist training services to existing industry personnel and proprietors;
- advisory and business development services to industry; and
- training for unemployed people to enhance their prospects of finding employment.

Among CERT's success stories is its Customer and Information Skills Training Program for Tourism Advisers. This training certificate program is a six-month part-time course designed to upgrade the professional skills of tourism advisers and their knowledge of Ireland's tourism industry. The program is also fully adaptable to meet the needs of other target groups. These markets include new entrants to the industry, and seasonal personnel in tourist information offices and centres, heritage centres, and attractions.

IMPLEMENTATION

CERT's Customer and Information Skills Training Program for Tourism Advisers was created in 1989 at the request of Bord Failte (the marketing board for Ireland) and the regional tourism organizations. A working party consisting of a CERT representative, tourism organizations, and potential participants developed a training program, delivery mechanisms, and resource materials. The program design was based on the training needs identified and recorded by the working party.

CERT and Bord Failte supplied the resources to develop the pilot program for southern Ireland. The International Fund for Ireland later supplied additional funding. At this point, the Northern Ireland Tourist Board (NITB) participated in the program.

As tourism advisers are competent in at least one major foreign language, this program did not address the issue of language development.

Training is spread over a six-month period. Program delivery is varied and each portion builds upon the other. The program delivers training in four specific ways:

- **On-the-job training**—A workbook outlines on-the-job training procedures. Supervisors verify the progress of participants.
- **Off-the-job seminars**—Up to three 3-day seminars take place during the program to prepare participants for their self-study and assist them in using the program workbook.
- **Distance learning/self-study**—Participants are to devote 6-8 hours per week to distance learning. Employers are expected to allocate this study time to participants as part of their working week.
- **Familiarization field trips**—The field trip themes and destinations are directly linked to the off-the-job seminar topics. Field trips are planned around national, regional, and local tourism attractions. Regional and local familiarization trips are integral components of the self-study workbook. A one-week intensive regional familiarization trip is required and organized with a specific regional tourist organization and a registered tour guide.

CERT staff supplied trainers and speakers for the integrated program, which is divided into three distinct categories:

Tourism skills and knowledge (36 hours)

Profiling tourism, Ireland as a tourism destination, and cultural studies in Ireland.

Tourism retail, information, and service skills (64 hours)

Teaching skills in sales, promotion, merchandising, information, and office procedures, as well as setting and monitoring standards in a tourist information office.

Quality and customer orientation in tourism (32 hours)

Improving skills in customer welfare, customer service skills, and general communication.

Successful completion of a written assessment, assigned project work, and industry assessment leads to national certification. Staff supervisors must also complete a standard industry experience assessment report form. The form has a marking structure and evaluates the employee's professionalism/work preparation, technical skills, standard of finished product, related knowledge, and interpersonal skills.

RESULTS

The Customer and Information Skills Training Program for Tourism Advisers was evaluated through two surveys. Overall, participants and employers were very satisfied with the program. Eighty-nine percent of participants felt the program improved their understanding of north-south relations in Ireland and fostered an informal network of friendships with colleagues across the border. Employers noted that staff were better motivated, more knowledgeable about the country as a whole, had greater interpersonal contact between offices, and improved their merchandising and sales skills.

By surveying program participants, CERT developed an advanced program for supervisors who identified training needs in:

- staff training and induction
- recruitment and selection skills
- retail sales and merchandising skills
- marketing skills.

To date, this new program has trained 60 supervisors.

Statistics show remarkable growth in Ireland's tourism industry. Visitor numbers, investment, growth in output, and employment are all on the rise. In 2000, employment in tourism industries is estimated at 180 000.

Through programs like the Customer and Information Skills Training Program for Tourism Advisers, CERT will build a qualified workforce capable of meeting international standards.

WTTC HUMAN RESOURCE CENTRE COMMENT

CERT's working relationship with industry is an example for any country wanting to establish a tourism training agency. Limited funds need to be maximized through cooperation and partnerships. CERT's investment in training has paid off through its successful placement of graduates, reports of employer satisfaction, and development of new programs to meet the needs of industry and employees.

At the 1999 conference Tourist Office 2000, Bord Failte invited CERT to speak to delegates about servicing the visitor. CERT's message stressed investing training in front line staff. As its research has shown, customer levels of satisfaction or dissatisfaction will continue to be influenced by the expertise of staff and staff relationships. CERT's training challenge is how to develop these skills through participation in training programs. To create a dynamic organization, one must establish a business environment that empowers employees to provide a quality product or service tailored to customer satisfaction.

KEY TERMS

training agency   familiarization field trips
national certification   professional development
distance learning   career planning

 **www.cert.ie**

DISCUSSION QUESTIONS

1. It is important for tourist information staff to develop friendships with colleagues across provincial and state borders, in neighbouring cities, and in other centres in the same city. Explain the benefit of these alliances and the impact they have on the staff members, and on the visitors.

2. Other than familiarization trips, what are ways to teach participants about the geography, history, and culture of a country?

3. How might you motivate staff to complete training programs such as this?

United States
The International Ecotourism Society

Submitted by: Megan Epler Wood

EVALUATING ECOTOURISM GUIDELINES FOR NATURE TOUR OPERATORS

… Guidelines have been developed to ensure that ecotourism operators are achieving guest expectations, and that ecological standards are consistently applied and monitored.

LEARNING OUTCOMES

1. Evaluate why it is important for ecotourism businesses to have established guidelines.
2. Analyze goals, objectives, and methods of study in developing ecotourism guidelines.
3. Recognize why independent evaluation by a neutral source is essential for programs to have credibility in certification.

OVERVIEW

The International Ecotourism Society (TIES) is an international membership organization dedicated to sharing knowledge and distributing information about ecotourism. Its 1 700 members come from over 55 different professions and live in more than 100 different countries.

TIES defines ecotourism as "responsible travel to natural areas that conserves the environment and sustains the well-being of local people." Since 1991, TIES has been involved in ecotourism education and training programs, and it is one of the first institutions in the world to offer ecotourism-accredited training in the field.

In 1993, a group of conservationists, tour operators, and academics drafted a set of performance standards for the nature-based tourism industry. The document, called *Ecotourism Guidelines for Nature Tour Operators,* was created in response to the growth of ecotourism. The growth in ecotourism fuelled the debate about a need for ethical standards in fragile ecosystems. *Ecotourism Guidelines for Nature Tour Operators* provided guidelines on: what should be required of nature tour operators; how ecotourism-related services should be delivered; what objectives ecotourism services should have; and who should benefit from ecotourism.

TIES *Ecotourism Guidelines for Nature Tour Operators*:

- Prepare travellers, before departure, to minimize their negative impact while visiting sensitive environments and cultures.

- Prepare travellers for each encounter with local cultures and with native animals and plants.

- Minimize visitor impact on the environment by offering literature and briefings, by leading through example, and by taking corrective actions.

- Use adequate leadership and maintain small parties to ensure minimum group impact on destinations. Avoid areas that are undermanaged and overvisited.

- Ensure managers, staff members, and contract employees know and participate in all aspects of company policy to prevent impact on the environment and local cultures.

- Give managers, staff, and contract employees access to programs that will upgrade their ability to communicate with and manage clients in sensitive natural and cultural settings.

- Be a contributor to the conservation of the regions being visited.

- Provide competitive, local employment in all aspects of business operations.

- Offer site-sensitive accommodations that are not wasteful of local resources or destructive to the environment and that provide ample opportunity for learning about the environment and for sensitive interchange with local communities.

Ecotourism Guidelines for Nature Tour Operators was the first set of international guidelines developed for the ecotourism industry that focussed on practical steps for running operations. Following the development of these operational standards, TIES launched a pilot initiative with the Ecuadorian Ecotourism Association (ASEC). The project, called Green Evaluations, was initiated in 1995, and tested how well ecotourism operators in Ecuador were meeting the standards.

IMPLEMENTATION

Ecotourism Guidelines for Nature Tour Operators

The approach used to create *Ecotourism Guidelines for Nature Tour Operators* served as an example for developing future standards, or rules, in delivering a true ecotourism product. In fact, the process for creating these early guidelines set the framework for all future guideline-setting work by the society.

Research began by uncovering "best practices" (examples of good things) that had already been happening within the ecotourism industry. This research was collected by surveying operators in the industry, non-governmental organizations (NGOs), travel departments, and ecotourism conference participants. Research also included input from consumers of ecotourism products. The surveys were compiled and presented to three focus groups, which included representatives from the ecotourism industry, the academic community, and conservation organizations.

The focus groups took place in San Francisco, California; Washington, DC; and San José, Costa Rica. TIES's executive director drafted the initial guidelines, which included information collected during the focus group sessions. The results were sent out for review to all participants in the focus group process. A final 20-page document was published and is distributed by The Ecotourism Society (renamed TIES) for a small fee. More than 5 000 copies have been distributed worldwide, in both Spanish and English.

The Green Evaluations

The Green Evaluations program began in Ecuador in 1995, to test if guidelines were being followed. To ensure that evaluations were objective, TIES chose not to be involved in the design of the survey, or in interpreting data. Instead, a request for proposals was sent to academic institutions involved in tourism and recreation research. The request for proposals invited outside companies and institutions to submit a bid for conducting the required research. Ten proposals were received, and Clemson University was selected. Structuring research in this way supports the society's belief that independent evaluations of tour operators by a neutral source should be mandatory if an ecotourism certification program is to have any real credibility.

It was decided that consumers should be surveyed to collect objective information on how well ecotourism operators were meeting standards. Initially, a three-month survey time period was considered; but with input from tour operators in Ecuador, a 12-month survey process was deemed appropriate. Extending the survey time allowed for smaller operators to be included, as they needed more time to fulfil the required number of survey responses. Clemson researchers established a sampling framework, and the principal investigator went to Ecuador to present the study's goals, objectives, and methods to local ecotourism operators. Thirty tour operators agreed to participate.

The primary reason for evaluating Ecuadorian tour operators was to develop and test a consumer evaluation program for nature tour operators based upon TIES guidelines. The specific objectives of this project were to:

- develop a process which evaluates the performance of nature tour operators using TIES's *Ecotourism Guidelines for Nature Tour Operators* in Ecuador;
- provide information that will enable TIES to market *Ecotourism Guidelines for Nature Tour Operators*; and
- implement the consumer evaluation program in Ecuador during a 12-month study period starting in April 1995.

In 1995, there was a border war in Ecuador which negatively impacted tourism numbers. Many operators complained that, after one year, the survey process was still not long enough. It was therefore extended to 15 months, officially ending September 1996. With funding from an international NGO (CARE-Subir), TIES hired an individual to work for ASEC as a local survey administrator. Survey response rates were low, so the local administrator worked with the local operators to increase the number of completed surveys. Each survey was returned in a sealed envelope from the clients, via the operator, to ASEC's survey administrator.

In March of 1996, an independent academic (from State University of New York, Plattsburgh) offered to interview tour operators in Ecuador to see how well the survey process was going. In his report to TIES and Clemson, he discovered that tour operators were not sampling their clients randomly as instructed, and that tour operators were using different techniques to distribute the questionnaire. While one in five clients were to be surveyed randomly, in fact some guides were giving surveys to all clients, while others asked for volunteers. Thus, one of the primary problems with the project was that the survey process lacked consistency.

RESULTS

The results from the surveys showed that Ecuadorian tour operators were largely meeting ecotourism standards:

- Nearly 88 percent of the tourists were receiving good pre-departure information.
- Visitor information and education materials, and briefings on trails, in campsites, and in fragile zones, did take place more than 80 percent of the time.
- More than 80 percent of the operators were using local transportation services.
- More than 70 percent of the operators were using locally-owned restaurants.

Nearly all tour operators seemed to provide enough guides to manage the tour group. These guides appeared to do an excellent job in explaining how to minimize impact on the environment and local cultures, with nearly 80 percent of the guides frequently or always communicating these concerns.

Problem areas surfaced when evaluating local accommodations. Less than 50 percent of the respondents felt that local lodges were providing adequate educational materials, minimizing their waste stream, providing locally-made goods on property, or reflecting local cultural motifs in their architecture. It was also unclear how well contact with local cultures was being managed. It appears that ecotours in Ecuador still minimize contact with local cultures, with less than 20 percent of respondents feeling they were either having contact "quite a bit," or "a lot." However, in over 75 percent of the responses, the travellers judged whatever contact did take place to be unintrusive.

The two key areas where "average" performance was noted were tour operator contributions to conservation and local development. Both were rated as just average over 60 percent of the time. Just under 60 percent of those observed were using guides, food, and craft vendors from local communities.

The Ecuadorian Ministry of Tourism, ASEC, and several Ecuadorian universities have expressed interest in another round of ecotourism evaluations. It was concluded that more surveying needed to be done by survey professionals to ensure quality control in the process. Using students from local academic programs could solve this problem.

Objective evaluations are also needed. The International Ecotourism Society is working with a coalition of NGOs around the world to develop an international sustainable tourism and ecotourism accreditation program to standardize the process of certifying ecotourism. The Green Evaluations program provided valuable information on how to design certification programs. As a result, TIES understands how certification programs need to be designed to be effective, and has shared this information with other groups to encourage consistency. The complete *Ecotourism Guidelines for Nature Tour Operators* and the Green Evaluations study are available on TIES's Web link.

WTTC Human Resource Centre COMMENT

In designing programs to meet the rapidly changing needs of the ecotourism professional, The International Ecotourism Society used a neutral source for evaluation. This approach was essential for the ecotourism certification program to have any credibility. It is generally recognized that program sponsors and funding sources can rarely act completely independently or autonomously.

This good practice illustrates how data can be collected for the benefit of travel suppliers and tour operators in a non-intimidating manner. Feedback is essential for suppliers to get travellers' repeat business, and for operators to be recommended favourably via word of mouth. It is six times more expensive to attract a new customer than it is to retain a current one.

KEY TERMS

ecotourism	ethical standards
nature tour operator	sampling
guidelines	ecosystems
guest expectations	non-governmental organizations (NGOs)
evaluation	request for proposals
accredited training	

 **www.ecotourism.org**

DISCUSSION QUESTIONS

1. Discuss why TIES developed guidelines for running ecotourism operations as the first step in creating certified standards?

2. How useful are the survey results for developing an international code of ethics for all nature tour operators? Explain.

3. As the ASEC local survey administrator, you are given the task of making sure local operators have their clients complete the Green Evaluations survey. What could you tell local operators to convince them that participating in the survey was to their benefit?

Australia
Kingfisher Bay Resort & Village
Submitted by: Alanna Baxter

ECOTRAINING

… Building value and reputation in an ecotourism destination resort by investing in employee environmental knowledge, professionalism, and motivation.

LEARNING OUTCOMES

1. Describe an approach for instilling ecotourism values in employees through education and awareness.
2. Identify a system of laddered training.
3. Note how a company culture may be strengthened through incentive-based professional development programs.

OVERVIEW

Kingfisher Bay Resort & Village is an award-winning development on the Queensland Coast of Australia. It is located on Fraser Island, which is the world's largest sand island and a United Nations–designated World Heritage Site. Kingfisher Bay Resort & Village has been built to strict environmental standards. The resort is a destination for nature study, boating, snorkeling, beachcombing, and bushwalking and protects its natural assets with high environmental management standards.

Kingfisher Bay Resort & Village received Advanced Accreditation status by Australia's National Ecotourism Accreditation Program (NEAP) Committee, which gives assurance that the best ecotourism practice standards are employed. Developed by industry for industry, NEAP identifies genuine ecotourism operators and performs on-site inspections to ensure that the certification criteria are continuously met. Currently, only 13 other Australian resorts have attained advanced accreditation.

The nature-based tourism market is demanding and competitive. Well-educated guests who expect to learn something from their ecotourism experience typify the clientele. They arrive with expectations that resort staff may not be able to handle. For management, it is a challenge to build profitability and reputation, while protecting both the natural environment and resort market share.

Courtesy of Kingfisher Bay Resort–Fraser Island, Queensland, Australia.

The Kingfisher Bay Resort Junior Eco Ranger program is designed to show children how to care about the environment in a fun way.

To ensure resort staff provides guests with a true island experience, management designed a staff training program that focussed on the natural environment. Developed in 1999, the Environmental Activities Program teaches staff what it means to provide a true ecotourism product.

IMPLEMENTATION

All resort employees and new managers begin the training program by enrolling in the eco-induction session. This induction process includes a three-hour training session that explains the key ideas of ecotourism. The training session includes an overview of the history of Kingfisher Bay Resort & Village and the unique geography and topography of Fraser Island.

The eco-induction session:

- improves staff knowledge of ecotourism and Fraser Island;
- reviews staff expectations; and
- provides a basis by which to identify individual competency levels.

Staff members receive a badge upon completing the induction session. This session is the prerequisite to level one of the Environmental Activities Program. Staff is encouraged to continue with the program and successfully complete the next three levels. A red tick on the ecotourism-trained badge indicates each successful level completion. The badge reinforces guiding qualifications, provides an incentive for staff to complete all levels through attending seminars and workshops, and stimulates guest discussion on ecotourism.

Level one training provides employees with the knowledge and presentation skills necessary to deliver at least seven of the 23 different interpretive activities conducted on-site.

Interpretive activities include a bird walk, an interpretive tour, or a night walk. Training is conducted through information sessions and guided activities.

Level two training further develops individual interpretation abilities, knowledge levels, and presentation skills deemed necessary to conduct the majority of all 23 interpretive activities. These activities include both walking tours and static presentations, such as slide shows and guided tours.

Level three training develops competency to deliver guiding services up to level four, whereby the guide is deemed competent to deliver all interpretive programs.

In the Environmental Activities Program, rangers present weekly seminars averaging one hour. Training tools used in the seminars include: videos, whiteboards, overhead projectors, slides, role-playing, nature walks, examples of flora, and audiotapes. Throughout the resort there are approximately 20 qualified trainers from various disciplines. All rangers conducting training have train-the-trainer qualifications (which they obtain through in-house courses), and the majority also have workplace assessor qualifications.

All training is on company time. The program enables employees to develop more flexible skills. By completing additional training and progressing through program levels, staff members are able to fill more roles. For example, if a ranger is absent, a porter who has attained a certain level of competency may host a bird walk. Pay levels are directly related to skill levels. Should employees wish to increase their pay level, they must increase their individual knowledge and proficiency levels.

RESULTS

By receiving basic interpretation skills training in the Environmental Activities Program, staff at Kingfisher Bay Resort & Village appreciate the values of ecotourism. Although higher levels of the program are not compulsory, 98 percent of staff members have attended the eco-induction seminar since January 1999, and 63 percent have continued to further their knowledge by attending the tutorials and seminars offered throughout the program.

Since developing the program, existing rangers have further developed their skills and sought to obtain the highest accreditation. Several key staff members have also completed entry-level training qualifications to become more confident in the delivery of these programs. Both absenteeism and staff turnover have decreased throughout the organization. Furthermore, the ranger department receives good guest comments 98 percent of the time.

WTTC HUMAN RESOURCE CENTRE COMMENT

With so many ecotourism products to choose from, visible accreditation credentials such as logos allow visitors to make more educated travel choices. Kingfisher Bay Resort & Village has outstanding natural attractions that have made the island an important ecotourism destination. The product is dependent on the staff's ability to interpret the natural surroundings to guests. An accessible, modularized training program builds professional competence and morale, and ensures a quality guest experience. This generates both business and environmental sustainability.

KEY TERMS

ecotourism
World Heritage Site
accreditation
incentive

competency levels
interpretation
motivation
nature-based tourism

 **www.kingfisherbay.com**

DISCUSSION QUESTIONS

1. Do you think that individual travel decisions are influenced by certification systems for ecotourism resorts and their employees?

2. What incentives are available for professional development at Kingfisher Bay Resort & Village? Explain how they work.

3. How does the laddered system of employee development at Kingfisher Bay Resort & Village help maintain and support the resort's environmental accreditation?

Canada
Remote Passages Marine Excursions

Submitted by: Kati Martini and Don Travers

WHALEWATCHING AND ECOTOURISM IN-HOUSE STANDARDS FOR BOAT OPERATORS AND GUIDES

… An example of a soft adventure tourism operator minimizing risk to both guests and employees by developing an in-house training program.

LEARNING OUTCOMES

1. Recognize the circumstances where a company must develop its own in-house training system.

2. Evaluate the role of training guidelines, standards, and regulations in limiting risk in an adventure product.

3. Recognize a four-stage training program which builds employee qualifications, skills, and practice while on the job.

OVERVIEW

Remote Passages Marine Excursions is an adventure tour company based out of Tofino, British Columbia (BC). The company offers whalewatching from rigid-hull inflatable boats (RIB's), and operates sea kayaking day trips along the west coast of Vancouver Island and throughout Clayoquot Sound. Remote Passages Marine Excursions (Remote Passages) provides guests with a safe, soft adventure experience, and offers a range of information about the surrounding area's history and culture.

To provide a safe product, the company developed a comprehensive set of in-house standards and operating requirements for RIB's. Federally, only basic standards are in place for the operation of motorized vessels under five tonnes, even though most whalewatching operations use this category of vessels. Currently, no training or commercial licensing requirements exist for operators of vessels under five tonnes.

Several years ago, the Department of Fisheries and Oceans (DFO) and the Canadian Coast Guard began collecting input from industry and researchers who operated coastal wildlife-viewing operations. At the time, a range of topics was covered, with nothing specifically defined. Thus far, the process has evolved to address only guidelines, standards, and potential legislation related to wildlife viewing practices. Driver guide training and proficiencies for watercraft operations were not addressed. Other legislation which affects all operators is the requirement that safety equipment be kept aboard all vessels, as regulated by Canada's Department of Transportation (DoT). It is possible that DoT will eventually address vessel operations. To date, no operator in the area has been approached regarding such a process.

Therefore, it has been the commercial operator's responsibility to develop company standards for training of vessel operators/guides on vessels under five tonnes. Remote Passages took advantage of the provincial standards-based training programs developed for sea kayaking to minimize the risk and liability to its sea kayaking operations. With no guidelines in place for operators/guides on motorized vessels under five tonnes, Remote Passages developed its own standards.

IMPLEMENTATION

Standards and Training

Remote Passages designed its in-house standards and requirements "from scratch." These include:

- a comprehensive set of in-house standards and operating requirements which have been refined over a seven-year period;
- a one-on-one, multi-skilled training program based on senior guides mentoring trainees;
- a training program to ensure new guides develop and maintain professional boat handling skills and customer service skills;
- flexible entry points into the training program to accommodate new employees with various levels of prior experience; and
- curriculum and techniques to interpret the natural and cultural history of the Tofino and Clayoquot Sound areas of BC.

The Remote Passages training program takes two months to complete. A portion of this time is spent in commercial activity. Before entering the training program, an applicant is required to volunteer 30 hours aboard a vessel operating regular commercial trips.

Volunteer status—minimum 30 hours of training

To be accepted as a volunteer, some background in small- or large-vessel handling and basic seamanship and navigational skills are required. The applicant must be keen to learn more about seamanship and navigation and show an interest in improving their knowledge of the marine and surrounding wilderness environment.

Successful volunteers are those who show an aptitude for boat handling and working well with other staff and with the public. A successful *volunteer* is invited to continue in the training program. He or she then works through the additional three levels of Remote Passages' guide-training program, from *on-board trainee* to *assistant guide*, and finally to *first level guide*.

On-board trainee—minimum 70 hours of training

On-board trainees work with a senior guide at all times. At this level of training, employees gain an overall understanding of vessel operations and company touring programs. Trainees learn about engines and instrumentation through hands-on practice and study manuals. Study manuals were developed in-house and incorporate the "Tofino Whale Watch Operators' Guidelines."

On-board trainees must pass a practical, hands-on two-hour exam with their instructor. Senior guides review skills and proficiency before the employee is able to advance to the next level.

Assistant guide—minimum 150 hours

As an assistant lead guide, the employees are in control of their own vessel, but under the on-site direction of a senior guide. Throughout their training, the employee gains:

An understanding of:
- all navigation gear (compass, GPS, radar)
- "rules of the road"
- "vessel procedures" document.

Practice in:
- handling vessels
- emergency procedures involving radio operation, flares, and boat drills.

Continued study of:
- equipment, vessel handling, and local charts
- interpretive programs.

As well, the employee receives VHF licensing.

At this level, the trainee must seek clearance to operate in fog on a case-by-case basis. Assistant guides are promoted to the next level after senior guides are satisfied with their proficiency with equipment and guiding skills, and the guide has completed the mandatory number of hours as assistant.

First level guide—minimum 700 hours

The first level guide continues training in all components of the assistant guide training program. To complete this training section, the employee must show proficiency in:

- the use of navigational equipment;
- identifying waypoints and programming GPS;
- handling vessels in rough seas and fog conditions;
- removing and replacing props at dock and at sea;
- engines, alarms, and servicing water separators (able to address minor problems such as burned-out trim solenoids or non-starting engines);
- reading and understanding local charts;
- identifying weather conditions unsuitable for running a program; and
- knowledge of program materials.

Trainees are also evaluated on their leadership and teamworking abilities. First level guides are required to attend additional training courses and must keep their first aid and cardiopulmonary resuscitation (CPR) certifications current.

Further progress as a guide is based on accumulated sea-hours and a number of other factors, including:

- **Qualifications**—additional related seamanship courses, first aid and CPR, and VHF qualification.
- **Skills**—interpretive skills, mechanical knowledge, ability with navigation equipment, and knowledge of local waters.
- **Other**—ability with languages, understanding of programs, and ability to work with others (especially mentoring new guides).

Certifications

Remote Passages guides are also required to obtain a wilderness first aid "Essentials for Leaders" certificate, which is financed jointly by the company and guide. This requires substantial commitment from both the company and the employee, but has proved a valuable asset in developing confidence and leadership skills in the guiding staff. Because the course is difficult to hold annually in a small location like Tofino, guides are asked to maintain basic first aid and CPR skills until an opportunity to take the course becomes available.

Associations

The Whale Watch Operators Association Northwest (based in Washington State and southern Vancouver Island) hosts a Web site featuring issues relating to whalewatching. A group of local Tofino whalewatching operators reviewed the guidelines featured by the

Northwest Association in 1998. Some useful parallels and distinctions to local practices were cited regarding safety equipment aboard vessels and wildlife viewing.

The Northwest Association's document did address driver training in terms of number of hours on the water (approximately 30 hours). Local Tofino operators noted this and a higher standard was adopted (50 hours). As Remote Passages' training hour requirements are beyond even these, the company made no changes to its guide training program. It is the responsibility of the operator to ensure that reference materials and training information, relevant to safe operations, are made available to the guides.

There is no formal whalewatching association in the Tofino area—though informal meetings are held periodically between operators. During the meetings, local operators review behaviour on the water. Remote Passages' owners actively participate in DFO wildlife-viewing workshops, focussed on developing general guidelines and standards.

Ethics

Operators in the Tofino area have adopted a set of voluntary whalewatching operator's guidelines. The guidelines address "on-site etiquette" for commercial boats viewing whales and other coastal wildlife. The guidelines are specific to various species, and include items such as: the slow approach (detailing speed and distance when approaching wildlife); working in rotation with other vessels when viewing whales; and viewing proximity and speed of travel when leaving the whales. Additional information outlines appropriate behaviours during whale migration and in feeding grounds.

These voluntary guidelines are introduced to guides during their training with Remote Passages. In addition, more stringent in-house standards are developed to best address public safety and protection of area wildlife issues as they arise. These standards are posted and distributed to crew, and monitored for compliance.

Employment

While interviewing applicants, Remote Passages asks candidates about their long-term career plans. To recover training costs, the company requests a guide to commit to working a minimum of two seasons for the company after their training is completed. Remote Passages estimates that it spends approximately $1 000 in wages and training costs per new employee. Training also requires a substantial commitment of the owner's time, senior guide's time, and other resources such as gas and engine time.

If an applicant shows proficiency and an aptitude for guiding in the initial 30-hour volunteer period, he or she is then invited into the extensive, 220-hour structured training program.

RESULTS

Remote Passages' training program has resulted in:

- a reduction in marine incidents during the operational season;
- a reduction in risk perception by insurance underwriters;
- the development of effective training standards, easily adaptable to applicants with a diverse range of skills and experience;

- a high staff return rate season-to-season, important in a remote area with a small population base; and

- increased customer security and satisfaction.

Remote Passages has developed a reputation as a preferred industry entry point for potential guides. This is largely due to the quality of the up-front training and monitoring provided. Requests for entry into training programs are increasing yearly.

Taking on new trainees is done very conservatively. Extra effort is required from senior guides during a training-in period. There are financial costs to the company as well. New guides generally start in an on-call or part-time capacity, moving into full-time by peak season.

WTTC HUMAN RESOURCE CENTRE COMMENT

Adventure companies require highly skilled staff willing to work on a seasonal basis. Smaller companies operating out of remote locations must be particularly careful to choose qualified employees who are conscientious and dedicated. Safety issues are of particular concern both from a business perspective and as a moral obligation. Remote Passages' boat operator/guide training program has produced results which enhanced profitability while helping employees develop and improve individual skills.

KEY TERMS

standards	marine tour operator
soft adventure	liability
ecotourism	mentoring
whalewatching	leadership
wildlife viewing	peak season

 **www.remotepassages.com**

DISCUSSION QUESTIONS

1. If you were interested in working for Remote Passages Marine Excursions as a driver guide, what would you do to better your chances of being hired?

2. Why do you think standards and guidelines have not been developed for commercial motorized vessels under five tonnes? Explain your reasons.

3. After reading this good practice, what questions would you ask marine tour operators (under five tonnes) before you agreed to purchase a whalewatching adventure?

New Zealand
Sky City

Submitted by: Julie Berry

SKYCITY

Minimizing Legal Risk Through CARE

. . . Setting up a customer-management training program that helps staff to anticipate problems and intervene effectively when working in drinking establishments.

LEARNING OUTCOMES

1. Recognize why a drinking establishment should create a friendly environment that discourages overconsumption of alcohol.
2. Discuss the role staff plays in diffusing confrontational situations.
3. Explain how a company adapted a program developed in another country to fit its situation and locality.

OVERVIEW

Sky City never sleeps. The excitement of gaming is alive 24 hours a day, 7 days a week in Sky City. New Zealand's most popular entertainment and leisure destination is called "a city within a city." Located in the heart of Auckland, this multi-faceted entertainment destination needs a staff of 2 500 to manage the property's gaming facilities, 344-room hotel, four restaurants, theatre, convention centre, and Sky Tower.

Sky City was New Zealand's first casino following the 1990 change in government legislation, which permitted the operation of casinos throughout the country. Licensed for 24-hour operation, Sky City soon found itself to be a highly popular social venue. Staff was challenged with handling customers who were either drunk when they arrived, or who had too much to drink while on-site.

After just a few months in operation, Sky City recognized the need to ensure appropriate management of alcohol consumption to retain the integrity of its alcohol licence. New Zealand's legislation holds drinking establishments responsible for the subsequent actions of their patrons.

Management reacted by closing all bars on property between the hours of 3 a.m. and 11 a.m. An eight-member team was established to find a better solution to the challenge.

IMPLEMENTATION

Sky City management bought the New Zealand rights to a training program originally developed to help drinking establishments minimize the risks associated with serving alcohol. Controlling Alcohol Risks Effectively (CARE) was purchased from the Educational Institute of the American Hotel & Motel Association (AH&MA).

After some adaptation, Sky City's eight-member team successfully implemented a host responsibility scheme to benefit employees and patrons alike. Sky City adapted the program to New Zealand's laws and conditions. Next, a training procedure was designed which prepared each team member to instruct other employees in the four-hour program.

All front line staff was informed of the program through team briefings. A flyer was circulated to outline the objectives of the program, and to explain how the program would be delivered. Staff then worked with their supervisors to arrange appropriate times for attending training sessions. Attendance was, and remains, mandatory for all employees who interact directly with guests.

The program is based on a "traffic-light system" for identifying low-, medium-, and high-risk patrons. Staff are shown how to work together to be responsible hosts and encourage guests to choose non-alcoholic drinks if necessary. The program also illustrates how staff can professionally handle conflict situations and make judgement calls when telling patrons they can no longer be served.

The four-hour seminar covers:

- Alcohol Service and the Law
- Checking Identification
- Alcohol and its Physical Impact
- Intervention.

Information covered is appropriate for servers, bartenders, managers, and others who are involved in serving alcohol, or in supervising others who serve. The four-hour program is made interactive through role-playing and discussions.

A written exam is given immediately following the seminar and takes about an hour to complete. This comprehensive 45-question exam consists of two parts (true or false and multiple choice) and tests the employee's ability to apply the knowledge gained during the training. Employees must score 75 percent to pass. Those achieving 90 percent pass with distinction. Employees receive a certificate and a manual for reference while on-the-job. Through performance reviews, supervisors are able to systematically track employee activity in putting to practice the newly learned procedures.

RESULTS

Over 1 800 employees have participated in the training program. These employees came from a variety of departments including security, conferences, food and beverage, and gaming. Of the 1 800 employees, 50 percent completed the training program with adequate marks and an additional 45 percent passed with distinction.

After completing the program, staff is better qualified to:

- state the effects of too much alcohol;
- explain the legal restrictions that affect alcohol sales;

- state the establishment's alcohol policies and procedures;
- carry out identification checking procedures;
- describe how alcohol affects the body;
- identify behaviour that may indicate intoxication levels;
- monitor and control guests' alcohol consumption; and
- intervene tactfully to prevent possible problems from arising.

WTTC HUMAN RESOURCE CENTRE COMMENT

Word of Sky City's success has spread throughout the industry. Other New Zealand organizations, as well as overseas establishments, have contacted Sky City with an interest in adopting the program. Sky City was able to purchase materials off-the-shelf and adapt them to suit its needs. Here again, investing in training has demonstrated how Sky City's commitment to responsible host policies and to enhancing staff skills results in financial benefits for the operation.

KEY TERMS

risk management
gaming
legislation
conflict resolution
responsible host

overconsumption
liability
staff performance reveiws

 **www.skycity.co.nz**

DISCUSSION QUESTIONS

1. Provide a list of establishments, other than gaming, that could benefit from implementing a similar program.

2. What could management do to make sure that employees continue to put into place the training learned in this program? Discuss several strategies for keeping staff motivated and alert.

3. What kinds of safety mechanisms should management have in place to support staff in reinforcing on-site rules about alcohol consumption?

Index